Chatto

By John Sandifer

By John Sandifer

Tracking T.J. The life and times of Thomas Jefferson Sandifer. Copyright 2011.

One Tough Ombre, the 90th Infantry Division in Europe. Copyright 2012

Chatto's Promise, an Apache Saga, ISBN-10-1508894388, ISBN 13-9781508894384, Copyright 2015

All rights reserved. No part of this book may be reproduced or transmitted in any form or by any means, electronic or mechanical, including photocopying, recording, or by any information storage and retrieval system, without permission in writing from the copyright owner.

This book was printed in the United States of America.

Contents

List of Illustrations		6
Introduction		8
Chapter 1	Fort Marion	12
Chapter 2	Growing Up Apache	20
Chapter 3	Chatto's World	28
Chapter 4	Bounty Hunters and Invaders	33
Chapter 5	The Lure of Gold	39
Chapter 6	Pushing Back	44
Chapter 7	Janos	49
Chapter 8	The Bascom Affair	53
Chapter 9	Yankees and Rebs	62
Chapter 10	Tubac	67
Chapter 11	Love	69
Chapter 12	Pinos Altos	71
Chapter 13	Apache Pass	73
Chapter 14	The Warrior Chatto	78
Chapter 15	Camp Grant Massacre	83
Chapter 16	Nantan Lupan	85
Chapter 17	Slaughter at Salt River	91
Chapter 18	Broken Arrow	96
Chapter 19	John Clum	106
Chapter 20	Victorio	112
Chapter 21	Going Separate Ways	117

Chapter 22	The Scout	124
Chapter 23	Cibeque	127
Chapter 24	Kidnapping Loco	136
Chapter 25	Aliso	142
Chapter 26	Casas Grande	144
Chapter 27	Crook Returns	150
Chapter 28	Chatto's Raid	154
Chapter 29	Lordsburg	162
Chapter 30	Sheridan	170
Chapter 31	Escape and Surrender	172
Chapter 32	The Interval	177
Chapter 33	Tiswin Trouble	187
Chapter 34	Chasing Geronimo	198
Chapter 35	On the Trail	209
Chapter 36	Ulzana's Raid	219
Chapter 37	The Crawford Affair	224
Chapter 38	Geronimo Meets Crook	227
Chapter 39	General Miles	231
Chapter 40	Bear Valley	234
Chapter 41	Gatewood	238
Chapter 42	Going to Washington	242
Chapter 43	Geronimo Surrenders	248
Chapter 44	Stab-In-The-Back Letters	253
Chapter 45	Welsh Goes Public	261
Chapter 46	Mount Vernon	269

Chapter 47	Fort Sill	275
Chapter 48	Mescalero	286
Epilogue		294
Bibliography		297
Index		301

List of Illustrations

Chatto, 1
Fort Marion, 12
Apaches at Fort Marion, 14
Herbert Welsh, 16
Chatto, 17
Cradleboard, 20
Apache Raiders, Geronimo, 31
Mangas Coloradas, 34
Miners near Silver City, 39
Jacob Snively, 41
Union Cavalry, 45
Geronimo, 50
Lt. George Bascom, 54
Cochise, 56
Chiricahuas, 59
Confederate Cavalry, 64
Puberty Rite, 70
Dragoon Mountains, 73
Field piece 1885, 75
Fort Bowie Ruins, 76
Gen. George Crook, 85
Crook and mule, 87
John Clum, 106
Juh and Geronimo, 108
Clum and Apaches, 109
Naiche, 111
Victorio, 113
Lozen, 114
Dahteste, 114
Nana, 122
Chatto-scout, 125
Cpt. Asa Carr, 128
Dandy Jim, 131
Loco, 141
Captain Crawford, 151
Bonito, 155
Peaches, 159
Roadsign, 162
Judge McComas, 164
Charllie McComas, 167
Gen. Sheridan, 170
Scouts, 172
Lt. Davis, 188
Davis' Scouts, 201
Mickey Free, 214
Chiricahua Mountains, 216
Ulzana, 220
Chihuahua's Wife, 229
General Miles, 231

Lt. Gatewood, 238
Kayitah, 240
Secretary Lamarr, 245
Train to Florida, 249
Warriors at Ft. Pickins, 251
Geronimo at Mt. Vernon, 262
Senator Dawes, 263
Col. Langdon, 268
Mt. Vernon Barracks, 269
Grover Cleveland, 276
Pawnee Bill Poster 279
Buffalo Bill, 280
Show Scene, 281
Geronimo dressed for show, 282
Elderly Chatto, 287
Freddie Kaydahzinnie, 288

Introduction

I've often heard that "the end justifies the means" and when I was a reporter for KING TV, in Seattle, one of my bosses introduced me to a new phrase; "situational ethics." I presumed he meant it's okay to bend or break the rules, lie if you have to, if it's good for our side. Don't get me wrong. I thought the management at KING TV was exceptional. But I didn't really trust that guy very much after that. I certainly thought back to those phrases while looking into the life of Chatto, a Chokonen Chiricahua Apache, and how his life went.

Researching subjects, gathering information is a legacy from fifty-seven years as a broadcast journalist, beginning in 1957 at the little AM radio station operated by Washington State College (now University) and ending whenever that comes. After a career that took me to most of the major markets in the Pacific Northwest, with a stint at ABC TV Network in New York City, working as Editor, Reporter, Anchor and Producer, after retirement, I am still keeping my fingers in with occasional writing, radio and recording projects.

But, you know, I am a snowbird too. I live part of the year in my native Washington State and the rest of it in Buckeye, Arizona, getting away from the grey and wet in Washington. Travelling parts of the Southwest occasionally to soak in the geography, the weather and the history, I could scarcely avoid the ancient civilization of the Apaches and their relentless fight to preserve their lands from incursions of Spaniards, Mexicans, American miners, railroaders, settlers and troopers. The viciousness of the fighting was not the exclusive domain of the natives. Mexicans and Americans treated the Apache as less than human, wild animals, to be killed at will.

The Chatto thing came up because, as a painter, I was looking for a picture of Cochise and there aren't any. Cochise never had his photograph taken. There was a general fear among some Indians that if your image went into a small box, it stayed there. Several internet sites had a photographic portrait allegedly of Cochise, but it was really Chatto, often mistaken for Cochise in the strength and handsomeness of his face.

Looking at his photograph I thought this face begged to be painted. I do watercolors. It's another kind of research and recording of places and events that I enjoy. Chatto, the watercolor portrait, turned out pretty well. In fact, I sold it to a lady at the Catitude Art Gallery in Avondale, Arizona, for more than I had received for most of my other paintings. She said it went with her southwestern décor. But then, she wanted to know more about the subject. I said I would give her a write-up on some of the basics of Chatto. And that's how it started. She got her quick overview, but the more I looked, the more I got caught up in Chatto's world.

The Indian strongholds of old are scattered over the map of south-central and south-east Arizona, along the rivers and streams, in the many mountain ranges and canyons. The names of their chiefs are preserved in street and road names, colleges, cities and counties. Today they are a source of pride, yesterday a symbol of dread.

I found myself visiting Tombstone, Benson, Safford, Lordsburg, Silver City, Pinos Altos, Las Cruces, the Dragoon Mountains, the Mogollon Rim, the Chiricahua Mountains, and the San Carlos, Fort Apache and Mescalero Reservations…all territories associated with Apaches and especially the Chiricahuas. My experience with Apaches was limited to watching Jeff Chandler as Cochise in a movie called "Broken Arrow." It's so easy to see a cowboy movie and think you know something about Apaches. There was a lot to learn.

This was not written as a history, but it comes close. You won't find footnotes indicating every source. In general they are contained in the works listed in the bibliography. Historians have done an admirable job providing some of the same information for researchers. This is just a story about the Apache Wars emphasizing the role and actions of one Chiricahua warrior. It is based on the facts available and does not deviate from them except to the extent that I have employed literary license to provide snatches of dialogue that help with the story and are in context with it. And where gaps appear in the record, I have created some events in ways that were most logical to me.

One of the latest books about Geronimo was written by the football coach at my Alma Mater, Washington State University. Mike Leach's work was valuable because Chatto was near, with and sometimes against Geronimo for almost his entire life. You can tell Geronimo's life without Chatto, but the reverse is not true. For a day-by-day, play-by-play account of the Apache leadership, you can't beat historian Edward Sweeney's volume "From Cochise to Geronimo." Other historians like Dan Thrapp, Angie Debo and Evelyn Ball have dealt intensely with Geronimo, Victorio, Cochise and Mangus Coloradas, all part of Chatto's life. Also, Alicia Delgadillo's massive compilation of Apache prisoners, based on research by Gillette Griswold at Fort Sill, was very valuable in determining interrelationships and affiliations.

I read about the Apaches themselves, the six main tribes and their hundreds of bands, then about their great chieftains: Mangas Coloradas, Cochise, Geronimo, Victorio, Nana and more. A great deal has been written about them. Chatto is sort of a figure in the background. He shows up in most written articles or books about the more famous chiefs, but the full-fledged Chatto remained a mystery. I couldn't figure this out. He was an acknowledged chief of the Chiricahuas at one time. Historian Edwin Sweeney listed him among the chiefs, including Victorio, Nana, Juh and Chihuahua, who fought alongside Cochise and Mangas Coloradas. He staged one of the most God-awful raids in Arizona history. He was one of the Indians with whom the government sought to negotiate over the locations of Indian reservations. He was one of the first Apaches to meet face-to-face with a U.S. President. Yet little is known about him. In the literature he is variously described as brave, daring, intelligent, a leading spirit, erstwhile, enigmatic, an honored scout, a servant to his people and to the American government, but also a blood-thirsty murdering renegade …sort of an Apache Jekyll and Hyde.

A big thank you goes to Freddie Kaydahzinne, the Curator at the Mescalero Apache Tribe Culture Center, for spending many hours going over Apache traditions and some of the stories and songs he learned on his grandmother's knee. Kudos also to Chick Sandifer, Rich Martin, and Larry Cali for editorial advice and copy editing.

I think the essence of Chatto's life was one of broken or unfulfilled promises. We have all heard about the hundreds of Indian treaties made and broken by the United States in its quest for manifest destiny; 350 by one count. But it just seems to me that Chatto had more than his share; not just treaties made by his tribe, but promises to him personally and perhaps promises he made to himself. If he was severely screwed-over, we must also include the fact that he did considerable screwing himself. He didn't think of his actions as crimes. They went with being an Apache during a time when most of the white population wanted the Apaches eradicated down to the last man woman and child. He was a bad guy and a good guy. It depends on the viewpoint. This is his story.

CHAPTER 1   Fort Marion

As he entered the gray old fort, the diminutive Herbert Welsh passed below a large overhead escutcheon at the entrance. The fading crest was the Coat of Arms of Spain. He adjusted his glasses and read the crumbling stone words which declared that the fort was built by King Don Ferdinand IV in 1756, to protect the village of Saint Augustine, Florida. Since then the deteriorating bastion had flown the flags of the Spanish, English, Confederate States of America and, now in 1887, the United States.

Fort Marion, St. Augustine, Florida

He was coming here to see Apache prisoners who had been jerked off their reservation or captured in the wild and imprisoned. Passing through the entrance to the fort, Welsh, accompanied by an Army Captain, John Bourke, found himself in a passage as dark as the fort's history. The Spanish, expert torturers that they were, had installed four dark dungeons where unfortunate prisoners had once been hung on heavy chains or torn apart on the rack.

He noticed the lightly colored sea-shells protruding from the Coquina shell-rock walls, found only on the east coast of Florida and quarried only two miles away. To the right were three dim chambers where prisoners were once confined and to the left, a guard room. The place smelled musty.

Welsh had asked Captain Bourke to come along and got special permission from the War Department. Bourke, the former aide to General George Crook was very familiar with Chiricahua Apaches and sympathetic to them. He was an immaculate journalist, recording, in detail, his dealings with the Apaches over a long period when he was assigned to the Apache Wars.

Continuing forward into the small open courtyard, Welsh glanced at the ragged humanity around him, at the 12 foot-thick upper walls of the fort, the casemates, the entrance to an ancient chapel, the bastions and watch towers. There were tents all over the place. He was greeted by the lanky Commander and Civil War veteran, Lt. Colonel Loomis Langdon.

Colonel Langdon, though suspicious of do-gooders for the Indians, was cordial.

"May I offer you a tour of the Fort, Mr. Welsh?"

"Thank you, Colonel, I have only limited time, but think it essential to get a look about and still be able to interview some of your prisoners."

"I understand," said the Colonel, "We are pleased to have members of the Indian Rights Association visit us and anxious for you to understand our situation."

Colonel Langdon left Mr. Welsh in the hands of two Lieutenants named Conkling and Smith, who were in direct charge of the prisoners and Welsh followed them to the ancient ramparts. There was scarcely room to walk. Tents were pitched tightly all along the walkway. Inside the tents Indian women were sewing or stringing beads, playing cards or preparing to cook. He saw pieces of stale bread, meat and other scraps lying on the stone. He made a note that the prisoner's rations included bread, sugar, coffee and beans and, every two weeks, potatoes or onions, but no fresh vegetables or fruits.

Apaches at Fort Marion, 1885

As an ice-breaker, Lt. Smith told about the man who delivered meat for the Indians. He had a good scare on his first delivery. The Apaches were whooping and running toward Mr. V.D. Capo with knives. They had their knives out to divide the meat. Mr. Capo thought they were after him. He almost fainted. Lt. Smith chuckled.

On a parapet, Mr. Welsh looked out over the waters of St. Augustine Inlet, and loosened his tie a bit because it was very muggy. St. Augustine had a warm humid climate with hot summers and no dry season. In the summer it rained 40 percent of the time and the temperatures stayed in the mid-80s.

"How many Apaches are imprisoned here?" he asked of Lt. Conkling.

"447, sir. 82 men and the rest are women and children."

"I have correspondence which indicates this Fort can accommodate no more than 75 prisoners," said Welsh.

"Yes sir. It's a bit tight here."

Welsh asked how they dealt with all the human waste. He was led to a casemate where a stream of water flowed across the rock surface and fell down the outside wall to a small stream which flowed into the Matanzas River and, less than a mile away, into the ocean. He made a mental note of the highly porous stone of the fort and its capacity to trap and transfer disease in the hot, humid climate. He formulated, in his mind, a line that would appear in his subsequent report; "The danger of contagious disease attacking these Indians and spreading from them to the inhabitants of St. Augustine is, in my judgment, a matter worthy of prompt and serious consideration." His warning would be borne out in tragic proportions.

"How many of your prisoners have died, Lieutenant?"

"22, sir. 14 of them have been children. We do the best we can."

"Disease?"

The Lieutenant nodded. "Or natural causes. There has been no violence."

Welch knew this. He had in his briefcase a statement written by a young Chiricahua at Carlisle School in Pennsylvania, who had lived at Fort Marion. It said, "I will not forget the first death among us. Though I knew that old people sometimes died because of their years, I had not realized that it could happen to the young. A girl passed away, my people said, from the heartbreak and loneliness. Men took her body away in a box…a terrible thing to us. Whether she was buried, we had no way of knowing. That to us was much worse than death caused by violence, and it was the first of many, many, that were to follow. In Florida the dampness and the mosquitoes took toll of us until it seemed that none would be left. Perhaps we were taken to Florida for that purpose; from our point of view shooting would have been much less cruel. James Kaywaykla, Chiricahua Apache Prisoner of War and Carlisle student."

Welsh toured the dungeons. The Lieutenants assured him none of the prisoners were housed there and the dungeons were used only for storage. The officers told Welsh the Indians preferred to be out in the open air or in their tents, surrounded by saddles, shoes, clothing, wood chips and assorted trash. He would state in his report, "It was, in fine, an Indian camp lifted from the mountains or plains of Arizona and transported intact to the narrow confines of Fort Marion." He looked at the clothing worn by the Apaches. It was dirty and ragged for the most part and he would later comment that, even in Florida, people needed coats in the winter. The more he observed the conditions, the more disturbed he became.

"Thank you Lieutenant. Now I would like to speak to Chatto."

"We'll take you to the Chapel and arrange for him to meet you there."

As Captain Bourke split off to inspect more of the fort and talk to military men, and Welsh headed for the chapel, the Lieutenants tried to impress him with their efforts to keep the fort clean, for keeping the savages in line through military precision and providing them an opportunity to be like white men. Indeed, Mr. Welsh had similar goals. The stated objective of the Indian Rights Association, since its founding in Philadelphia in 1882, was to "bring about the complete civilization of the Indians and their admission to citizenship." Welsh just didn't believe that this was the way to do it.

Herbert Welsh

Born to a prosperous Philadelphia merchant and philanthropist, Herbert Welsh had studied art in Paris, but found himself a full time advocate for the rights of Indians after visiting the Sioux reservation in 1882. He was a founder of the Rights Association, now operating out of a new office in Washington D.C., where he, and a limited staff, lobbied Congress and advised the Board of Indian Commissioners. This trip was part of the mission, keeping in contact with Indians,

Indian Agents and doing field trips to reservations, settlements and, yes, prisons.

He asked, "Why is Chatto here? He and the other Apache Scouts who served the United States?"

Lt. Smith was quick to respond, "Sir, those decisions are made at a much higher level than us."

Welsh nodded. "It just seems such a shame that men who came in from the war-path, who put their lives on the line to round up hostiles were, themselves, rounded up and shipped here like cattle."

"Well, Chatto did commit murder," responded Lt. Smith.

"That has never been proven, Lieutenant. And he was at war." said Welsh, as he took a seat in the dim chapel and waited for the Apache.

Chatto

Chatto entered the chapel and strode confidently to the white man. Although not tall, he looked strong; barrel chested, with a bull neck. Still in his early thirties, his hair was black and long, in the Apache style. He wore a white linen shirt, a vest, a tie and trousers. Welsh later described him as looking like "a decent white man."

"See, I am dressed as you are," said Chatto to Welsh.

It was his way, thought Welsh, of telling me he has been a good Indian, going along with the ways of the white man and hoping for an escape from this steamy hell. After exchanging pleasantries Welsh got into his formal interview.

"What are conditions like here?"

Chatto thought for a moment. "Hot. Wet. Crowded. The white guards are not cruel. But they look down on Apaches. They have done some things for us."

Welsh took notes as Chatto explained aspects of life at Fort Marion. He said visitors were curious to see the Apaches and paid well for souvenirs both the men and women made inside the fort. Little white boys were told how to handle a bow and arrow and were rewarded if they could shoot a dime out of a forked stick at 20 paces. They got to keep the dime. The Army provided a huge bathing tub and the Indians used it now and then. Some of the local lads came into the fort to bathe with them. The Apaches held on to their burial customs, wrapping corpses in blankets and placing them in niches, covered with branches, at a secret burial ground on North Beach.

Their discussion moved to the working conditions at the fort. Chatto complained most strongly that there was no work.

"I want to work. All of us want to work," he said.

Instead of a pocket watch, Chatto carried a silver medal on a chain. In his hands he had papers: two honorable discharges from the United States Army.

"We pick up trash. We cut weeds. That is no work for the people."

Welsh knew. He had asked the Lieutenant while making the rounds of the fort. The Lieutenant had said, "The men don't do anything. There's not much for them to do." Welsh thought about their previous lives in the mountains, on the plains, hunting, riding, running, raiding. This sedentary life was punishment in the extreme. Promises that were made to the Indians and broken, he thought, made it even worse.

Welsh changed the subject. "How do you get along with Geronimo?" he asked.

"I think Geronimo wants to kill me."

"Because you were a scout?"

"Maybe he is still angry about that. It started when I was working for the Army and Geronimo and some others, many others, were drinking too much tiswin at Fort Apache and got themselves into trouble there. But he is not here."

"I know," said Welsh. "But there is some talk about bringing all you Chiricahuas to one prison. You would see him again. You would be living in the same place."

Chatto rubbed his chin and thought a moment. "Geronimo is an old man now. I think he would not be able to do much."

"Okay, now, I want to talk about the arrangements you had with the white leaders before you came here," said Welsh.

Chatto nodded, "The Great White Father promised me that I would be free if I did not fight with the whites. I promised I would do good. They promised me my land and house and tools and money. I kept my promise. They broke theirs and I was put here against my will."

"I agree with you, said Welsh. "Those Apaches who lived peacefully on the reservation and those Apaches, who served as scouts for the Army, should not be living in prison with other Apaches who stayed on the war path. For me to help you, I need to know your story, from the start."

CHAPTER 2   Growing up Apache

At his birth, he was named Pedes-klinje and a cradleboard ceremony was performed and his ears were pierced. His mother said to him, "It is so that you will hear important things and obey them." Boy babies were specially cherished because they represented future warrior strength. The Apaches needed warriors. Theirs was a warrior nation where raiding was the main industry. Pedes-klinje would go through a series of traditional ceremonies essential to mark his passage from birth to death as an Apache. For one thing, he told Herbert Welsh, he was not permitted to cry. Not only would it show weakness, but worse, it might alert an enemy. When he cried, Pedes-klinje found himself in his cradleboard, hung out on a tree, until he cried himself out. He soon learned crying was useless.

His sister, Gotsi, was born nearly three years before Chatto. Then, it was seven years before his brother Gonaltsis came along.

Gonaltsis was also called by his Apache name, Janokla, and still later by the Spanish name Patricio. He was followed by another sister, Bahnahtsi.

As the boys began to walk in new moccasins, their parents directed them to follow a trail of pollen leading to the east. This symbolized a long and successful life. A bag of pollen was often carried by the Apache for ritual purposes. Their seasons were marked by the migration of animals, the blooming of desert flowers and the growth of grasses. In the spring the adults cut their hair to encourage health and vitality.

Each day they were awakened before sunrise to train for their life-role. Everything in the world was filled with spirits and powers that affected Chatto's life; the moon, the sun, the plains and mountains, the animals, the trees, and Ussen, the great giver of life. Each of those entities had medicine that he needed to survive. The tribe would teach him how to call upon these powers through elaborate and frequent ceremonies, some of which could go on for days. Those who had the power, Apaches like Geronimo, Lozen and Pedes-klinje, himself, could predict the future, tell the location of enemies and even stop bullets.

Those who got this power likely climbed to the peak of a high mountain without food, without water, and they stayed there, praying to Ussen and waiting for what Freddie Kaydahzinne called "a transformation" a trance-like state during which they would be filled with the power of the giver-of-life and learned to talk to the rain, the clouds, to living plants; the knowledge to be one with nature. Chatto said his power often came to him accompanied by a twitching of the muscles of his neck, back or legs. The twitching would tell him something was amiss and he could deal with it.

In the decade of the 1850's many births among the Apache bands produced the maidens and warriors who would frame Chatto's life. His older sister Gotsi, his younger brother Gonaltsis and his little sister Bahnatsi were among the closest. Cochise's oldest son, Taza and his second son Naiche were second cousins. Taza was one year older than Chatto, Naiche one year younger. Growing up, he respected but often resented them; they were tall like their father, very handsome and athletic. He almost always lost in competitions with those two. The Warm Springs boy Bonito, at almost the same age and build as Chatto, was a great rival. He and Bonito would wrestle like Mountain Lion cubs, learning and practicing the skills they would need as adults. They challenged each other almost every time they met. Bonito usually won and that spurred Chatto to run farther, wrestle quicker, hunt harder and do all in his power to build himself up for future successes.

Chatto knew well Cochise's daughters Naithlotonz and Dashdenzhoos. Ihtedda, destined to be one of Geronimo's nine wives was born the same year as Gotsi. Future warriors and scouts Kaydahzinne and Nahdozinne were always in the mix when spear throwing contests were held. Dutchy, who would spend long days with him on the trail, was the same age as Chatto, along with the warriors Kayitah and Noche. They included Martine, the Nedhni who would be his brother-in-law one day and Jose First who would ride with him often. Many of his playmates were destined for fame or notoriety during the Apache Wars. They were all peers and would be friends, compatriots, warriors and sometimes enemies.

When the Bedonkohe band visited the Chokonens, the boys played with another cousin, Mangas, the son of the Great Coloradas and the same age as Chatto, Taza and Naiche Mangas would come with Fatty, the son of Chief Gordo and Toclanny who would, one day, be regarded as the best tracker in the tribe.

As boys, they and most of the men, wore deerskin shirts, leggings and moccasins that covered much of their lower leg. These were sewn by the men themselves and each was prepared to sew new ones if needed when out on raids. They always wore a loin cloth and sometimes an ornamented deerskin cap. Later, with trading and raiding, they began to wear white cotton tunics and pants, like the Mexicans. Often their tunics were fringed or beaded for decoration. Girls and women wore calico skirts and dresses.

On many nights Pedes-klinje and the other boys learned the history of their band from Mano Amarilla—Yellow Hand. Stories were very important to the band. With no written language the oral histories told the boys who they were and why the adults did the things they did. The Yellow Hand stories helped put things into context. Each story had some central theme; care for the family, honor the tribe, praise and obey Ussen—the giver of life, build strength and retaliate like no tomorrow for injustices. Sometimes the old man would ramble but each time he told a different story so that the boys would come to know ancestors, grandfathers and fathers, uncles and others who had performed extraordinary deeds or had fallen in the many raids and battles of the band. The history leading up to Pedes-klinje's rough life was pitted with tragic stories.

Pedes-klinje would be trained for only one thing: war. To Apaches raiding and stealing and the killing in war were not crimes. They were a natural part of life; of survival. When the Apaches weren't at war with the Spanish or Mexicans, they were often fighting each other. In fact, their failure to unify would be their downfall one day.

Pedes-klinje could ride a horse when he was 5 years old and bring down game with a bow and arrow before turning 10. He got his Spanish name Chato (Flat Nose) when a horse kicked him full in the face when he was a little boy. Names were highly valued and thus not over-used. Children were taught not to use a person's name to their face out of respect. Thus nicknames having to do with their physical features, age, or some other phenomenon were used to avoid saying a name. Cochise was 'Having the Strength of Oak." Geronimo was "One Who Yawns." His friend Dutchy was "Yellow Coyote." Thus Chato was known for his flat nose and not his name, Pedes-klinje. The second "t" was added to his name by whites many years later.

The horse was important to his Apaches, but not all important. Not like the Comanches who were the best horsemen in the world. An Apache would as soon eat a horse as ride one. They stole mounts from anyone, raided on horseback against other tribes and traveled by horse.

But they were not devoted to their horses. After all, they lived in the most dried out areas of the country, a wasteland with little support for either man or beast. In this environment they didn't want to be seen high in the saddle by an enemy. They were much more effective on foot, hiding in the bushes, blending in with the terrain, becoming invisible, sneaking to the attack. They became, in the words of an admiring commentator, "one of the toughest human organisms the world has ever seen."

As part of his preparation, Chatto's father, Culto or Jose Mangas, would say, "Race to the top of that hill and back. Fill your mouth with water and do not breathe through your mouth." That happened almost every day. Soon he was racing to the peaks of high mountains to build his wind and legs. Apaches became legendary for their stamina on the run. Chatto could trot 50 miles without stopping. Other times adults would throw him into cold streams, or the boys would bathe in the coldest water available before dawn, because this shock to the system provided strong hearts. He and the other young boys were encouraged to attack wasp nests to show their bravery.

He learned that retaliation and revenge were cultural obligations. One old Apache told an author, "Revenge is part of our philosophy." And he learned the concept of collective guilt. That is, if one Mexican offended an Apache, all Mexicans were liable to pay the price. It was not such an alien concept. Americans also painted most Indians with the same brush.

When not playing war games or 'Mushka" the popular game of throwing spears at a wooden loop for accuracy, Chatto and the boys hunted. They could follow the chase at eight or ten years old. Buffalo were on the northern plains. Deer and elk were high in the mountains. The boys learned never to approach a deer except against the wind. They would spend hours sneaking up on grazing deer, crawling long distances on the ground, and holding brush in front of them for camouflage. His father, Culto said, "When you skin the deer, turn his head to the East, the source of life." Because the deer was so valuable to them, they would try to kill several before the others in a herd ran away. Later the hide of the deer would be soaked in water and ashes and the hair removed so the process of tanning could begin and the buckskin became soft and pliable.

For Apaches like the Kiowa and some of the Mescalero who ranged up as far as Amarillo, in the Texas panhandle, the buffalo (American Bison) was their department store. They hunted buffalo on horseback, killing them with spears and arrows. Every part of the buffalo was used; his hide for lodges, robes, bags, shirts, skirts, bedding, leggings, shoes, dog and horse harnesses. His offal was dried and burned as fuel. His horns became ornaments, tools and utensils. His hoofs made strong glue. His hair was braided into cords and ropes. His bones were used for flint punches, awls, needles, skin scrapers and dressers, hoes, spades, knives, beads and ornaments, his sinew for sewing moccasins and binding arrowheads and spear tips. His bladder and intestines carried water. His brains contained effective chemicals for tanning hides and making them pliable.

Chatto's father had buffalo robes and used hides on his wickiup, but he had bartered for them. Chatto saw very few buffalo. Hardly any bison crossed the Pecos River, which ran south in West Texas and, on the rare occasions when they did, they never went farther west than the Tularosa Basin, in New Mexico, many days ride from his village.

Chatto's band depended primarily on the deer, but they also killed wild turkeys and rabbits from horseback using clubs. Geronimo said in his life story, "I have killed many bears with a spear, but was never injured in a fight with one. I have killed several mountain lions with arrows, and one with a spear. Both bears and mountain lions are good for food and valuable for their skin. When we killed them we carried them home on our horses." The skin of the Mountain Lion made the best arrow quivers, said Geronimo. In the lowlands the boys hunted antelope, jack-rabbits, quail and even field rats that could be dressed and cooked over an open fire.

Most of the hunting was done with a bow and arrow. Chatto fashioned his bow, as he had been taught by the elders, from the hardest, most pliable wood that could be harvested or traded. He fashioned the three-and-a-half foot bow with a sharp flint knife, dressed it down with sandstone which was notched to the shape of the bow. Using the powerful glue made from horse, cattle or buffalo hoofs, he glued a laminate of thin bone strips to the front for additional strength and resilience. Finally he rubbed the wood with buffalo or deer brains rendering it pliable and toughening the wood from splitting. He made the bowstring from braided sinew, tying one end permanently to the top and making a loop to be strung onto a notch in the lower end of the bow. It would be strung only when it was to be used. He made a strong leather cuff for his left arm so the bow string would not lacerate his arm when he shot.

His two-foot arrows were made mostly from stiff reeds and, like the bow, scraped with a flint knife, dressed with sandstone, then passed through a hole drilled in a shell or rock to assure they were uniform. Then he would cut a small notch to fit into the bow string and a larger, longer notch on the business end of the arrow where a flint or metal arrowhead would be glued and bound with rawhide. Three feathers were glued and tied to the other end for stability in flight.

Apache boys were expected to be accurate enough with a bow and arrow to bring down ducks in flight. They played a game to see how many arrows they could put into the air before the first one hit the ground. Many warriors could have seven arrows in the air at once. Their bows were powerful enough to shoot an arrow clean through a deer.

He learned every desert flower, cactus, bean and berry that would sustain life. His mother, sisters and most of the women in the band had their own upper grinding stone and maybe two of them, one coarse stone to start corn or bean flour and the other a finer one to finish it. The larger bottom grinding stones (mutates) were community property, placed here and there in the camp for the use of all.

The men taught him to make spear shafts from the beautiful Mescal plant and drink the fermented sap "Pulque" which, when distilled, becomes Mescal or Tequila. He ate the roasted heart of the Mescal, but preparing it was women's work. His mother and sisters dug the mescal plant from the ground using sticks and trimmed off the leaves, like the layers of an artichoke. The heart of the plant was placed in a rock-lined pit, where fire had heated the rocks and where grasses were laid onto the plants and dirt heaped onto the pit for twelve to 24 hours. Then the agave hearts were unearthed, cleaned up and either eaten or stored. Roasted mescal was a great gift.

He learned how to extract precious water from desert cactus and plants. His tribe used the Mesquite tree to build wickiups and corrals, they crushed and ate the beans, used the limbs to fashion weapons and sewed with the thorns. They utilized every part of the tree. His father said, "The Mesquite is the tree of life to the Apache."

Growing up, one of the important things Chatto learned was; there was a price on his head. The Mexicans had been paying for Apache scalps for more than 20 years by the time he came along. As a youth under 14, his scalp was only worth 25 pesos. Still, it was his scalp. His father said, "Remember the father of our great chief, Cochise, was scalped by bounty hunters. Don't trust Mexicans or Whites." The Mexicans had always been cruel, as were the Spanish before them. They became less a threat after the Americans won their war with the Mexicans. But now the Americans claimed the Apache lands as their own and they were brutal too. To them, Apaches had no say over the land.

CHAPTER 3   Chatto's World

Herbert Welsh knew the history of many Native American tribes. He was a dedicated student and wrote and lectured extensively on the subject. There was no doubt in his mind that Chatto was a pure product of a stone-age culture that had been at war for more than 300 years when he was born in the Arizona Territory, in 1854.

There were many and tragic events long before Chatto's time. The chronology formed the backdrop for the drama that would be his life. Apache wars had been fought with other and more powerful tribes like the Comanches, then the Spanish, then with the Mexicans who won independence from Spain, then with the United States and its miners and settlers and ranchers and its Army. The war with the United States was full blown as Chatto made his appearance into the world.

His Apache nation had once controlled an area larger than France, spanning territories from Oklahoma and Texas to New Mexico and Arizona and the states of Sonora and Chihuahua, Mexico. His was only one of six main tribes within the Apache nation, each occupying significant territory. Chatto's Chiricahuas ranged from east Arizona to mid-New Mexico and into the northern provinces of Mexico. The Mescalaros lived from south central New Mexico to Texas, The Western Apaches occupied central to northern Arizona. The Jicarillos controlled north New Mexico and into Colorado, the Lipan were in south Texas and the Kiowas, or Plains Apaches, existed in Oklahoma and the Texas panhandle. What they had most in common was language. It was an Athabaskan (also called Apachean) language similar to that spoken by Alaskan and Canadian natives, whose ancestors had crossed the land bridge from Siberia to Alaska.

Each of the large tribes had numerous bands living along the rivers, mountains, plains and canyons of the southwest. The bands were usually small because the land would not support great numbers of people. Chatto's was the Chokonen band of the Chiricahua. His chief was Cochise. Other Chiricahua bands included the Chihenne or Warm Springs band, the Bedonkohe, and the Nednhi.

With a chief as respected as Cochise, Chatto saw all of the great Apache leaders pass through his camp. His uncle Mangas Coloradas of the Bedonkohe, visited often. His daughter Dostehsey had married Cochise. Coloradas often brought Geronimo, a medicine man who was gaining a strong reputation for his powers to see into the future. From the Warm Springs tribe he would see old Nana and the impressive Victorio. The strong chieftain Chihuahua and his brother Jolsanny (Ulzana) came from another branch of the Chokonens and many times stayed for weeks. Chief Loco from the Chihenne band was a frequent visitor and one of Chatto's favorites was Zele, the renowned warrior who would be close to Chatto as he grew up and entered the warrior ranks. Chatto couldn't have known it at the time but he would follow many of these leaders, raid with them, track others, oppose some and become a target of several.

Near the time of his birth, their nation was dwindling. The Apaches were regarded by invaders as sub-human, a wild race of primitive people best dead. His uncle, the magnificent chieftain, Mangas Coloradas was 61 when Chatto was born, Cochise was 49 and Geronimo was 25. Each had suffered horrific losses and indignities at the hands of the invaders that made them implacable enemies of Mexicans and Americans and stern teachers of survival and retaliation to new generations.

Chatto's people had been run down, tortured, ambushed, tricked and murdered through their history. The depravations visited on the Apache had been returned by his people against all invaders and they became known for their ingenuity, strength, skills and endurance. And for their cruelty.

The Apache, once buffalo hunters on the plains, were, centuries ago, pushed by Comanches into the deserts of New Mexico and Arizona. The Comanches were the first Indian nation to adopt, breed and train the Spanish horse. One U.S. Army general said they were the finest light cavalry in the world. They were among the first to accumulate modern firearms through trade or raids. With use of the horse and firearms, they became as powerful in their world as Genghis Kahn had been in his. The Apaches were forced to move away from them and adapt to a different life style in a hostile land where agriculture was next to impossible and hunting, gathering and raiding were essential ways to survive.

When the Spanish came looking for gold in the late 1500's, fighting between the Spanish and the Apache started and never stopped. The Spaniards saw the Apaches, at best, as a source of slave labor and at worst as a pestilence. The Spanish, in their arrogance, thought if they subdued the Apaches, made Christians of them, and bent them to the power of the church; the natives would be a constant work source for the crown.

The Spanish built a series of forts along their Mexican northern frontier, called Presidios. The most prominent was Janos, others included Chihuahua and "San Augustin del Tucson," the first Spanish settlement in what would become Arizona. Each of these forts was put in place to protect Spanish missionaries while they introduced a new and confusing religion to the hostiles. When the Indians failed to respond, the Spanish sent out punitive missions against the Apache, killing hundreds and taking more hundreds as slaves.

The Apaches, always hardy and warlike, retaliated against the Spanish. They killed thousands of Spaniards, destroyed settlements, ranches, villages and mines. They killed priests and stole thousands of horses and cattle.

In 1786, the closest to peace the parties achieved was when Viceroy in Mexico City, Bernardo de Galvez, offered peace and subsidies to Apaches who would settle down, and continued war for those who wouldn't. Friendly Apaches were provided with food and supplies. Within five years many of the Apache bands were at peace with the Spanish. The great future leader, Mangas Coloradas was born during this time (1793) and things stayed peaceful until after the turn of the century.

In 1821, Mexico wrested its independence from Spain. Mexico, as an independent country, had far less money to support its soldiers at the forts and less to spend on the Apaches. In 1831 the Mexican government cut off food rations and other subsidies. The Apaches reacted by departing the presidios and going back to their hunting-gathering-raiding lifestyle. The Mexicans responded by declaring war on the Apaches and turning loose the army on them.

With no central leadership, the Apache tribes acted differently. Some negotiated with the Mexicans, others fought with them. With each band numbering 100 to 500, the raiding parties were small unless bands got together for larger forays. The Apache would be at peace with one Mexican town and at war with another.

Photo by C.S. Fly, Tombstone, AZ 1886, National Archives

The Chiricahuas, who were Chatto's forebears, raided from New Mexico and Arizona Territory into the Mexican provinces of Sonora and Chihuahua. They were often led by a chief the Spanish called Juan Jose Compa. Compa was mostly after livestock, but participated in raiding settlements in which men were killed and women and children taken as slaves. Compa could read and write Spanish and he was willing to negotiate, but was best known for his raiding.

The Mexicans willingness to pay money to have Apaches killed resulted in an industry of bounty-hunters, including prominent American ones who preyed on peaceful and innocent Apaches.

CHAPTER 4   Bounty Hunters And Invaders

The years counting down to Chatto's birth saw increasing violence. In 1835, the governments of Sonora and Chihuahua put bounties on Apache scalps; 100 pesos for each scalp of a male over 14 years of age, 50 pesos for the capture of an adult female and 25 pesos for a child under fourteen. The bounty for one Apache male was sometimes more than many Mexicans and American workers could earn in half a year. One of the early Apaches to lose his scalp was the father of Cochise.

In 1836, as Texans and American adventurers were fighting the battles of the Alamo and Goliad and eventually defeating General Santa Anna at the Battle of San Jacinto, other American frontiersmen were attracted to the Mexican bounty on Apaches. One such was John Johnson an American trader living in Mexico.

In 1837, Johnson invited the Chihenne band, whose warriors had stolen a herd of cattle near Moctezuma, to a trade meet near the mining town of Santa Rita, about 15 miles east of Silver City, New Mexico. Johnson showed up with 17 men. There was food and drink. The natives were all gathered around a blanket when Johnson and his men suddenly opened fire with rifles and concealed cannon loaded with scrap iron, glass, and a length of chain. They killed 20 Apaches, including Chief Jose Compa, and wounded several women and children. Mangas Coloradas was thought to have been there and witnessed the massacre. He became known for his hatred of the white man. The Mexican government gave Johnson a reward of 100 pesos and official thanks.

Mangas Coloradas, National Archives

With the death of Compa, Mangas Coloradas (Red Sleeves) became the most prominent Apache leader. His brother, Culto (and sometimes Jose Mangas) was Chatto's father. Coloradas was a striking man, at least six feet in height, unusually tall for an Apache. He had a powerful body and an enormous head. Anglo Americans regarded him as the greatest Apache leader of the mid-nineteenth century. Indian agent Edward Wingfield called him "a noble specimen of the genus homo. He comes up nearer the poetic ideal of a chieftain than any person I have ever seen."

Cochise, Victorio and Geronimo would take their lead from him. He would be noted for uniting parts of the Apache nation. Juan Jose Compa had been a special hero to him and others of the Mimbreno Apaches. Shortly after Juan Jose's death, Coloradas and his inflamed warriors avenged the treachery by constant raids, slaughtering trapping parties and attacking supply trains to the region. In one attack the enraged Apaches massacred a party of 22 American trappers. From that day forward, no American was safe from Mangas Coloradas in the Gila River country.

A main target was the rich copper mines at Santa Rita. The crude ore was shipped to Chihuahua City, Mexico, for processing. In 1838, in retaliation for the Johnson outrage, Apaches severed the mine's supply line. The 300 to 400 inhabitants of Santa Rita fled south toward the Janos presidio, 150 miles away. The Apaches killed all but about six of them enroute. The Apaches cleared the area of its white and Mexican inhabitants. The Franciscan missionary effort in southern Arizona came to an end. The priests were recalled and the two remaining missions in Arizona, Tumacacori and San Xavier del Bac, were deserted.

Another American scalp hunter came on the scene in 1839. This was James Kirker, a large disheveled Irish immigrant seen mostly in a greasy buckskin shirt. A one time friend of the Apache, Kirker became a bitter enemy with the start of the Mexican bounty program. Kirker had been an illegal fur trapper near Santa Fe, using the copper mines as storage pits for his furs. For 15 years he escorted ore trains to Chihuahua, Mexico, based on an alliance with Chief Juan Jose Compa. It involved selling Mexican goods, stolen by the Apaches, to buyers in Texas and Louisiana. This was such a good deal for the Apaches that they named Kirker an honorary chief.

While the Apaches hated Mexicans, they also depended on them for horses, cattle, foods and whiskey. These were obtained by trading and raiding. Soon the Mexicans upped the bounty on Apaches. Now it was 250 pesos for live male adults, 200 if the man was dead and 150 for women and children. The scalp had to be given to local governments for verification. The state paid out almost $18,000 for scalps and prisoners in 1849.

Mexican officials called on Kirker to try to pacify the Apaches. The Mexican government authorized a private army led by Kirker. It had over $100,000 in financing. Kirker didn't pacify. He killed. Gathering up a hodge-podge force of Indians, escaped slaves, Americans and Mexicans, he slaughtered Apaches at random, including friendly ones and groups negotiating peace. On several occasions his scalp-hunting army attacked peaceful Apache villages, including

Chatto's, killing from 50 to one-hundred men, women and children and selling their scalps in Chihuahua City, which became known as the "Scalp Capital of America."

When the Mexicans were short of money to pay for scalps, Kirker retaliated by selling Mexican military secrets to the United States, which seemed to be nearing a war with Mexico over disputed territory in Texas and elsewhere. Mexico declared him an outlaw and offered a $10,000 reward.

Kirker claimed that he and his men had killed 487 Apaches for their scalps, but authorities figured that many of those hair-pieces came from unfortunate Mexicans too. After a stint as an Indian fighter for the U.S. Army on the Colorado-New Mexico border, Kirker disappeared with a wagon train headed for California.

In 1845, Congress made Texas a state, over the objections of Mexico. The location of the border remained in dispute. By 1846, the Texas border dispute was an excuse for Americans to resort to military force and whet their insatiable thirst for westward expansion.

In June of that year, General Phil Kearney, under the expansionist President James Polk, led the Army of the West containing 1,586 troops from Fort Leavenworth, Kansas toward Mexico by way of Santa Fe. He was to be prepared to invade Mexican territory from the north as other armies hit the Mexicans from the south through the Gulf of Mexico. In the event of war, he would take possession of New Mexico Territory for the U.S.

Kearney told Mexican residents in New Mexico Territory they would be better off under the American government. For one thing, he said, this new government would do a better job of fending off Apaches, who rustled their herds and carried off their women. In the heart of Apache country on the Gila River, he met and negotiated with Mangas Coloradas who promised safe passage and assistance to the Americans, especially if they were going to displace the hated Mexicans.

When the Texas border conflict grew into the Mexican-American War, the United States took the disputed territory in Texas and didn't stop until it had gained most of the Apache homeland in Texas, New Mexico and Arizona Territories.

All this was only part of the pattern taking shape in Chatto's world. At the start of the Mexican-American War, the Apaches sided with the Americans. They wanted the Yankees to push their old enemies out. Many bands promised American soldiers assistance. Cochise supplied wood and gave Americans safe passage through his lands. These events would forever change the world of the Apache. As U.S. troops were sent west to enforce the new borders and protect miners and settlers, Indians got in the way and became expendable.

In 1848 the Mexican War was over. With the signing of the Treaty of Guadalupe Hidalgo, American troops began to arrive in the southwest in greater numbers to secure the borders and establish control. It began a long-running debate about what to do with the native inhabitants. Should the United States make peace with Indians and kill them if that didn't pan out? Or, should it make war on the Indians and force treaties on a vanquished foe?

The Government decided to try a series of peace treaties first and kill Indians if those didn't work. Mangas Coloradas and seven other chiefs signed a treaty in 1852 at Santa Fe, which was remarkable for how much it gave the United States and how little the Indians got from it. Included in its eleven major provisions was a promise by the Indians to acknowledge the power and authority of the United States Government, to obey the law and stay at peace, including no raiding into Mexico. They were to allow free passage over their lands and let the whites determine which lands were theirs, and treat white people with respect and kindness. For this, The United States promised periodic gifts and that the Government "shall so legislate and act as to secure the permanent prosperity and happiness of said Indians." The papers were worthless almost before the ink was dry. The prosperity and happiness never came. The Apaches were in the way of westward expansion. U.S. General, J.H. Carleton probably typified Anglo opinion when he called for a war of total extermination against Apaches.

Many of the agreements with various tribes were never ratified by Congress or were simply broken. The peace was uneasy. U.S. military officers like Major George Forsyth found the Apaches were not worthy of treaties because they were "cruel, crafty, wary, quick to scent danger, equally active to discover a weak or exposed place, tireless when pursued, patient in defeat and merciless in success." General George Crook would call them "The Tiger of the Human Species." As white men encroached on Apache culture and territory by 1849 the so-called Apache Wars were beginning. They would last 40 years.

CHAPTER 5   Lure of Gold

To Chatto's Apaches gold had little meaning. It was too soft to make good bullets or arrowheads and otherwise practically useless. For its trading value with the white-eyes, gold could be picked up from the ground, but never dug from beneath the surface, because that was an intrusion on Mother Earth. Not so for the whites.

The California gold strike, in 1849, had proven what riches might be found in the West. Prospectors combed every gorge, river and peak. A river of miners and prospectors flowed through Arizona Territory. It was the quickest way to the California gold fields. Many wanted to prospect their way through Apache lands. Unfortunately for the natives, the miners successfully discovered veins of gold, silver and copper and stayed put to play them out.

Miners near Silver City, NM

The miners were rough tough types, many with criminal backgrounds. Hundreds of gold, silver and copper camps and towns began to spring up. Many disappeared almost as fast as they rose, but others grew into substantial towns and cities. Tombstone was one of these and it owed its name to the Apaches. Other miners told a scrubby prospector named Ed Scheifflin that probably all he would find in the surrounding hills was rocks. And those rocks would be his tombstone when the Apaches caught him. So when Scheifflin found silver in abundance, he named his mining claim "Tombstone," to poke fun at them. Within two years the place was crawling with miners, cowboys, merchants, whores and lawmen.

Prospector William Parsons wrote, "It was a mad furious race for wealth, in which men lost their identity almost, and toiled and wrestled, and lived a fierce, riotous, wearing, fearfully excited life; forgetting home and kindred; abandoning old steady habits; acquiring restlessness, craving for stimulant, unscrupulousness, hardihood, impulsive generosity, and lavish ways."

Many of the camps and towns were on the traditional and sacred stomping grounds of the Apache, like Gila City, Wickenburg, Safford and Tombstone Arizona, Pinos Altos, Silver City, and Santa Rita, New Mexico. One source said one in every four persons in Arizona was a miner by the mid-1800's.

If it weren't the miners it was the cattlemen intruding into the hunting grounds of Chatto's people. Ranchers from Texas, California and Mexico drove their herds of longhorn cattle through the best of the grasslands. They claimed it was free range; open to any rancher who wanted to use it. The miners and cattlemen were followed by the merchants, settlers, railroaders, gamblers and gunslingers, all of whom hated Indians. All were driven by the idea that the native peoples of the country had no right to interfere with the destiny of a white, Christian nation.

Chatto was still in the crawling stage when Colorado had a major gold strike. A torrent of prospectors, estimated at 100,000 struck out for the west as eastern newspapers published banner headlines about the new El Dorado. During the same time economic conditions in the United States forced the issue. The financial panic of 1857 meant a large pool of jobless workers and farmers, who lost their land, were ready to head west to start anew.

An essential difference and basic conflict of aims between the Americans and the Apaches was that the Americans looked upon the land for its potential to be exploited for economic gain and they felt that they needed to completely dominate it as part of the process. The

Apache looked upon the land as a gift from Ussen that was to be preserved except to the extent it was to be utilized for survival.

The first big strike in Arizona happened in 1858 at Gila City, (now Yuma) when Jacob Snively found gold. Snively had spent considerable years as a soldier for the Republic of Texas, commanding troops against the Mexicans and rising to the rank of Colonel. Snively would later lead a company of Arizona Scouts to fight Apaches during the Civil War. At one time he headed for California like other gold rushers, but eventually worked his way back to Arizona. An engineer/surveyor by trade, he set off what was to become a fever of prospecting for gold, silver and copper in Apache country.

Jacob Snively and friend, 1859

Within months of the Gila City claim, Snively was leading a group of 12 men who left Tucson, prospecting the upper Gila River, which flows from the continental divide in western New Mexico 650 miles across Arizona to the Colorado River at Yuma. They made a strike at Pinos Altos and began another gold rush. Prospectors found a rich gold vein at Santa Rita about the same time and in the same vicinity. These mining claims were in smack-dab in the traditional haunts of the Chiricahua and Mescalero Apaches. Apaches who saw the white men digging in their hunting grounds or sacred places, moving dirt, diverting streams, hauling supplies and getting drunk, tried to drive them away. Miners who saw Apaches riding or roaming considered them vermin that required killing.

Snively reportedly led a mule loaded with 60 pounds of gold which he claimed to have panned in ten days from a nearby canyon. He was exploring near present day Wickenburg when about 150 Apaches, likely including Chatto's father, Jose Mangas, attacked his party. Snively died with numerous arrows piercing his body. His companions fled for their lives. They left his body to be picked clean by vultures.

The Chiricahuas, who had not gone on the warpath against Americans for many years, finally did. It started when Chief Mangas Coloradas approached miners working new claims near Silver City at Pinos Altos. Mangas told miners, who were just beginning to unearth what would be $8,000,000 in gold, silver, copper, lead and zinc, that the Pinos Altos (High Pines) was holy ground to the Chiricahua. He told them to look for the yellow iron someplace else. The miners laughed at him. Then they tied Coloradas to a tree and flogged him to within an inch of his life. This was an act that was deeply painful and embarrassing to a tribal chief and to his warriors. This and the earlier massacre that killed Juan Compas developed in Mangas a fiery hatred of white men, carried with him always and passed along to Chatto's generation.

The miners became bolder. When Chatto was 6, thirty miners launched a surprise attack on the encampment of his uncle Mangas Coloradas on the west bank of the Mimbres River, which runs near Silver City. This was in December, 1860, and the miners were retaliating because Indians had stolen a few cows. It was called the Battle of the Mimbres River. The miners killed four Indians, wounded others, and captured thirteen women and children. These were little friends of Chatto. He was old enough to understand when his elders told him the children became slaves. He felt his own hatred for the white man grow.

CHAPTER 6 Pushing Back

Retaliation was key to the Apache culture. So, as they were being pushed around, assaulted and killed, they pushed back. American newspapers created sensational headlines from most Apache counter attacks. One such incident happened in the spring of 1851, at Tucson. The immigrant family of Royce Oatman stopped in the middle of the desert when their oxen broke down on their way to Fort Yuma. They were attacked by Tonto Apaches. The Indians killed Oatman and his wife along with four of their children. A son, 14 year old Lorenzo, was left for dead but survived. The Indians kidnapped daughters Olive and Mary Ann Oatman. When reported in the papers it created frenzy among the white settlers. The children were eventually traded to the Mojave Indians. Mary Ann died less than two years later, in 1853, and Olive was finally rescued in 1856, after 5 years of captivity. She was never quite the same.

The Santa Fe Weekly Gazette reported that the action between American troops and Jicarilla Apaches in 1853, "was one of the severest battles that ever took place between American troops and Red Indians." It was severe because the Indians were getting even for an unauthorized cavalry attack at Cieneguilla, and they won a four-hour battle with superior tactics. Apaches and Utes dominated because they could shoot 4 to 5 arrows per minute, while the troops, struggling with their cap and ball muskets, could only get off two shots in the same amount of time.

In December, 1853, the year before Chatto's birth, the Americans completed the Gadsden Purchase, in which they bought land south of the Gila River that they had not taken in the war with Mexico. This put the traditional lands of Chatto's band under U.S. control for the first time. In return for ten-million dollars, the United States received nearly 30,000 square miles of additional Apache land in southern New Mexico and Arizona. With prospecting, mining, plentiful range for cattle and the prospects of a coast-to-coast railroad going through, Americans continued to enter the territory in even greater numbers.

Most inhabitants of the region, even resident Mexicans, welcomed the change from Mexican to American control. They had felt isolated and neglected by a government in far-away Mexico City. Now they would have the protection of the U.S. Government. They would have markets for ore, cattle and grains. And the Apaches would be neutralized.

So, when Chatto was born, in 1854, the influx of white people had become a river of humanity and it naturally increased the incidents and misunderstandings with the Apaches. The history of his tribe, leading up to his birth, was punctuated by violence against and by his people. And he had many years of it ahead of him before he would, individually, seek peace.

East of Chatto's village, the Mescaleros were also at war with the Americans. They ambushed Company B, 1st Dragoons, on the Penasco River, New Mexico, in mid-January 1855, killing two privates and Captain Henry Whiting Stanton, for whom nearby Fort Stanton was later named. U.S. troops retaliated in a series of campaigns that destroyed Mescalero villages and harried the tribe until it agreed to settle on a reservation between the White Mountains and the Pecos River.

Union Cavalry

A full contingent of U.S. troops rode into southern Arizona in late 1856, when Chatto was two years old, to assure possession of the region and to suppress the Indians. His Apaches continued to raid. They didn't think of it as making war, but the Americans did. With increasing pressure on them most of the tribes, the Jicarilla, Chiricahua, Mescaleros and Tontos all went on the war path. Though fiercely independent, even to the extent of fighting each other, the Apaches often put large numbers of warriors in the field for a common cause; keeping foreigners out of their territory and retaliating for violence committed against them. They waged war with large parties, often using clan members. By 1856, authorities in horse-rich Durango claimed that Comanche and Apache raids in their state had taken nearly 6,000 lives, abducted 748 people, and forced the abandonment of 358 settlements over the previous 20 years.

Apache raiding reached monumental proportions into the early months of 1856. The U.S. Government abandoned the idea of pursuing treaties and ordered the Army to whip the Indians first, and then sign treaties with the subjugated foe. The army's Mogollon Attack in 1856 was an example of this strategy and how the innocent suffered with the guilty.

General John Garland ordered a two pronged attack on the upper Gila River and Mogollon mountain areas, where Chatto's band lived. In April of 1856, a detachment of troops led by one of General Garland's commanders, Lieutenant Colonel Daniel T. Chandler entered the rugged Mogollon Mountains of Arizona, about 15 miles southeast of present day Flagstaff. They were searching for hostile Apaches.

What they found was peaceful Indians living in the village of Chief Delgadito and Itan. Chandler ordered his men to attack it anyway. They killed dozens and scattered the rest. Chandler's destruction of the camp increased the retaliatory raids of the Coyotero, Mimbres, Mogollon, and Chiricahua Apaches. In November, a band of Apaches operating in Zuni and Navajo country committed one of their more spectacular murders when they killed the Navajo agent Henry

Linn Dodge. The Americans thought of it as a terrible crime by Apaches. On the other hand, they exonerated Colonel Chandler in the killing of peaceful Apaches.

Many of the U.S. Army officers sent into the southwest Indian wars would soon appear in the Civil war. The army, not yet engaged in that great conflict and having little to do after the Mexican-American War, practiced strategy and tactics against Indians, sending out frequent expeditions. If a soldier was ambitious and wanted an increase in reputation and rank, his best chance was in combat. The only combat after the Mexican war was against Indians on the frontier.

In May, 1857, one of these expeditions, coming out of Fort Filmore, New Mexico, was led by Colonel Benjamin Louis Eulalie de Bonneville, deep into Apache country to avenge the Navajo agent's death. He split his command of 800 men into two prongs, one coming out of Albuquerque under Colonel William Loring, under whom my great-grandfather would fight in the Civil War as a Confederate. The other column marching from the Fort was commanded by Lt. Dixon Miles. Loring was first to make contact with the enemy, a band under Chief Black Knife (Cuchillo Negro), herding 2,000 sheep. Loring attacked and killed seven warriors, including the highly regarded chief and scattered the rest.

The Miles column, moving more slowly, took a month before coming across an Indian encampment on the Gila River. His surprise attack caused serious damage to Chatto's tribe, killing 42 warriors and capturing their women and children. Can you imagine losing 42 citizens in one day in your town? Lt. Miles lost two men. In a separate expedition, Captain Richard Stoddert in Ewell's command attacked a Coyotero camp near Mount Graham, killing 24 during the assault. Ewell was wounded. He was recovered in time to fight for the south at Gettysburg and Spottslyvania Courthouse.

An ominous pattern was developing in the Southwest. Throughout the Gila River country, warfare was steadily increasing in a series of raids and counterattacks by both whites and Apaches. Chatto's world was aflame.

CHAPTER 7   Janos

Even as a toddler Chatto was being trained how to survive in the wilderness, how to stalk, how to kill. For practice, he had his cousins and Gonaltsis, his smaller brother, whom he picked on a lot and ordered around unmercifully. The periodic raids by his elders were becoming full-blown battles in his youth. The skirmishes were not limited to his band. They were spread throughout the Apache nation: The Tontos, Yavapai, San Carlos, Chiricahuas, Mescalaros, the Jicarillos, Lipan and Kiowas were all fighting skirmishes or pitched battles with the whites. The whites had decided there were only two ways to deal with Apaches; feed them or kill them. The majority favored extermination. Chatto, Gonaltsis and their sisters, Bahnahtsi and Gotsi, were often jerked up out of camp in the middle of the night to escape oncoming troops. Chiricahuas ran for Mexico when the U.S Cavalry was in hot pursuit.

In the spring of 1858, when Chatto was 4, there was great excitement and anger in his camp when the story reached them about Geronimo's tragedy at Janos. Geronimo and several men went into the Mexican presidio of Janos to trade for goods and drink some whiskey. Geronimo loved whiskey. Geronimo, the Spanish name for Goyathlay, or "One Who Yawns," was a Bedonkohe who, along with his mother, went to live with the Nehdni after his chieftain father died. Geronimo had married a Nehdni girl named Alope within the band at 17, the first of nine wives he would have.

Geronimo, cropped C.S Fly 1886 Photo

While Geronimo and the other men were away, a company of 400 Mexican soldiers from Sonora led by Colonel José María Carrasco rode into their camp. It was a slaughter. When the men returned to their camp, Geronimo found his mother Juana, his wife Alope and their three children butchered. Almost one-hundred Apaches had been killed. Geronimo was the only one whose entire family was wiped out. His grief knew no bounds. Survivors said he said he just stood out in the wilds for the longest time, not moving, just staring to the horizon, grieving and hating. Geronimo hated all Mexicans for the rest of his life and would make them pay dearly for the treachery of those Mexican soldiers.

Chatto remembered that Geronimo came to his camp after first visiting Mangas Coloradas asking if he and his band would go on the war-path against the Mexicans. Mangas said he might, but wanted to know whether Cochise would also join in. Chatto knew that something important was up when Geronimo entered the camp of his chief. There was great ceremony with the greetings. Geronimo was forceful in his arguments to Cochise and his war council. He said that he would fight in the front of the battles and die if need be, but the Mexicans deserved death for the massacre at Janos. Cochise promised to take it to his warriors. They had the choice. He couldn't order them into a deadly conflict. They agreed. Geronimo next went to Juh, his cousin and lifelong friend from the Nednhi band and successfully recruited him and his warriors. All told he brought a force of 200 warriors to bear against the Mexicans.

The Apaches moved 120 miles south into Mexico and the "land of the fire ants," at Arizpe. They camped north of the city where eight Mexican soldiers rode out to talk to them. There was no talking. "These we killed," Geronimo was quoted as saying, "to draw more soldiers from the city." And more soldiers did come the next day, setting off a pitched battle. The Apaches captured their supply wagon with guns and ammunition. And now the Mexicans came in force with about 100 soldiers on foot and mounted. The Apaches engaged in a set-piece battle. True to his word, Geronimo was in the front as his warriors charged into the Mexican troops, firing their newly acquired rifles from the supply wagon, raining arrows on the Mexicans and using clubs at close range. Geronimo told an author years later, (throughout the fight) "I thought of my murdered mother, wife, and babies, of my father's grave and my vow of vengeance, and I fought with fury."

Indeed he must have. Geronimo was in the battle for two hours killing Mexicans right and left, including two Mexican soldiers who had just gunned down three of his warriors. He killed one with a spear and the other with his knife. Cochise was amazed and rewarded Geronimo with a new wife, his cousin She-gah. At that time Geronimo already had three previous wives, two of whom, Alope and Nanathatlith, had been captured and killed by Mexicans. With Janos avenged, the large war party broke up and the Bedonkohe, Chokonen and Nednhi bands went their separate ways. Yellow Hand told the story in front of the night fire.

Geronimo wasn't finished. He stayed on the war path with 25 or 30 warriors hitting Mexican targets wherever they found them.

Geronimo paid a price for his exploits, he later told writers, "During my many wars with the Mexicans I received eight wounds, as follows: shot in the right leg above the knee, and still carry the bullet; shot through the left forearm; wounded in the right leg below the knee with a saber; wounded on top of the head with the butt of a musket; shot just below the outer corner of the left eye; shot in left side, shot in the back."

Some of the Apaches began consolidating their forces through inter-tribal marriages and allegiances. Chiricahaus celebrated the marriage of Cochise to the daughter of Mangas Coloradas, Dos-The-She. It was one of those power marriages for Cochise, now 56, and the taking of one of his many wives. For 7-year old Chatto it was a special occasion. There was face-painting, and games and gifts. Warriors and women danced for Cochise and songs filled the desert mountain sky. Already Cochise was a hero figure to Chatto, and well he should be. His name meant "Having the Strength of Oak" and his demeanor supported it. Cochise was becoming, under the tutelage of his now father-in-law Mangas Coloradas, one of the most powerful Apache leaders. Chatto was awed by his physical presence; almost six feet tall, muscular, with classical features and long black hair. His father told him this marriage would join the Mimbreno and Chokonen bands and make them very strong against the white soldiers.

Another marriage brought Apaches from separate bands closer. This was between Chief Juh from the Nedhni Chiricahuas, another six-foot tall, 225 pound warrior. He married the sister of Geronimo. Even though Geronimo was a Bedonkohe Apache his mother had taken him to live with the Nedhni band at a young age. It was a good time for Geronimo. His wife Cheehashkish gave birth to a boy. They named him Chappo. Juh and Geronimo combined forces. Since Juh had a stuttering problem, Geronimo often acted as his mouth-piece, giving others the impression that Geronimo was the chief. Geronimo was always a medicine man. His powers to foresee the future would become legendary among the Apaches.

CHAPTER 9   The Bascom Affair

1861 was a tumultuous year for Chatto's Chiricahuas. Early in the year his chief, Cochise, would go on a murderous campaign of retaliation for the stupid actions of a young army lieutenant named George Bascom. It may have been the single most important factor in a long campaign of terror that would snatch him up in the whirlwind. Meantime, the first shots of the Civil War, at Fort Sumter, South Carolina, would affect the Apaches thousands of miles away; it would reach into the hunting grounds near Tucson, the mountains of New Mexico and into his own wickiup. Both Confederate and Yankee troops would attack Apaches wherever found. It started with the first moon in January, when Chatto was turning seven years old.

Yellow Hand lit a new pipe and was starting a story when Chatto interrupted. "Why does Cochise hate the White-Eyes?"

Chatto's question surprised Yellow Hand. "He didn't always," Yellow Hand said. "For many seasons Cochise welcomed the Americans on the land. He provided them with food and firewood. But have you not heard about 'Cut the Tent?" he asked.

"I know Cochise escaped the Pony Soldiers through a hole in a tent. But I want to know more," replied the boy.

"Then listen and I will tell you."

Yellow Hand retraced the events that turned hatred of Mexicans toward the Americans; that united Cochise, Geronimo and Mangas Coloradas into the leaders of a vast killing machine and set off eleven years of war. What version of the story he told is unknown. Time and the re-telling have produced several versions. But the essentials remain the same. This is one.

On January 27th, 1861, a band of Coyotero Apaches raided the "squalid" ranch of John Ward, an often drunk Irish immigrant living with his Mexican mistress, Jesusa Martinez, southeast of Tucson. She was widowed and the mother of a 12 year old boy variously known as Felix Ward, Felix Telles and Mickey Free. While Ward was away from the ranch, the Coyoteros plundered the ranch-house, stole 20 head of cattle, which was most of Ward's livestock, and kidnapped his stepson.

Ward rode the 12 miles to Fort Buchanan and reported to Lt. Colonel Pitcain Morrison, "It was Apaches, Chiracahua Apaches," he yelled, "led by Cochise." Morrison assigned an inexperienced 24 year old Lieutenant, George Bascom, who had graduated next to last in his West Point Class three years previous, to lead an investigation.

Lt. George Bascom

Fifty-four troopers from the 7th Infantry and an interpreter named Antonio rode out with Bascom and John Ward. They snooped around the Ward ranch and returned to the fort saying that horse and cattle tracks pointed eastward, toward the Chiricahua Mountains. That was known as Cochise country. Morrison ordered Bascom to ride the nearly 150 miles across the desert to Apache Pass to retrieve the boy and the cattle and to punish the Indians for their crime. John Ward would ride along. Some said Ward expressed more worry over his cows than the whereabouts of the kid.

Bascom and his command made it to the remote Apache Pass, between the Dos Cabezas and Chiricahua Mountains on February 3rd. There they found Sergeant Daniel Robinson, leading a wagon escort detachment, and drafted those men to his cause. This gave Lt. Bascom 67 troopers plus Ward and the interpreter. Sergeant Robinson had intelligence on the location of Cochise's winter encampment near the Butterfield Overland Mail Station at Apache Pass. It was no secret; Cochise was at peace with the whites at the mail station.

Riding to the station, Bascom met the station master, Charles Culver, and stagecoach driver James Wallace. Both said they knew Cochise, and could get messages to him, if that's what the Lieutenant wanted. Lt. Bascom told them his men were riding to Fort Bliss, along the Rio Grande. The lie was calculated so that the Indians would not get word that the soldiers were in the area for any other reason. In fact, U.S. troops often passed this way in transit from one place or another.

"I need water for my horses and a good place to camp," said Bascom. "Then, I'll send my interpreter over to Cochise's camp to see if he wants to meet, while we're here."

"Fine, said Mr. Culver, "If you go another mile and a half, toward Goodwin Canyon. You can camp there."

From a hillside, Cochise's scouts were watching the Army arrival at the mail station. If Cochise received an invitation he gave no response. Becoming impatient, Lt. Bascom asked a reluctant Mr. Wallace if he would ride to the Indian camp and again invite the chief to a pow-wow.

Cochise sculpture, National Park Service, Ft. Bowie, AZ.

Late the next day Cochise rode into Bascom's camp. The chief was not anxious about it. He brought his brother, Coyuntwa, with him and two nephews and his wife and two children. It was Apache custom to greet visitors. Lt. Bascom invited Cochise and his party into his tent. Once inside, soldiers quietly surrounded the tent and Bascom hardly waited past the greetings when he accused Cochise of the Ward kidnapping and demanded the return of the boy and the stock.

"We do not have them," said Cochise, through the interpreter.

"You have them alright," said Bascom, "and it will be well for your tribe to return them immediately."

Again Cochise responded. "My people do not know of a raid. We did not raid the ranch. We did not take cattle or the boy."

"That's not the truth," Bascom shot back.

Yellow Hand shook his head slowly. "That's the one thing you don't want to do with Cochise. You never want to accuse him of lying.

Cochise is very proud of making his word good. He is known for his sense of honor. Apaches hate liars."

In spite of this slight from a green-horn soldier, Cochise, suspecting the Coyoteros were responsible for the kidnapping, offered to travel to their village, maybe 100 miles away, and attempt to return Mickey Free. Bascom didn't understand that the Coyoteros were not obliged to do what a Chiricahua requested.

"Fine," said Lt. Bascom. "And all of you will remain here as my hostages, until the boy and the cattle are returned. You are under arrest." As that was interpreted Bascom motioned for his soldiers to move in on the Apaches.

Cochise reacted quickly and instinctively. Drawing his knife, he turned, cut a hole in the tent and escaped through the hole. His brother, Coyuntwa, was right behind him. Lt. Bascom yelled behind them. "Get him. Shoot him. Shoot them down." Cochise ran, pushing his way past soldiers as troopers fired fifty or more shots at him and wounded him slightly in the leg. Then he disappeared. His brother, Coyuntwa, stumbled and fell. Soldiers caught him and dragged him back to the tent where the others were captive.

Only hours later Cochise appeared at the crest of a hill overlooking the mail station. Mr. Culver, along with Wallace and a Mr. Welch, another worker at the station, climbed up the hill where Cochise stood.

"The pony soldiers have taken my family and friends", said Cochise, "I want them released."

"We'll see what we can do," said Mr. Culver, "but I caint promise nuthin."

"Then you," Cochise said pointing to Wallace, "will stay with us until my people are free."

Cochise's warriors took Wallace and walked him away. Welch and Culver walked back down the hill. While crawling over a corral railing, Welch was shot by a soldier who later said he thought the

Indians were sneaking up to attack. There would be no negotiating this day.

Bascom, sensing an attack from the Indians, moved his men from their camp back to the stagecoach station and its rock walls.

The next morning a meeting on neutral ground was arranged and the negotiations didn't go well. Cochise demanded the return of his relatives. Bascom demanded the return of Mickey Free and it was a stalemate. Not long after they parted company soldiers were exchanging gunfire with Apaches and both sides took casualties.

Again, Cochise tried to keep the peace. The next morning he brought Wallace, his arms tied to his side, to the crest of a hill, where he could be seen. He asked for his family back in exchange for the stage-driver.

"I'm not going to negotiate with Indians," fumed Lt. Bascom, "and I'm not going to exchange prisoners."

"Then what?" asked his Sergeant.

"Then we'll do what he have to do." said the Lieutenant.

Cochise upped the ante. He sent for reinforcement from the other bands, including Geronimo and Mangas Coloradas. When they arrived he sent them to attack a wagon train coming through Apache Pass. The wagons were burned, and two white men were taken captive. They were L.C. Jordan and Walter Lyons. Eight Mexicans, who were part of the wagon train, were hideously killed. They were tied to the wagon wheels upside down. Fires were built under their heads, boiling the brains and exploding their heads; a favorite method of slow death for a pissed-off Apache.

Near dark, on the same day, the East-bound stage reached the Apache Pass summit, and Indians, lying in ambush, fired on it. They hit the driver, King Lyon, in the leg and a passenger in the chest. And they wounded the lead mule. That stopped the coach.

The conductor was Mr. Culver's brother. He yelled at a passenger, "You, Buckley. Come with me." Culver jumped from the coach. Buckley was right behind him.

"Quick, we gotta cut the harness away from that mule, or we're all dead men."

They managed to get the harness off the lead mule.

"Jump aboard!" yelled Culver. "Drive, drive!"

King Lyon, leg bleeding, drove the stage full speed down the twisty, dusty trail to the station. There the civilians and soldiers remained in a state of siege.

Two days later, Cochise had Mr. Wallace placed in view of Bascom's men at the station. Then they removed him, leaving a stick in the ground with a message attached to it. A soldier was sent up the hill and brought back the message, written by Wallace, informing Lt. Bascom that Cochise now had three white captives to exchange for his people.

Meantime, Bascom had sent out riders headed for three destinations; to Tucson to ask the Overland Stage Company to send a stage coach to transport wounded passengers, to Fort Buchanan asking for medical aid and to Fort Breckenridge asking for reinforcements.

Cochise sent the women and children of his band deeper into the Chiricahua Mountains for safety. At night, as snow fell, Apaches danced the war dance.

Fort Buchanan immediately dispatched Surgeon Bernard Irwin and 15 mounted infantrymen to Apache Pass to treat the wounded. Fort Breckenridge sent two companies of mounted infantry.

Cochise struck February 8th. Warriors attacked a detachment of soldiers watering their horses at Apache Springs, wounded some of them and drove off all of Bascom's animals. Then he turned his attention to the soldiers holed up around the Overland Mail Station. It was clear that he would lose many warriors in an all-out attack and he got wind that Army reinforcements were on the way. Discretion being the better part of valor, Cochise pulled back and, leaving his family as Army hostages, he disengaged and left the area.

Surgeon Irwin's group travelled 65 miles in 24 hours fighting a running battle with Apaches for about seven miles. He arrived at Apache Pass on February 10th. The Breckenridge Dragoons arrived without incident four days later.

On February 15th the Dragoons rested. On the 16th they patrolled, but found no Indians. On the 17th they found Cochise's abandoned rancheria and set it afire. On the 18th they found the bodies. Mr. Wallace, Mr. Jordan and Mr. Lyons were full of holes from lances. They were mutilated almost to the point of being unrecognizable.

It may have been Surgeon Irwin who first suggested hanging the captive Indians in retaliation, but it was Lt. Bascom who did it. Yellow Hand paused, rubbed his forehead and continued, "His men marched all of the Chiricahaus to the area where they buried the Americans, and hanged them from Oak trees. Cochise lost his brother, two nephews and four warriors who were captured by the pony soldiers from Fort Breckinridge. They left them hanging from the trees. That is why Cochise hates the white eyes."

"But his wife is here," said Chatto.

"Yes. They did not hang his wife or children. Much time later they released them."

On his return to Fort Buchanan, Lt. Bascom was highly commended for his handling of the situation and shortly promoted to Captain. He would die in a Civil War battle in New Mexico one year later.

Mickey Free, the kidnapped kid, was never returned to his step father and mother. He was adopted and raised by a White Mountain Apache called Nayundiie to be a warrior. In 1872 he met the chief army scout, Albert Sieber, and joined the Apache scouts at Camp Verde. Within two years he was promoted to the rank of sergeant. Since he remembered English from his days in John Ward's home, he served as an interpreter.

Cochise, in a white-hot anger, led his warriors on a relentless campaign of terror that killed 150 whites within the first 60 days of the Bascom hangings. As Chatto was becoming a warrior, the death toll would grow to 5,000 or more in the next eleven years and leave southern Arizona a burned-out wasteland.

CHAPTER 10   Yankees and Rebs

In April, 1861, Union and Confederate forces fired the first shots of the Civil War at Fort Sumter, South Carolina. By early summer the conflict was forcing the United States to withdraw forces from the southwest territories. The Apaches noticed U.S. soldiers were not being seen as regularly. There didn't seem to be as many of them in the forts or on the wagon trails. As the fighting grew in the east, the nation ignored Arizona. Many of the Apaches thought they had won. They had driven out the pony soldiers. This meant they were free to attack miners, farmers and ranchers and they did so with gusto. They wanted to drive all the Anglos away from the land.

What Chatto's people had no way of knowing was the wealth, power and ambition of the United States. The white soldiers would be back, representing a culture that was bound to assimilate or eliminate any other that stood in its way.

The Apache had no real knowledge of the Americans who had whipped the British twice, the Spanish and Mexicans once, bought millions of acres from France and stood among the world powers. It had incorporated 33 states by 1860 spanning the continent from the Atlantic to the Pacific.

Geronimo described his first sight of white men when he noticed a small contingent surveying the land with some funny looking equipment. He said he rather liked them. But their government had pushed the Kickapoos out of Illinois, the Seminoles out of Florida and the Creeks out of the southeast. The "Indian Removal Act" of 1830 gave Americans a legal basis to uproot any tribe so that whites could take over their lands. And these curious surveyors seen by Geronimo were the first trickles in a flood of white men. The Americans had sent an expedition under Lewis and Clark across the continent to discover the wonders of the west. Within 25 years settlers were crossing the Oregon Trail to arrive on the Pacific Ocean.

The Americans had invented a way to remove seeds from cotton with a gin as far back as the 1700's. By 1803 they had categorized most chemicals and made a chart to understand them. They were using a Frenchman's, system to capture pictures on metal plates. Robert Fulton had invented the steamboat in 1807 and steam locomotives were chugging between Baltimore and Ohio by 1828. They dug a tremendous canal near Erie, New York, to open up eastern trade. Americans could talk to each other over long distances thanks to a telegraph invented by Samuel Morse in 1844. Within four years they could send their messages across the ocean by transatlantic cable. By 1851 they had a machine that would sew clothing better than the best Apache woman. They knew how to mass produce steel for rails, boats and weapons.

And of weapons, they had plenty. While the Apache was still fighting with bows, arrows, spears and clubs, the Americans had improved on European rifles with rifled barrels for accuracy, percussion caps for reliable ignition and breech-locks for easy and fast loading. In 1836 Samuel Colt invented his revolver. The Springfield Armory in Massachusetts debuted the Springfield rifle in the mid-1860's. It would be followed by Remington, Sharps, Browning, Winchester, Marlin, Henry and Smith and Wesson within the quarter century leading up to the Civil War. The Apaches didn't know these things. Their people didn't even have the wheel.

As the War Between the States heated up, the white people in southern Arizona declared themselves for the Confederacy and rebel troops began to occupy strategic points. In response, the Union raised a volunteer force of Californians to march the 900 miles through Arizona to recapture the territory and to reinforce the Union army in New Mexico. They built camps along the way and left men to garrison them. Now the Apaches had four enemies; The Rebels, the Yankees, the Mexicans and other Indians. If the U.S. or Confederate troops found Apaches along their route, they attacked. It was automatic.

Confederate Cavalry

In an early engagement the Confederates found an Apache camp at the foot of Mount Gray, New Mexico. Quietly the troops surrounded the camp and opened fire at day break. 250 Indians scattered into the hills as the soldiers burned their wickiups and all of their dried mescal and other foodstuffs.

The Apaches began stashing preserved foods, hides, blankets and weapons in caves and canyons along their travelled routes. Often they would place stone direction markers out on the trail, pointing out to warriors and their bands where to find sustenance.

The Apaches retaliated when they could. The Apaches, who were often outnumbered, preferred to move quietly under cover to the attack. Their ways were described years later by U.S. Army Captain, John Bourke. He wrote that Apaches were more effective when they attacked and scattered, than when they fought in groups. In his journals he wrote that Apaches were likely to attack in groups of two or three, sneaking up to military posts or other targets and waiting, sometimes for days, for the appropriate time. They were usually camouflaged with grasses, bodies rubbed with clay or sand. Then they would stampede a herd or kill a herder or two and preferably with an arrow so as to make no sound. They would be many miles away by the time a body was discovered.

Bourke had studied the Apaches closely. He said it was almost impossible to catch Apaches because of their skills and stamina. "He will dodge and twist and bend in all directions, boxing the compass, doubling back like a fox, scattering his party rather than moving in file and not, perhaps reuniting for miles." He said seventy-five miles a day was nothing for an Apache warrior. Their lungs were strong and their legs were sinewy and powerful. "He could strike a match on the bottom of his feet."

During the early Civil War years, the Apaches in New Mexico had it tougher than those in Arizona. New Mexico was a war zone where Union troops were successful fairly rapidly in driving the Confederates out. With nothing left to do, in order to keep soldiers occupied, the military commander, Major James H. Carleton turned his forces against the Apaches in a war of extermination.

Carleton seems to have been a rigid personality and a vicious enemy. His orders to subordinates, including Captain Kit Carson, were to locate the Indians, Mescaleros, Mimbrenos and Navajos, kill all the men and capture all the women and children.

With minor set-backs here and there, he decimated the tribes and sent 350 Mescaleros to the arid Bosque Redondo (Round Wood) area where Fort Sumner was being built, the place where Billy the Kid met his end. It was flat and dry, the water was alkaline and not fit to drink, wood was scarce, there was no hunting allowed and sparse rations. Carlton ordered that any Indian trying to escape would be shot on sight.

With the reluctant but brutal subjugation of the Navajos, by Kit Carson, Carlton ordered 8,000 of these traditional Apache enemies on "The Long Walk" to the Bosque Redondo also. It was an eighteen-day, 300-mile death march ordered by the army, during which 500 ill-clothed and starving Navajos died, struggling across the desert. It combined, on one reservation, peoples who hated each other and destroyed each other's crops, stole their horses and killed one another with abandon.

Carleton was so cruel and strict with the Indians that the Indian Commissioner for the State, Dr. Michael Steck and a federal judge, Joseph Knapp, argued that it was cheaper to feed the Indians than to kill them, and that the policy of annihilation resulted in continued violence. They called upon Carleton to loosen up and when he refused, because he was the virtual dictator of New Mexico, they went to Washington D.C. to seek relief.

Nearing war's end, with New Mexico suffering one of its worst years due to unfavorable weather, plant diseases, insects destroying crops and the Mescalero's dying from starvation and illness, they began to sneak away in small then larger groups to return to their mountains. They preferred to starve at home, or be gunned down on the way, than to stay at the horrible Bosque Redondo. For once, the army didn't chase them. By now Steck and Judge Knapp's complaints had set off an investigation that confirmed their charges that the Fort Sumner reservation could not sustain an Indian population. Soon Carleton was transferred to another theatre or all the Mescaleros could have perished.

CHAPTER 11   Tubac

Yellow Hand rubbed his hands together and settled in before the blazing campfire. Tonight he was telling of the attack at the Presidio of Tubac in 1861.

"We saw Confederate troops at the Presidio. We were 200 strong and we ran circles around them. There were Mexican bandits on the other side of the fortress. Many whites ran away while the moon was high, and we burned Tubac. The flames could be seen many miles. The next day or two, some settlers whose houses burned, left." These settlers became known as the Ake party; 24 men, 16 women and seven children.

"When they were trying to escape to the Rio Grande," Yellow Hand recalled, "we had 100 Apaches. They were in seven wagons and two buggies and driving 400 head of cattle, 900 sheep and horses and goats."

"Was my father there?" asked an attentive Chatto.

"Yes. And he fought bravely. The white eyes circled their wagons at Cooke's Canyon. The fight started. We fought hard. They fought hard and they had repeating rifles. All day, till the sun went away we battled. We killed four men and wounded eight. We took all their cattle and sheep and herded them away." The old man chuckled to himself and watched the smoke rise. "Now go get sleep. Tomorrow maybe I will tell you more."

Most likely Chatto didn't hear that Confederate soldiers got the livestock back. In fact, the soldiers took up the chase, knowing the Apaches could not travel fast with so many cattle and sheep. They caught up in the Florida Mountains, just south of Deming, New Mexico and less than 20 miles from the Mexican border, and attacked. In a running fight eight of the Apaches were killed and the livestock was recovered. The bodies of the warriors, in Apache tradition, were partially wrapped and deposited in cavities created by the removal of rocks or trees. They would not be mentioned again, for the Apache did not speak of the dead.

Many stories were told of Cooke's Canyon. This was one of several deep mountain passes or canyons that were ideal spots to ambush any party trying to get through. Cooke's Canyon, was the best pass on the trail from Las Cruces, New Mexico to Tucson, Arizona. It became littered with the bones and skulls of settlers, Mexican herdsmen and travelers, many of whom had been killed, mutilated and left scattered all over the floor of the canyon.

There were dozens of stories like this. Chatto and his friends could hardly wait for the chance to ride with the men, which they could do at 14 or earlier if called upon. Meantime they listened and learned of the Apache way.

CHAPTER 12   Love

For Chatto, not all was war games and hunting. As a youngster, Chatto's eye was caught by a young girl, Ishchosen, perhaps two years younger than he. Trying to impress the young maiden on one occasion, he almost broke his leg jumping off a running horse. However she didn't seem that impressed and his courtship was not going well. He talked to old Amarillas about it.

"Yes, I have seen her," said the grey-haired story-teller. "And I have seen you. Why do you pull her hair? Why do you push her and throw rocks at her?"

"I need to show her my strength," reasoned the youngster.

"That is not strength. It is weakness. You do not treat women that way." Yellow Hand shook his head. "Watch your father. Watch your chief, Cochise. They receive much respect from their women because they give respect. You need to learn."

Chatto followed the advice and watched the warriors. Apache men went to live with the families of their wives. That's why his Bedonkohe father brought him here to live with the Chokonens. Their mother-in-laws were powerful influences. A man never spoke to his mother-in-law. It was the tradition. It was true, his mother and the wives of Cochise obeyed their men out of respect and love. Their lives were hard because they did much of the physical labor around the village; skinning, tanning, grinding, cooking, erecting lodges and tearing them down again, packing, caring for the children and pleasing their men. Chatto came to a conclusion; he would have his woman obey him out of respect and everyone else follow him out of fear. That seemed like a plan.

Mescalero Puberty Rite, painting by Rudolph Treas 1930-1969

When Ishchosen was 12, the tribe held puberty rites for her and other young girls and Chatto believed she was the most desirable female in the tribe. The puberty rite which lasted four days was of great importance in Apache society; essential to a girl's vitality. It strengthened her ability to bear healthy children. Chatto enjoyed the special foods set out for many friends and relatives. He watched the wickiup from afar when he knew Ishchosen was being bathed by the women and dressed in decorated clothing with bright beads and fringe. He listened intently as a tribal singer sang to her at her wickiup, and wished he could see her perform the ritual dance. At night he and other masked dancers came and were joined by other men and women dancing together. This continued for four days and nights. The puberty rite was so important that Apaches escaping army troops would still stop for the ceremony. Though many Apache men had two, three or four wives, Chatto only wanted one; Ishchosen.

CHAPTER 13   Pinos Altos

While the U.S. Army was away fighting at such places as Bull Run and Fredericksburg, Apaches had a field day driving miners and settlers back. And the campfire stories came thick and fast. One of the largest attacks was at Pinos Altos, where, earlier, Mangas Coloradas had been flogged so severely.

Pinos Altos straddles the Continental Divide at 7,080 feet. Only six miles from Silver City, it is 2000 feet higher in elevation. From here you can see to the horizon and it's easy to see why it was a sacred place to the Chiricahua. The Battle of Pinos Altos happened on Sept 27, 1861.

Infuriated by the discovery of gold at Pinos Altos and the influx of miners and Confederate soldiers on their sacred land, Mangas Coloradas and Cochise attacked the town in force with 300 warriors. But Pinos Altos had formed two militia companies; the Arizona Guards and the Minute Men, just for this purpose.

The assault completely surprised the town's population. Many miners, at their camp, were trapped in their diggings and subsequently killed. Some survivors stayed underground, too afraid to venture out, thus contributing nothing to the town's defense. The Arizona Guards and the Chiricahua battled at long range till about noon, then the Indians came running in, trying to set fire to cabins and buildings and fighting miners hand to hand.

Captain Tom Mastin ordered his Arizona Guards to retreat and set up a defensive line in the center of town. There, Mastin saw an old cannon, used for decoration in front of Roy Bean's store, and ordered his men to roll it out. They stuffed it with nails and other debris and fired it at the groups of Apaches directly ahead. Many natives went down wounded and dying. The others stopped, and then retreated. Mastin had saved the day, but lost his life in the process, cut down by an Apache bullet.

Confederate troopers mounted up and chased the Apaches, but the Indians disappeared like so much smoke.   Pinos Altos taught the Apaches that having pitched battles with opponents, who possessed cannon, was not a good idea. After the Battle of Pinos Altos, the Apaches changed tactics. They reverted, almost exclusively, to guerilla war.

Today there is little left: two main streets and maybe 75 standing buildings, most of which cannot be seen through the thick timber. The "historic tour" takes you over a dirt road past old abandoned cars, a few foundations, piles of trash and old houses where weeds have hidden the fences. There's a re-built saloon, still serving meals and the old opera house, both the worse for wear, a small gift shop and museum that was once a school, and a three-quarter scale replica of Fort Webster. Still, the place reeks of history.

CHAPTER 14 Apache Pass

It was almost Chatto's time to ride with the great chieftain, Cochise. And there were momentous actions taking place as he trained and waited and while Cochise retaliated for the Bascom Affair.

Confederate soldiers occupied southern Arizona and their captain, Sherod Hunter issued orders to lure the Apaches into peace talks and exterminate the adults. The order was never enforced. Hunter's men found themselves too busy skirmishing with Union troops. Still, the Apaches were caught in the middle on occasion.

The home of the Chokonens, the Dragoon Mountains, is approached by vast flat-lands that look like barren desert, but grow Mescal, Spanish Bayonet, Palo Verde, Cholla, Nopal, Mesquite and Pitahaya…called the candelabrum cactus which attains great heights. Cochise took 100 warriors to the Dragoon Springs to ambush a detachment of Confederate troops that had ridden out of Tucson to forage and round up some stray cattle. Cochise found them in a small valley and his warriors rained arrows and rifle shots on them. Four Confederate soldiers died and were buried near the Dragoon Springs stage station, where they remain today in the little graveyard near the ruins of the station. The Apaches took their horses and cattle.

Dragoon Mountains; Cochise Stronghold, Authors Photo

Only a few days later Captain Hunter ordered his men to get revenge and get back the captured herd of cattle and horses. This was known as the Second Battle of Dragoon Springs. The Confederates succeeded, recapturing most of the stolen animals and killing five of Cochise's warriors for no loss of their own.

This was followed one month later by the Battle of Apache Pass, July 15, 1862. This time it was Union troops commanded by Col. James Henry Carleton. They were trying to find and engage Confederate soldiers reported at the pass in the Chiricahua Mountains. Instead, he found Mangas Coloradas and Cochise with 500 Apache warriors protecting the critical watering hole. It became one of the largest battles ever between Americans and the Chiricahuas.

Tired, low on water and realizing a retreat would cost many men, the Yanks chose to fight. Apaches were behind almost every mesquite tree and boulder and they made it hot for the Americans. Private John Teal was holding off the Apaches in his sector almost single-handedly with his carbine. It was he who apparently fired the bullet that hit Mangas Coloradas as the chieftain was about to kill a cavalry scout. The bullet hit Coloradas in the chest, wounding him.

The Yankees would probably have been wiped out if they had not brought artillery with them. They retreated to the mouth of the pass, regrouped and brought their field pieces into play. Many Apaches had not seen artillery before. It spooked them. They held their positions until nightfall, then fled. With all the shooting, it was surprising that only two soldiers were killed and three wounded. The Apaches lost ten. The Chiricahua rode all the way to Janos, Mexico, with the wounded Mangas Coloradas and there forced a Mexican doctor to cut the bullet out.

U.S. Fieldpiece at Fort Bowie Visitor Center, Author's photo

The army's main column reached the Apache Pass mail station about 10 days after the battle. Realizing the importance of the pass and its water supply, the army started building up its defenses right away. The U.S. Army started construction of what was to become Fort Bowie. The springs there were the only reliable source of water for 50 miles in any direction. Building of a wall which surrounded tents started in July 1862 on a hill overlooking the springs and the site of the battle. It was named for the California Regiment's commanding officer, Col. George Washington Bowie. Over the next six years the army expanded the fort on a flat plateau 300 yards away and erected not less than 35 stone and adobe buildings to serve as the nerve center for the military campaigns against the Chiricahuas.

Today, you can travel, as I did, on the dirt and paved Apache Pass Road between the Dos Cabezos and Chiricahua Mountains and find a parking strip and trail head. It's only a mile or two hike on a maintained trail down to the creek, amid cottonwoods, tough evergreens, brittlebush and prickly pear to the site of the battle, the ruins of the old Butterfield station, a small graveyard and then uphill to the first fort site. In a meadow-like setting lie the ruins of walls and foundations and a small tourist center filled with artifacts and displays explained by friendly U.S. Park rangers. You touch a stone wall and wonder if Geronimo touched the same stone almost 130 years ago.

Ruins at Fort Bowie, Author's photo

In January 1863, Coloradas had recovered from his chest wound when gold miners in Pinos Altos asked him to come into town and talk peace. He should have known better. Instead, they grabbed him and took him to Fort McLane and General Joseph Rodman West of the California Militia, whose standing orders were: "Punish the Gila Apaches, under that notorious robber, Mangas Colorado."

Coloradas walked directly to Brigadier General West.

"I have come. Where will we talk?"

"I'll tell you where we'll talk, Chief," snapped the General. "Okay, men."

Soldiers with rifles immediately surrounded Coloradas and clapped manacles on his legs and wrists. He was hustled into a wooden hut.

General West walked away, telling his Sergeant, "I want that Injun dead."

Very soon soldiers heated bayonets in a fire and entered the hut.

"How do you like this, you red bastard?" said the Sergeant. With that he applied the hot bayonet to Coloradas' legs. Others followed in turn.

Coloradas writhed in pain and smelled of his own seared flesh. Rising to confront the soldiers he yelled, "I am no child to be toyed with!" They were his last words.

Two soldiers shot him at point-blank range. Coloradas slumped to the floor. The soldiers took out their pistols and each put a bullet through his head.

Soldiers then decapitated Mangas Coloradas, boiled the flesh from his head and sent the skull to the Smithsonian Institute. Word of the events went almost immediately to the Apache village and the place went crazy. The death was one thing; the mutilation of his body was another, because Apaches go through the after-life the way they were at death. Chatto, shocked and saddened, mourned his uncle for thirty days as was the tradition. Cochise and Geronimo plotted their revenge.

CHAPTER 15   The Warrior Chatto

Chatto's father Culto, or Jose Mangas, died sometime after 1857. He had been blamed for burning a ranch house in the Sonoita Valley and killing the owner, a William Wordsworth. He was also part of the Apache ambush of the Ake party coming out of Tucson and going through Cookes Canyon. He could have been one of the eight Apaches killed there.

At the death of his father, Chatto would have followed tradition. His father's wickiup was burned. The women would have dressed the deceased in his best clothes, painted his face and wrapped him in a colorful blanket. His horse would be saddled and a funeral procession be made to a secret place of burial with family carrying his armaments out in front with the horse trailing behind while the people sang of his deeds of valor. The body would have been deposited in a cave or another hidden place. The horse would have been killed and his property burned. Thereafter little would be said of him as a sign of respect and for fear his ghost would return. Every effort was made to erase the memory of the dead Apache. His name would not be spoken.

After Chatto's father died, the 52 year-old Cochise became a father figure to him. Chatto was binding a flint arrowhead to a shaft with deer sinew when Cochise approached him.

"We have lost many warriors fighting the Californios at Gray Mountain two months ago and at Doubtful Canyon last month. We have buried 31 brave men and 20 more are wounded. You are becoming a man. One day you will be a chief if you are strong. You have strong medicine. It is time for you to ride with the men"

Chatto swallowed hard. He was not yet 12 years old. "I want to be a chief."

Cochise continued "I promise, you will, but you must build your courage and endurance. Tomorrow we ride to Fort Buchanan. It is small, only a few buildings, but we will destroy it. You will ride far to the rear with old Yellow Hand. You will do whatever he tells you.

If there is trouble, you will turn and ride swiftly to camp." With that he turned and walked away.

The next day Cochise attacked the U.S. Army post at Fort Buchanan in Southern Arizona. It was February 7, 1865. Chatto rode at the back of the party, being covered with dust. His job was to act as a servant and do anything the warriors wanted done. It was the first step in his apprenticeship which, to the Apaches, was a formal procedure.

The Battle of Fort Buchanan was really a small skirmish. The outpost, at that time, only had about 9 men. Two of them were out surveying, two were cutting hay and another was hunting. That left only Corporal Michael Buckley and three privates to hold down the fort. Fort Buchanan wasn't much of a fort. It didn't have walls and was just a collection of adobe buildings. It was one small link in the U.S. Government's initiative to round up all the Apaches in Arizona and New Mexico and stick them on reservations. It was just another target in Cochise's campaign to retaliate for the Bascom affair.

Chatto was in the rear, as instructed, but saw the action start twelve miles from the Fort. He watched as the Chiricahuas spotted, ran down and killed the two surveyors and a Mexican boy with hatchets. Then Cochise's warriors moved closer to the Fort and Chatto watched as they sneaked up on Corporal Buckley sitting on the porch of a cabin. A warrior shot, but it was badly aimed and hit Buckley in the hip. Buckley was able to draw his pistol and he killed the sniper. Chatto moved closer and saw the soldier duck inside the cabin. 75 other Apaches surrounded the building and a soldier fired from a window, killing another of his tribesmen. In his first few hours of raiding he had seen five human beings die violently. He felt slightly sick at his stomach, but he also felt an exhilaration he couldn't explain. Firing through port holes, the Americans managed to push the Indians back. Yellow Hand yelled at Chatto, "Keep your head down!" Chatto couldn't. He watched warriors set fire to the building. Pretty soon the roof was caving in. Inside, Corporal Buckley ordered his men to charge through the fire and the enemy and run for the hills. Apaches chased them as they fired wildly.

"Let me go!" begged Chatto.

Yellow Hand held his hand up. "No," he said in a strong voice, "You stay. You will have your chance. Today, you stay with me."

The warriors eventually gave up the chase. Buckley and his men marched on foot to army camps near Santa Ritas Mountain and safety. Private George English, the soldier that was hunting before the attack, was never heard from again. The hay cutters responded to the sound of shots at the fort, but laid low when they spotted Apaches looting and burning the buildings. They too walked to Santa Ritas. Later, the army proudly pointed out that Fort Buchanan was the only American military post conquered by Indians during the war against the Chiricahua. Chatto had heard, at the campfires, what it was like. Now he had his first taste of the things of which stories are made. For the next four raids, Chatto worked his fingers to the bone, cutting and packing firewood, boiling water, brushing trails left by the horses, repairing broken weapons, doing every chore the warriors wanted done.

He was a true apprentice beginning the four raids that could lead to warrior status. Why four times? It was a magic number to the Apaches. The first time out Chatto worked hard to meet the demands of the warriors and ate the most inferior food. He was not expected to complain about it. Through the second and third expeditions he was a servant, cooking food, tending to the horses, retrieving anything the party wanted. He did not speak unless spoken to. And he learned all the sacred names for everything pertaining to war because war was a religious experience. After the fourth time out, if he was brave and had shown courage the council would vote whether he could become a warrior. Even one vote to the contrary would send him back for more training. He would be a lowly warrior at first and would not achieve higher rank until he proved worthy.

Under the tutelage of Yellow Hand and other older men, if he performed his assigned chores well, he could become not only a warrior, but a man who could take a wife. He found an Agave with a long stem and cut it and honed it for a new lance. He split the upper shaft and fit a small knife into the slit, binding it with horse-hide. He took the intestine from a horse Yellow Hand had butchered and made a water bag from it. It would hold two gallons of water; enough to last for days but not too much to weigh him down. He fashioned additional arrows for his quiver and made a good club from a Mesquite limb. Soon he entered full-fledged into the world of raiding, capturing cattle, shooting at whites and Mexicans. He became proficient.

After his seventh raid with Cochise, the chief summoned Chatto to his wickiup. There, the great chieftain handed Chatto his first rifle, which had been taken from a stagecoach outrider. It was a Winchester Model 1866, which fired the same .44 caliber rim fire cartridge as the Henry rifles carried by many warriors.

"Here are ten bullets," said Cochise. "Use five of them to practice firing and hitting a small target. Save the other five to get more bullets." With that, the chief tapped Chatto on the shoulder and pointed him to the tent flap.

Chatto aimed down the rifle barrel. He fired off imaginary bullets, "Pyoo Pyoo!" He rubbed the rifle clean and shined the wooden stock. He carried it with him as if it were a baby. He slept with it.

The band went to Sonora for a series of horse and cattle raids in February. Chatto packed his Winchester along and looked for the opportunity to use it. It happened when a unit of Mexican troops attacked the Apaches. Chatto snapped off two shots, hitting nothing and then escaped into the hills with all except for his brother Gonaltsis.

Gonaltsis was captured by the Mexican troops and led away tied up in ropes. Geronimo, who had the power to see into the future, said not to worry, Gonaltsis would return. And he did. After living for a time as a servant to a Mexican family in Chihuahua City, where they named him Patricio, Gonaltsis escaped and made his way into the Sierra Madre Mountains, home of the Nednhi band. With semi-frequent visitation between the Chokonen and the Nednhi, it wasn't a long time before the boy was returned to his band. Chatto had not known before how much he would miss his brother.

When the Civil War was over many soldiers and officers returned to the west, or entered it for the first time for a chance to make good or get rich. The only battles available for officers seeking promotion were against Indians. The Army built new forts in the Southwest and Union Generals like William Tecumseh Sherman, now Commanding General of the U.S. Army and Philip Sheridan, Commandant of the Department of the Missouri, began a program of total war against the Indians such as had been visited so brutally on the populations of Georgia and South Carolina.

Winter campaigning, destroying homes, livestock and stored supplies was one of the strategies that came out of the Civil War; a concept of total war invented or advocated by Generals Sherman and Sheridan. It was said of Sherman that his "entire life—and success—had been built upon the uncompromising use of force." To him was attributed the words, "Indians are a class of savage" who will soon "be displaced by the irresistible progress of our race."

General Philip Sheridan, now Commandant of the Division of the Missouri, which had oversight over most of the Indian campaigns in the west had helped conceive the strategy. It was a cruel strategy, aimed at women and children as much as warriors. Sheridan was known for his barbarity in carrying it out.

By 1866 many of the Apaches had been rounded up by the army. Chatto's Chiricahuas were too wiley for easy capture. And they could escape into Mexico any time U.S. troops got too close. Still, Chatto knew his tribe was wasting away from the killing and captures.

CHAPTER 16   Camp Grant Massacre

It was one of the worst crimes by whites in the history of Arizona. In February, 1871, five elderly Apache women walked into Camp Grant, a hot and bleak collection of adobe huts run by First Lieutenant Royal Whitman. It sat on the San Pedro River, only a few miles south of the confluence with the Gila River. The squaws asked about relatives who had been captured. Whitman, in spite of his reputation as a drunkard and loudmouth, treated them kindly and, before long, other Apaches from Chief Eskiminzin's band of Aravaipa Apaches, who wanted to live peacefully, and some Pinal bands were camping near the post and receiving rations of beef and flour. A substantial tribal camp built up. The Indians helped local farmers in their wheat and barley fields.

But not all the local farmers were friendly and the people in Tucson, with a long history of fighting Apaches, were down-right hostile. Whitman urged the Apaches to move along, maybe to the White Mountains. Their chief said, "No, that's not our kind of place, we know how to live in this territory, make our mescal, tend our cattle."

The Tucson townsfolk blamed every depredation in the territory on Apaches and two of them, William Oury and Jesus Elias, formed "The Committee for Public Safety" specifically to exterminate Apaches. They soon got their excuse to strike. When Apaches ran off some horses in early April, the Committee collected arms and ammunition from folks around town; they recruited nearly 100 Indians from the O'odham tribe and 48 or more Mexicans, and set off for the Aravaipa encampment.

When they got there, most of the Apache men were gone, out hunting in the mountains miles away. As the early morning darkness lifted, O'odham warriors leaped to the attack, stabbing, shooting, smashing heads with rocks, raping women and killing children. Members of the Public Safety Committee and the Mexicans stayed outside the village, picking off any Apache who tried to escape the carnage.

When Lt. Whitman was called to the scene, all he found was devastation. Wickiups were still burning; the ground was covered with bodies. All but eight of the corpses were women and children. Twenty-nine children were gone; captured to be sold into slavery in Mexico. A total of 144 Western Apaches had been killed and mutilated, nearly all of them scalped. The army buried the dead then sent interpreters into the mountains to tell peaceful Apache men, the husbands and fathers, that soldiers had not participated in the "vile transaction." It was no solace. It was their reward for being at peace with the Americans. Word reached Chatto's band within one day. The Chokonen were stunned and angry.

The eastern press made headlines of the massacre. President Grant got angry too. He wired Governor A.P.K. Safford, "If the perpetrators are not arrested and brought to trial, I will place Arizona under martial law." Going beyond his warning to Arizona residents, the outraged President, who thought his post Civil War peace policy would avoid this kind of violence, sent a peace commission to Arizona. It was led by General Oliver Howard and Indian Commissioner Vincent Coyler with instructions to establish a reservation system for Apaches and to work on a treaty with the Chiricahuas specifically. By the fall of 1872, they had designated five agencies—three in Arizona and two in New Mexico, and contacted many of the bands, most of whom agreed to resettle in exchange for regular food and supplies. And President Grant sent for his best Indian fighter, George Crook.

In October 1871, a Tucson grand jury indicted 100 of the assailants at Camp Grant on 108 counts of murder. Defendant William Oury told people it was "the killing of about 144 of the most bloodthirsty devils that ever disgraced mother earth." Most of the citizens agreed with him. The trial, two months later, focused almost entirely on Apache depravations; it took the jury just 19 minutes to reach a verdict of not guilty, and Tucson celebrated into the night. 144 murders; not guilty.

CHAPTER 17   Lupan Nantan

As the United States began to re-take the Wild West after the Civil War, the standing orders were to get the Indians onto reservations or kill them. Lt. Colonel George Crook was good at killing Indians. The Apache would call him Lupan Nantan-The Tan Wolf. He had begun fighting Indians fresh out of West Point, starting in California and Oregon. As a young lieutenant in the Northwest, he received his first experience with natives. He fought hard, but was disturbed at how the Indians were betrayed when the US Senate rejected 18 negotiated treaties, leaving them with no rights. It burned within him. General Sherman would later call General Crook the greatest Indian fighter in the history of the U.S. Army. He was also one of their best known advocates.

General George Crook, War Dept: Office of Chief Signal Officer

Crook established his credentials in the Civil War; at Bull Run, Antietam and Chickamaugua. In Grant's spring campaign of 1864,

Crook was an integral part of the push into the Deep South, initially moving to attack railroads and supplies between Virginia and Tennessee. After pitched battles at Cloyd's Mountain and New River Bridge, his forces joined in the Shenandoah campaign under General Phil Sheridan. He came out of the war with the rank of Major General and reverted to the regular rank of Major after the war.

Then, he returned to the Indian wars, against the Paiutes in the Northwest. Here, he started using Indian scouts to stalk Indians. He also noticed that the Northern Paiute used the fall, winter and spring seasons to gather food, so he adopted the tactic of attacking during the winter. Crook successfully waged a two-year campaign against the Snake Indians in the 1864-68 Snake War, where he won nationwide recognition. He was promoted to Lt. Colonel.

Meantime, in Arizona and New Mexico, the Apaches had been running amok. There had been recent violent incidents between the Yavapai and soldiers and settlers near Prescott, Tombstone, and Tucson and the death toll was rising. The Army needed help.

Now, in 1871, by-passing other officers, like the ambitious Nelson Miles, who wanted the post in the worst way, President U.S. Grant chose George Crook to head up the Department of Arizona and get the raiding Apaches onto reservations. He also gave Crook an extraordinary promotion from Lt. Colonel to Brigadier General, angering a number of full colonels next in line. He was to move, first, against the Western Apaches.

Crook was tall, athletic, sinewy and eccentric. He wore his hair close-cropped and parted his beard in the middle of his chin. He rode around on a mule named "Apache" wearing a pith helmet and an old canvas hunting outfit, just in case he wanted to hunt. He always wanted to hunt. He hunted endlessly. His men liked serving under him. He commanded by example. He was willing to negotiate rather than fight. If he had to fight, he fought hard.

Crook with his mule "Apache"

Crook's plan for the Yavapai and Western Apaches (Cibeque, Tontos, San Carlos, White Mountain) was to surround them with troops from several forts and then tighten the noose. This was going to be different than fighting Indians on the plains. The actions would be smaller, intense killing patrols in the high and dry mountains where water was scarce, the trails steep and narrow and the danger substantial.

On extended field trips, Crook took the time to try to understand the enemy and to have the enemy understand there was no place it could hide. He spread the word that the Apaches had about two-and-a half months to get onto reservations or he was coming after them. His Aide-de-camp Captain Bourke said, "There never was an officer so completely in accord with all the ideas, views, and opinions of the savages whom he had to fight or control. In time of campaign this knowledge placed him, as it were, in the secret councils of the enemy."

One of the first things General Crook did was start recruiting Apache scouts. He said "You need Apaches to find Apaches." He didn't have much trouble. Apaches were not a unified nation. Many tribes warred against each other, some hated the white man, others made peace, some had inter-tribal rivalries, and others had personal reasons for siding with the soldiers. All had considerable skills tracking down other Apaches. To most of the Apaches, the scouts were turncoats; traitors to be killed along with the pony soldiers. Crook appointed a German-born veteran, a prospector and rancher named Albert Sieber as Chief of Scouts. Sieber was stern with his scouts. If they got out of line he would kill them. But, he said, he always let them know he would kill them and that was fair.

Within a few days of assuming command in Tucson, Crook launched a 675-mile expedition into enemy territory. By the end of the year Crook had nine columns in the field; three from a camp near Prescott, two from Camp Date Creek, two from Camp Verde and others from Camps Apache, Grant and Fort McDowell. Crook told his forces to concentrate on subduing the Indians, not just on killing them. The troops destroyed weapons, clothing and food supplies. They confiscated or burned stores of cornmeal, dried meat, wild seeds and mescal. They forced the Indians out of the desert and onto higher, colder ground. Starvation and cold decimated the Indians.

Chatto was miles away and 17 years old when Crook took command. Little did he know that the two of them, mortal enemies at the start, would develop a friendship and call upon one another for help. His thoughts were far away from conflict with the white-eyes. Sometime after her puberty rites, the father and mother of Ishchosen presented her for her debut at the tribal love dance, a special time for young couples to pair-up. She was the sister of Martine, his boyhood friend and now a full-fledged warrior like him. This was Chatto's chance to seek her hand in marriage.

The dance would be held on the first full moon in a grassy meadow and continue for two days and nights and the whole village would be there. The chiefs came out to lead the singing. Ishchosen danced once around the campfire in the enclosure. Another eligible woman joined her on the second lap around the fire…then three on the third time around and then four women danced four times around. Behind them came the medicine men, stripped to the waist, with bodies brightly painted and dancing the sacred dances. More Apaches were joining the dance, funny dancers who delighted the crowd, then many tribesmen who linked hands and danced the circle around the campfire. After the old people tired, the young people took over and the Lover's Dance began.

Chatto stood in the middle of the circle with other warriors and Ishchosen was dancing with another maiden. The women were dancing two-by-two and the men followed their movements dancing forward to the center then back again. Chatto couldn't take his eyes off Ishchosen. They danced like this for two hours. Then the drum beat was increased and the warriors gathered at the center of the circle. It was time for the women to choose the man with whom they wanted to dance. Chatto held his breath and Ishchosen danced to him and they danced until daylight. At the end Chatto and the warriors gave gifts to the girls with whom they danced. Chatto's was a pair of beaded moccasins. Now Chatto knew he could talk to her father and make a bargain for her.

Captain Bourke reported that, at that time, for some reason, the Chiricahua had been specially exempted from General Crook's jurisdiction and he did not include them in his plans for the reduction of the other bands. Perhaps this was because the President was sending General Howard to the Chiricahuas to arrange a separate peace.

During the Western campaign, Crook went into the heart of Apache country to confer with as many chiefs as would come. That included Chiricahua country at Camp Bowie in Apache Pass. There, he called all the chieftains to a conference. Cochise was there, along with other powerful band leaders.

With the assent of the other chiefs, Cochise told General Crook, "We are at peace. We want to stay at peace. But there are many bad white-eyes who want to kill Apache"

Crook nodded. "The United States will protect the Apaches from bad white men. You must protect good white men from bad Indians."

The chiefs grunted their understanding.

Crook continued, "But I cannot, the Army cannot, protect you if the tribes continue raiding and killing people. You must know the

Indians can no longer live by raiding or on wild game. It is disappearing. Your people will be best off by seeking the safety of a reservation set aside for you and into which no white man can go without permission."

The chiefs looked to one-another looking for their reaction. It was stoic.

"We will help you," said General Crook. "The whites have many things to teach you. You can adopt the ways of the whites. You can farm and produce things people want to buy. I will work with you to find work and markets for your products. You will have a good life for your people. No more killing and being killed."

Geronimo piped up. "My people have killed Americans and Mexicans and taken their property. Their losses have been greater than mine. I have killed ten white men for every Indian slain, but I know that the whites are many and the Indians are few. Apaches are growing less every day."

In the days after the meeting with the white general, Chatto, Gonaltsis and others their age stayed close enough to the council fires to hear the elders discussing the general's message. Some were tired of chasing and being chased. They thought the idea of receiving free food and supplies was a good one in return for not raiding. More were suspicious. They said too many times the white man said one thing and did another and often at the cost of many lives. Chatto thought it was best not to trust the white-eyes and he saw nothing wrong with the way he was living right now.

CHAPTER 18   Slaughter at Salt River

When Chatto went to the father and mother of Ishchosen to offer ponies for her hand in marriage, He got a surprise proposition.

Her father said, "Ishchosen is not ready to marry now, but her older cousin who lives with us would be a good wife. If you will marry Nalthchedah first, then in one year or two, you can marry Ishchosen and you will only need to bring six ponies."

Chatto went away thinking about this. Nalthchedah was not bad looking and she was strong. She was the one dancing with Ishchosen at the lover dance. She was tall and statuesque and somewhat quiet, which was a good thing in a wife. What he really wanted was to marry Ishchosen. But he also needed the work and help from a wife. If marrying Nalthchedah was a condition of getting Ishchosen for his own, he would meet it. He married Nalthchedah.

It was a mistake from the get-go. After the couple had consummated the relationship and moved in to their own wickiup near Ishchosen's parents and learned many of the good things they liked about each other, then they started learning the bad things that drove both of them crazy. She thought he was too authoritarian. He thought she was too silent. She thought he was too driven. He thought she was too lazy. He wanted her as a servant. She wanted to be treated as a princess. He sometimes acted like a bully. She retreated and became unresponsive. Neither of them was very good at compromise. It was not what Chatto had envisioned, but he made up his mind to stick it out and put his best face forward for Ishchosen's parents to see.

Miles away, as expected, General Crook sent out massed troopers to put down the Western Apaches. He told subordinates the only way to control the Apache was to ferret them out in every hole and hiding place. One mission was to go after Yavapai Indians who had stolen horses near the village of Phoenix. It resulted in one of the incidents historians refer to in describing the violence of the so-called Yavapai War.

It was late fall in 1872. 220 men from the 5th U.S. Cavalry were under the command of Major William Brown. They camped at the base of the Superstition Mountains where an Apache Scout, Nantaje, told them of a secret cave in the Salt River Canyon where Indians sometimes hid. At daybreak, he led them to the trail down the side of the 1,200 foot canyon. The scout spotted the stolen horses, which meant the Indians were nearby. Brown sent his best sharpshooters to the top of the mesa on the edge of the chasm. He sent his other hundred men down the secret trail. Sneaking along, they could soon hear Apaches singing, laughing and apparently celebrating their raid, surrounded by sheer cliffs.

The sharpshooters edged closer, positioned themselves so that several could put warriors in their rifle sights and then they cut loose. Six Apaches went down. Others rushed into the recesses of the cave. Brown rushed 40 troopers to the front just as the Apaches started shooting back.

Maybe it's true, maybe not. Brown's after-action report said that he ordered a cease-fire and called on the Apaches to surrender. They yelled back at him, "You are a dead man, Tomorrow the buzzards will be eating you," words to that effect.

Brown argued back, "Send your women and children out. They will not be harmed." His answer came in the form of bullets. The soldiers fired back, but with both sides well sheltered, it was an impasse.

Then someone noticed that the roof of the shallow cave sloped downward toward the back. Brown ordered the soldiers to fire at the roof of the cave just above the mouth. A torrent of bullets splattered deep into the cave and the soldiers could hear the cries of wounded, frightened Indians, including women and children. The Apaches rushed forward to crouch behind a natural stone parapet, but still the ricocheting, shattering slugs were hitting them. Momentarily Brown stopped the shooting and called again for them to surrender.

A wailing chant rose from the cave and Nantaje said, "It is the death song; look out—here they come." About 20 warriors leaped up onto the rock parapet, firing rapidly. Half of them burst out the far side of the parapet and made for the tumbled rocks. Then the second line of soldiers opened fire, killing six or seven of the running men and driving the others back. Brown ordered his men to lay the heaviest possible fire against the cave roof and then prepare to charge.

Just about then other soldiers up on the crest of the mesa, directly above the cave, could see the Indians huddled inside. They started rolling boulders down on the Indians. Those boulders kicked loose a mass of stone which tumbled down into the cave and on top of the Indians, smashing bodies. When the stones stopped falling and the dust cleared, there were no more sounds coming from the cave.

Brown ordered a charge, but it was like charging a cemetery. Inside the cave was a horrible sight. Crushed bodies, some hardly recognizable as human, were everywhere. Scores were dead or dying, many of them women and children. Arms and legs protruded from rock piles. In all, 76 Apaches were killed that day; about 35 were still alive when the soldiers stormed the cave, but half of them were dying. The dead were left there. 18 captives were marched away. Years later, when a hiker came upon the cave and found the numerous skeletons on the floor of it, it became known as "Skeleton Cave." In 1925, a group of Yavapai along with a Maricopa County Sheriff, collected the bones from the cave, and interred them at the Fort McDowell cemetery.

In many lesser battles, Indian sources said General Crook's "War of Extermination" killed 250 Indians during his first year of campaigning. The other major battle in the campaign happened at Turret Peak, in central Arizona. A band of Tonto Apaches had attacked and killed three white men. Crook's scouts tracked them to a Yavapai stronghold on the mountain. Captain George Randall's command crept up the peak on hands and knees, trying not to make noise, about midnight. At dawn they charged into the Indian encampment. The natives were surprised, then panic stricken. Some of them jumped over a cliff, to their deaths. Others fought and 57 of them died. This was enough for those who survived. Within days; on April 6, 1873, they surrendered to General Crook at Camp Verde. Several of the soldiers who killed Indians at Turret Peak were awarded the Medal of Honor.

It proved that soldiers could find and conquer Apaches in their deepest hideouts. Crook's hard-ball tactics had paid off. Much of the success of Crooks campaign was due to the Apache scouts. They understood the movements of their people, even if they were from different bands. "The longer we knew the Apache scouts," Bourke noted, "the better we liked them."

By the spring of 1883, Yavapai and Western Apache resistance was all but broken and most of the Apaches were on reservations. The notable exception was the Chiricahua with their history of fierce independence. Chatto followed his leaders on continuing raids into Mexico for horses and cattle and he relished these times away from camp. For one thing he didn't have to deal with the sullen moods of Nalthchedah, who seemed to complain about everything, even the game he brought home for her. He was counting the days until he could go to Ishchosen and claim her as his true wife.

While life was free for the Chiricahua, it was slow death for the Western Apaches in captivity. The reservations were miserable dirty places. The Army herded Indians from different tribes, some of whom had been at war with each other for centuries, together like sheep in a corral. Many if not most of the Indian Agents were corrupt and cheated the Indians out of their subsistence rations. The nomadic Apache found themselves in one place all of the time, disease raged through their camps and hundreds died.

General Crook set about to meet his promises. He worked nearly as hard to promote a period of peacemaking as he had to subdue the Apaches. No other general, surely not the ones to whom he reported, would have dreamed of trying to help a vanquished foe as did Crook. He persuaded many of the fierce warriors to become farmers and found them good land. He encouraged the Indians to divert streams and dig irrigation ditches. He helped set up a system to market their beef and wool and produce.

He didn't wait for Washington to send tools and supplies. He rounded up old shovels and picks from camps and forts under his command and put the Apaches to work. Five miles of irrigation ditch took shape and soon melons and grains were growing on 57 acres of newly plowed ground near Camp Verde.

Arizona citizens didn't like this. They were still in their "exterminate them" mode. And profiteers who had gotten rich selling supplies to the military and general population didn't like this new era of peace. Nevertheless Crook had brought peace to the Arizona Territory. Crook remained in Arizona two more years upgrading military facilities and promoting humane treatment of the Indians.

Trouble was; Crook won his reputation as an Indian fighter and there was plenty of fighting left to do. This time it was against the Sioux in Montana and the Dakotas. Like the Apache, the Sioux were angry at the number of gold seekers invading the land that had been promised them forever. Although Phil Sheridan didn't like Crook very much and vice-versa, Sheridan still rated Crook as his best field commander. In 1874, Sherman and Sheridan sent Crook to the Great Plains to deal with Sitting Bull and Crazy Horse. When Crook was transferred to the Great Plains things started to go to hell in a hand-basket for the Apaches.

CHAPTER 19   Broken Arrow

Chatto was 18 when he first lived on a reservation. His chief, Cochise, and his tribe had been gradually driven into the Dragoon Mountains of Arizona and used them for cover and as a base from which to continue attacks against white settlements and Mexican properties. It was September, 1872 and Cochise had been talking to the Army off and on about sending the Chiricahuas to the reservation at Tularosa, New Mexico. Cochise had replied, "My people will not go away from their homes." His only white friend, Tom Jeffords, became a go-between. Jeffords had been an army man, but was running a mail-wagon business through Apache territory when he first made contact with Cochise. Jeffords helped set up a meeting between Cochise and General Oliver Howard who was sent to Arizona by President Grant, specifically to negotiate peace treaties.

"Did you know Tom Jeffords?" Herbert Welsh asked Chatto.

"Yes, I remember him. He was a tall man. Cochise liked his bravery because he came to our camp alone to ask our chief to stop killing his mail wagon drivers. They became friends and blood brothers. I think Jeffords was the only white man he ever trusted.

"And did Jeffords work out a meeting with General Howard?"

"Yes. Jeffords told General Howard that Cochise would not come to him. He had to go to Cochise to talk peace. Jeffords brought him."

"Were you at the meeting?"

"No, I was too young. Old Manos Amarillas, the story teller, told us about it. Cochise said 'We want peace. My people must be allowed to stay here in the Chiricahua Mountains, which has been their home and where the spirits are good."

"And they worked out a treaty?"

"Yes. Amarillas said Cochise came to the meeting with his youngest wife, his youngest son and his sister. General Howard wanted Cochise to take us to the reservation at Tularosa. Cochise said—'No, we won't go.' Then he said, 'Why not give us Apache Pass?' He said if we had Apache Pass, then we would protect the water springs and the roads and see that nobody's property was taken.

"But," queried Welsh, "The reservation he actually got was much bigger than Apache Pass. It went from the Dragoon Mountains through the Chiricahua Mountains all the way to the Mexican Border, hundreds of miles. And Tom Jeffords was appointed Indian Agent."

"Yes," Chatto smiled. "Cochise was a good talker."

With agreement on a number of other items, the ailing Cochise called off his war in 1872 and said, "I break the arrow. Hereafter the white man and the Indian are to drink the same water, eat of the same bread and be at peace."

In fact, it ushered in an era of peace. By late 1872, for the first time, every Chiricahua, was on a reservation; maybe 1300 of them. The Indians were ready for peace because they realized it was necessary for their survival. This was still a difficult concept for hothead warriors. For the majority, if the government treated them well, they were okay living where they did and not worrying about settlers and soldiers. Significantly, although the Chiricahuas agreed to stop raiding in the United States, nothing was said about raids into Mexico. Those continued. And they festered.

In June, 1873, Chatto rode with a Chiricahua war party consisting of members from all four bands as they plowed into Mexico and came back with cattle, plunder and even a small Mexican boy they captured.

Another raiding party entered Sonora and destroyed everything it approached. Chatto noticed Bonito was along on that one and they traded turns at tossing verbal jibes at each other. Also there was another dozen warriors from the Tularosa and Chiricahua reservation, raiding ranches, attacking travelers, killing at least ten people and stealing cattle. These were just two of dozens, maybe hundreds of raids into Mexico.

The Governor of Sonora complained bitterly and constantly about the raids. Tom Jeffords, now the Indian Agent, responded that maybe his Indians had been on some harmless stock raids, but had never killed anyone in Mexico. He disliked criticism that he gave the Indians a free hand and the newspapers hated him for being one source of continuing territorial troubles. General Crook tried to figure out how to force the Indians into some area where his men would have better control over them. The government was becoming convinced that the Apaches didn't need to be on multiple reservations…they should be on one or two big ones. Faced with being ripped up from his reservation, or a war to prevent it, Cochise ordered all Mexican raids to stop in November 18, 1873.

There, in the Chiricahua Mountains, Chatto returned to the parents of Ishchosen and got their agreement to take her as his wife. It was common for Apache warriors to have more than one wife, even to marry sisters. Geronimo would have nine wives, Naiche three. Chatto brought eight fine ponies to Ishchosen's father and one to her brother, Martine, and other gifts for her family to seal the deal. Following Apache tradition, he built a shelter for the two of them many miles from the main camp. He brought flowers from the desert and provisions to the get-away. Many warriors and their women danced at their ceremony and Ishchosen wore a buckskin dress with elaborate fringe and beadwork. After the celebration Chatto and Ishchosen disappeared to their honeymoon place. They stayed away many days.

Meantime, in furtherance of its policy of consolidating Indians, in 1872 the government set about building a huge new reservation in the hot, dry desert of Southeastern Arizona; San Carlos. True, it contained some mountains with oak and pine, rivers and creeks, but for the most part it was almost 3,000 square miles of desert in the lowest, hottest, most miserable terrain imaginable. It was chosen because whites believed Indians deserved no better and this was an ideal spot to keep an eye on them. It was also close to Tucson and a bunch of businessmen in Tucson were buying government supplies from Indian Agents and selling goods to the Army. San Carlos soon got the name "Hell's Forty Acres." Athough initially set aside for the Chiricahua, it would be packed with Indians from many different tribes, many of whom hated each other.

"It was not good," Chatto told Welsh, "We didn't want to go. We didn't have the same culture as the people there. We didn't speak the same language. We didn't even have the same God. The White-eyes wondered why we didn't get along and why we wanted to stay in the mountains."

The Chiricahua were content on reservations set up by the government on their traditional grounds; at Ojo Caliente for the Chihenne people, in the Dragoon and Chiricahua Mountains for Chatto's Chokonens. They were a mountain people. They had forests and rivers and wild game. For the Yavapai at Camp Verde, the labors of the Indians on an irrigation system were paying off with rich crops of melons, squash, beans and more. But all that changed in 1874 when the government made the final and stupid decision to close down smaller reservations and put all Indians on one or two big ones.

Unaware of government policies that would change their lives, Chatto and Ishchosen had their first child, a pretty little girl with coal black eyes, who would be called Maude. They were happy on the land, except for the presence of Nalthchedah, who was being a jealous pest. Chatto confronted her while she was grinding corn at the far end of the village. "You do not treat Ishchosen right. She is not your servant. She does not move to your orders."

Nalthchedah looked up at Chatto, almost expressionless. "I am your first wife. Remember that."

Chatto paused only briefly and replied. "You are my second choice. You remember that." He left her sitting and seething at the grinding stone.

Their land, the Chiricahuaua reservation in the Dragoons, was excellent land for grazing, lumbering, mining and building. The white government wanted it for that reason and also to make way for the Southern Pacific Railroad to run through the heart of Apacheria. This reservation and the one at Ojo Caliente and Camp Verde were soon on the chopping block. It's as if the government wanted the Indians to revolt.

Then, the government cut food rations to the Chiricahuas. Chatto agreed with the elders who said the only solution was to ride out and get livestock. He raided ranches with them far and wide. Tom Jeffords warned that he couldn't stop it. He said, "These people must have meat to live." Settlers and ranchers turned up the political heat over these raids. It added fuel to the demand among some whites that Tom Jeffords be sacked and the Indians be forced to move to San Carlos. In denying Jeffords a chance to explain his side, The Tucson Citizen newspaper said Jeffords, "is an aider and abettor of thieves and murderers [who] can under no circumstances use the pages of the Citizen to pardon the flimsy falsehoods of denial."

Like other agreements, the "Broken Arrow" treaty was too good to be true. The whites couldn't leave well-enough alone. Residents, especially those in the copper and silver mining business, didn't like the treaty. It kept Indians on lands they wanted for themselves. Meantime, since the Chiricahuas had not entirely stopped raiding Mexico, notwithstanding Cochise's directive to his people, those raids and the killings continued at a staccato beat. People said Jeffords looked the other way at this activity, that he was an "Indian lover." They wrote hot letters to their representatives in Washington and the politicians acted. The newspapers went after him with a vengeance. Tom Jeffords was removed as the Indian Agent.

Cochise was unable to bring his stature to bear. Suffering from a long illness, perhaps abdominal cancer, he died on the reservation in the summer of 1874. Chatto grieved as the band held elaborate funeral ceremonies in honor of Cochise. They hid his body in the deep chasms of the Dragoon Mountains and held the secret of his burial place tightly. His son, Taza became chief over the objections of the seasoned warrior, Eskinya, who thought he should succeed Cochise.

Chatto had his own ambitions but knew at 20 years old, he was not in a position to be chief. The "Broken Arrow" treaty with the Chiricahua had fallen apart.

"The Indian Agent from San Carlos, his name was Clum, came to us," said Chatto, "and he brought many pony soldiers to display his power. He told us we must move to San Carlos. We were split among us. Taza and Naiche had promised Cochise on his deathbed that they would honor the peace. So they argued against going to San Carlos, but then agreed to go in honor of their father."

The powerful sub-chief Eskinya said he would not go, he would rather die. Gordo, the Bedonkohe chief left and took about 20 of his people to Ojo Caliente. Four hundred or more fled to Mexico with Geronimo.

Sometime later Clum went to Ojo Caliente and forced Victorio, Nana and Loco and their Warm Springs Apaches to move to San Carlos. Juh and the Nedhni asked for two weeks to gather up their people. Clum gave them three days. They took their three days and gathered up their belongings and ran for Mexico."

"What about you?" asked Welsh.

"I could not agree to go. I hated the thought of San Carlos. Geronimo was also against it. Maybe 100 of his people went to San Carlos, but he had no trust for the whites. I packed my family and went with him. Nalthchedah didn't want to go to Mexico. So I took Ishchosen and Maude. We travelled far into Mexico and found Juh."

Juh welcomed his brother-in-law, Geronimo and the Apaches who travelled such long distances with him. It bolstered his forces.

Bonito was there. Typical of Bonito, he did not say "Hola" or "Como Esta" He just walked over, looked Chatto up and down and took a wrestling stance.

This was followed by a friendly shove by Bonito and a harder one in return from Chatto. They found themselves circling each other. This was going to be an amiable, but nevertheless serious contest of wills, skills and strength. Chatto had learned long ago not to wait in a wrestling match. He would make the first move with tactics drilled into him by Yellow Hand. He engaged Bonito by one arm with his left wrapped around the neck of his competitor, then moved quickly to plant one foot between Bonito's legs, then turning and placing his arm under the armpit of the other wrestler, lifted and fell backyards in a spinning motion that brought Bonito airborne and crashing to the ground on his back. It knocked the wind out of him. Chatto climbed on top and placed a punishing head-lock on the downed warrior, squeezing with all his might. He was proving a point.

It was over too soon. Bonito said "Enough!" and sagged to suggest his submission. Chatto got up and helped Bonito off the ground. He brushed away the dirt embedded in the Chihenne's shoulder and back. Bonito produced a half-smile and his hand. Their rivalry was becoming a friendship.

Meanwhile, back in the Chiricahua Mountains, Eskinya and his brother Pionsenay went on the war path to prove they would not be reservation-bound and that the leadership of the Chokonens belonged to them. Leading a small and murderous group of dissident warriors, Eskinya started with a raiding party of fourteen men into Sonora. They attacked a supply train killing three Mexicans. In another raid they stole 13 horses and some gold dust. Drinking whiskey bought from a couple of Arizona stagecoach station employees named Spence and Rogers and wanting more, Pionsenay made the demand, Rogers said "No." and Pionsennay gunned down the both of them and ransacked their cabin. They killed two ranchers along the San Pedro River, a farmer tending his crops and wounded another working on his irrigation ditch. Taza and Naiche felt obliged to take sides against Eskinya. His behavior violated the promises Taza and Naiche had made. They helped as army troops tried to run down the renegades.

The trouble with Eskinya came to a head with a shootout that erupted in camp. Naiche was married to Eskinya's daughter but, during the melee, shot his father-in-law through the head. Taza killed another of Eskinya's men and wounded one. Later he gunned down three more men who had been raiding with Eskinya. It was a battle for control of Cochise's band. Taza won, but was able to take only half of his Chokonens to San Carlos, maybe 300 of them. Clum settled them on a part of the reservation known as "The Black Hole." The Indian Agent turned Pionsenay over to the Sheriff of Pima County to be tried for murder, but the Apache escaped.

Chatto found that life was no bed of roses riding with Geronimo, Juh and the Nednhi. Juh was engaged in a full-out war with Mexican authorities and there was great bloodshed. Juh had the advantage. His warriors, including Chatto with his Winchester lever-action, were better armed than Mexican troops and they knew when and where they would hit next. They hit everything; wagons, stages and railroad trains, villages and towns, farms and ranches and they seldom left anyone alive. After each raid or series of raids, Chatto would return to Ishchosen and Maude, who were well taken care of by the village women in Juh's camp.

His raiding successes did not mean to suggest that Juh didn't suffer his defeats too. One of them happened in the winter when Lt. John Anthony Rucker's American troops crossed the border illegally, found Juh's camp, surrounded it and shot it to pieces. Ischosen and Maude were not injured, but it was a close call. Juh set off a series of raids to recover his losses. In a 12 month stretch Chatto and the other warriors killed thirty-nine men and wounded twenty-one in the Sahuaripa district alone. There were sporadic attempts to bargain peace with the Mexicans, but the conditions were so harsh that Juh settled on going deeper into the mountains and continuing his war with all outsiders. He suffered another setback when his sub-chief Nolgee brought 44 of his people to a Mexican feast that turned out to be another of those traps where the Indians get drunk and the Mexicans slaughter them. Juh lost 33 of his people on that occasion.

Chatto, Geronimo and Bonito were not attached to Juh at the hip. They staged their own raids. They moved back toward the U.S. border after an Army patrol destroyed their winter camp. Crossing the border with Mexico they stole twenty-one horses from a rancher named

Sam Hughes. Second Lieutenant John Anthony Rucker, with a company of Apache scouts and ten troopers, picked up the Apache trail at Crittenden and followed it through southeast Arizona to the Huachuca Mountains, across the San Pedro River, and across a part of the Chiricahua Mountains when he ran out of supplies. Chatto thought Geronimo had led them to safety once more, but in early January here came Rucker again, this time finding the Apache camp in the Animas Mountains of New Mexico. He set up a dawn ambush and launched it with first light.

Chatto, who had been dancing all night with other warriors, awakened from a deep sleep by the gunfire, grabbed his Winchester, yelled at Ishchosen to run with their daughter, then ran to the nearest rock formation and blasted away at the soldiers and their scouts. It appeared the odds were against him. He and the others fought a rear guard action, shooing the women and children away as they fought. As he fell back, he grabbed little Maude up in his arms and followed the pregnant Ishchosen into the brush and freedom.

Next day Chatto and Geronimo assessed their losses; ten men lost, Geronimo's nephew lost or captured, their herd of forty-five horses and mules captured and at least ten good rifles left behind. Geronimo railed at the Indian scouts who had helped to bring about this defeat. Revenge being as strong as it was to the Apache, Geronimo and Chatto started planning.

Geronimo persuaded Chatto, Bonito and forty to fifty others to join him on raids into southern Arizona to get even with Lt. Rucker. In Mexico they picked up more men from Juh and some Chokonens running with him. They re-entered Arizona through the Huachuca Mountains. On February 4th they hit the Thomas Hughes ranch along the Sonoita River, stealing fifteen horses and wounding a ranch hand. They rode those horses in attacks that killed ten men in the valley. Then they split up. Chatto led at least a dozen warriors in a separate war party going west and Bonito went south with Geronimo. Chatto and the western group found three Mexicans still sleeping and shot them in their bedrolls. They wounded rancher Bill Devers who died from his wounds, and one other man. The larger of the two groups, led by Geronimo, raided ranches down the Sonoita Creek and Santa Cruz River, killing one man and grabbing 45 head of cattle.

In the spring, Chatto, drifted back into the U.S. with some Chokonen followers and some members of the Chihenne and Bedonkohe bands. He turned up at Ojo Caliente, New Mexico, where Victorio had fled after leaving San Carlos after only three months at Hell's Half Acres. In July, 1876, the Indian Commissioner had granted asylum to those Chiricahuas who had gone to Ojo Caliente instead of San Carlos. Victorio greeted Chatto's band but wasn't happy about it. He blamed the Chokonens for his being sent to San Carlos in the first place. Chatto's people weren't the most polite of guests, demanding more rations and setting off feuds with Chief Loco's people. Chief Loco warned the government that many of these new men were young, excitable and might cause trouble. Still, it was a relatively peaceful time, which was good because it was time for Ischosen to give birth. It was a baby boy, Chatto's first son; Bedisclove, a true gift from Ussen. Chatto took the baby up in his arms and went outside the wickiup to yell and dance his pride to his fellows. They all told him it was a fine child; that it looked just like him.

Some trouble broke out when the Indian Agent at Ojo Caliente asked Chatto's band to bring in their families to be enrolled and counted. He flatly refused. The others followed suit. Routine counts of their Indians were one of the only ways the reservations had of knowing who was there. For instance, on January 6, 1877, Ojo Caliente had 521 Apaches, as indicated by rations handed out. A week later it had 672. That meant that more Apaches, namely Geronimo, had come to the agency. Not only had he come, he was using at as a base of operations for new Arizona raids.

CHAPTER 20   John Clum

The superintendent picked for the San Carlos reservations was John Clum, a graduate of Rutgers and member of the Dutch Orthodox Church, still in his twenties. This met a criteria established by President Grant that Indian reservation agents ought to be affiliated with churches. It was assumed that church people would take a more benevolent approach to the Indians than the Army or Indian Bureau. In fact, Clum did.

John Clum

Clum arrived at the San Carlos Reservation in early August, 1874. Apache scouts presented him with a gift the next day; the severed head of a Tonto Indian, Cochinay, a raider who they had tracked down and killed. It was soon clear to him that this was a violent world and it was run by the Army, which hated Indians and didn't care much for Indian agents either. He would expend great energy to get the Army out of the Indian business, once they were on his reservation, supposedly run by the Department of the Interior.

To his credit, Clum generally put the needs of the Indians above those of the U.S. Army. That put him almost constantly at odds with the Army. He didn't like the cruelty he witnessed, the corruption and graft that resulted in the disappearance of food and supplies intended for the Indians. It was common for Indians to receive few of their government supplies, while supply sergeants and private parties profited. Clum was also critical of harsh discipline and on the blatant racism displayed by officers and men. He was credited with running a pretty good reservation, given its environment, setting up a fair administration and enforcing rules using Indian policemen. He nagged the Indians to keep their housing and villages clean and thus avoid illness. He counted the Apaches twice a week when rations were handed out to know who and how many were there. The self-government instituted for the Indians by Clum was successful at San Carlos to the extent that it became another excuse for the government to close smaller, more desirous reservations.

Clum lost no time establishing his influence among the Apaches. He paid visits to Apache camps without soldiers. He fiercely defended Apaches against the military and he won their confidence. In turn, the Indians turned in their weapons, and checked them out again to go hunting. They set up a tribal police force and a court to try run-of-the-mill violations. Before long, the youthful agent had more than one thousand Indians living on his huge, dry reservation.

Clum also has his detractors. He was called brash, arrogant, difficult, cocky, headstrong and pompous. It was his job to get the Indians off the good reservations and onto "Hell's Forty Acres." This was in line with the Government's emerging "removal policy" which dictated that all the western Apaches and similar tribes west of the Rio Grande would be concentrated onto one reservation; San Carlos. During his second year on the job one of the most hellacious acts of the Apache Wars was visited on the Yavapais living peacefully, after their surrender, on the Camp Verde reservation which had been promised to them in perpetuity.

There, the Yavapais and Apaches built more than five miles of irrigation systems to cultivate the land and reap significant harvests. When government supply contractors became disappointed that the tribe was becoming self-sufficient, they complained and petitioned to have the reservation revoked. The government ruled in favor of the whites and against the Indians again, closing the Verde reservation and moving nearly 1400 Tontos and Yavapais to San Carlos. It fit in perfectly with the removal policy. Agent Clum favored it because it would increase his importance.

This was bad enough, but then the Army put the Indians through a punitive march of 180 miles, in the dead of winter, to the San Carlos reservation. Soldiers forced the Yavapai, and some Apaches at Camp Verde to walk down the Verde River valley then over the most primitive territory through the Mazatzal Mountains, the high cliffs on the northern end of the Tonto Basin and across the arid stretch of today's Highway 88, still known as Apache Trail. They purposely avoided wagon trails that ran through the area and forced the Indians to trek over the most difficult terrain. More than 100 didn't make it. Indians were swept down the rivers, they were injured on the trail, and they died from disease. The main culprit was Smallpox, brought to the Indians by the white man. It killed them like flies. Those who survived the long march from Camp Verde found themselves imprisoned for the next 25 years while whites took over their lands.

Juh and Geronimo

On the reservation the rules Clum enforced included no making or drinking of the Apache liquor, tiswin, no leaving the reservation, no dancing, and no swearing. Clum had problems with the Chiricahuas. Many of them, including Chatto, Geronimo and Juh, remained wild and free. The ones on the reservation, having come in with Taza and Naiche, hated it. They hated leaving the hunting-raiding life-style they had known for generations. They hated farming in a land not meant for farming. They hated the disease that wiped out many of their families. And they hated Clum. Juh's son, Daklugie said it was the worst place on earth. "There is no grass, no game. Nearly everything that grows is cactus. The heat is terrible. The insects are terrible. The water is terrible." What they loved was their mountains and the access they had to raid into Mexico and reap the rewards of plentiful sheep, cattle and horses. On the reservation they saw themselves as paupers and slaves.

Clum poses with Apaches

The San Carlos Reservation population rose to nearly 5,000 Indians. Even today the city of San Carlos does not suggest a vacation wonderland. It is the poorest Native American community in the United States. Entering from the south on Highway 170, you can do a loop through town on San Carlos Avenue, Cibique Circle and Apache

Avenue, where you will notice other street names like White Mountain Avenue and Coyotera Street. The streets are flat because the town is flat and more than 100 degrees many months of the year; where less than 2 inches of rainfall can be expected except during the flash floods that come with storms and an occasional tornado. You can see the poor. The average home is worth $48,000. The per capita income is $8,000 because of an unemployment rate that reaches 20.7%. Most of the population is under the poverty level.

At one point Clum recruited Cochise's son Taza and other braves for an authentic Indian show he wanted to take on the road to raise money. The money was intended to pay his way to the east coast to follow up on his engagement to a fair young maiden. The show was a flop, closing after three performances. But the entourage did make it to Washington D.C. Clum and his Indians toured the White House, went to a circus, cruised the Potomac and stood too long in a torrential rain, which gave Taza the sniffles. Next day Taza came down with pneumonia. Within 48 hours he was dead.

Still living at or in the vicinity of Ojo Caliente and raiding periodically into Mexico, Chatto saw the birth of his third child. It was a little girl and he and Ishchosen named her Naboka. Seeing to the needs of his growing family, Chatto found his movements more restricted than in the past. He helped some of the Warm Springs Apaches with their farming, getting ready for the growing season which was only a few months away. Geronimo would visit with him when he returned from his more frequent raids, mostly attacking ranches for horses and cattle.

When John Clum finally returned to San Carlos, after an extended stay away from the reservation, he tried to explain to Naiche what happened to his brother, but Naiche came away with the conviction that Clum had poisoned Taza and there was nothing he could do about it. Not yet, anyway.

Naiche, Son of Cochise

Once back on station, John Clum reportedly couldn't stand it that Geronimo, Chatto and other strong warriors were still out there free and wild. Getting word of the renegade's whereabouts, on April 21, 1877, he took 100 of his best Apache Police and tricked Geronimo into a meeting at the Ojo Caliente reservation in New Mexico.

Chatto shifted in his seat and told Herbert Welsh, "We thought we would pick up some government food rations there. And Geronimo thought he would be having a friendly chat with Clum."

Instead, Clum tongue-lashed Geronimo for raiding Arizona ranches and, at a signal, had the renegade medicine man, Chatto and his few braves surrounded by rifle-toting police. Geronimo, and Chatto were clapped in chains by the local blacksmith and taken back to San Carlos with most of their band. The U.S. Army was embarrassed and angered by Clum's maneuver. The capture made them look like idiots. It was the only time Geronimo was captured at gunpoint without a shot fired on either side. Clum crowed about this.

"I was released from my chains pretty soon after we got back to San Carlos," Chatto told Herbert Welsh, "and we went to the section of San Carlos where Nalthchedah was living among my people. But Geronimo was kept in chains and later in a guard house for a long time. He never forgot it."

CHAPTER 21   Victorio

No sooner did Clum have Geronimo and Chatto's people in hand than the Government ordered him to take all the Ojo Caliente Indians, Victorio and Nana's bands, to San Carlos. His troops swept the Ojo Caliente encampments and took 453 Chiricahuas on the unhappy 20-day trek to San Carlos. Several died from smallpox on the way, just as had the travelers from Camp Verde. 150 or so avoided the removal by fleeing north to Navajo country, south to Mexico or into the mountains of New Mexico. Victorio's people were paying a price for allowing Geronimo, Chatto and others to operate from their encampment.

John Clum resigned after two years on the job. His continuing battles with the army left him more than angry and frustrated. After Clum resigned, the military, saying that Geronimo seemed peaceable enough, let him out of the guardhouse and told him he was free as long as he stayed on the reservation and off the booze.

Victorio and his Chihenne band hated everything about San Carlos. He was angered by the broken promise that his people would live at Ojo Caliente forever. He was angry at contractors who stole their food. He was uncomfortable living near to the Chokonen, who he thought of as bad Indians. He was saddened by the lost of too many tribesmen, women and children to the white man's diseases. He was angered by the hostility shown his people by white citizens and their blue-coated soldiers. Then, Pionsenay dropped in on the reservation telling how profitable it was raiding in Mexico. This ignited a spark in the Warm Springs band. Within two months after Clum resigned, on September 12, 1877, Victorio escaped San Carlos taking 310 with him including the groups headed by Nana and Loco. They killed 12 ranchers along the way, and lost some men and thirty women and children to pursuing cavalry.

Two weeks later Victorio turned up at Fort Wingate, near Gallup, New Mexico and asked the military for a reservation nearby.

The Commander, a Colonel Hatch, opposed their staying. They would be a bad influence among the peaceful Navajos. They had to move along.

The Indian Commission didn't want to return them to San Carlos. It thought that would be a bad precedent. But then where? They considered Fort Sill, In Oklahoma, but it was filled with Plains Indians. In the end they decided to send them back to Ojo Caliente, north of Santa Fe, near the Rio Grande and surrounded by majestic mountains and verdant forests. This was great news to Victorio, Nana and the others. They pledged to stay peaceful if they could go home. By the last of October a troop of soldiers was escorting them to their old stomping grounds.

Victorio

Victorio and his people kept their promise and lived peacefully at Ojo Caliente. It was a land they loved. But that lasted less than a year when the government attempted to transfer them to San Carlos again, in October 1878. Sweeney wrote, "It was another in a series of incredibly stupid decisions made by federal officials in Washington."

In mid-July, 1878, as the military arrived to march the Chihennes to the place they dreaded the most, Victorio was fit to be tied, more than angry he was enraged. He promised he would die fighting rather than return to San Carlos. In fact he would. Nana stuck with Victorio and refused to go. Chief Loco protested the unjust decision, but he didn't want his children and tribesmen to suffer if the peace was broken. He and 172 Chihennes left with the military escort and arrived back at San Carlos in late November, 1878.

In his camp, Victorio had two of the most famous of the Apache women warriors, his sister Lozen and the Chiricahua, Dahteste, who was the wife of Chief Chihuahua. Victorio's sister rode with her brother and later with Geronimo to the very last. Lozen was scruffy. She cared little about her appearance. She dressed and fought like a man. She participated when hundreds of Chiricahuas retaliated in raids killing as many whites as possible. She got involved when the women of the tribe killed captives, crushing them under horse's hooves, beating them to death with clubs or rocks and even hacking them to pieces with knives. To Apaches, she had supernatural powers in battle and great healing powers, using songs and herbs. A road sign on the Mescalero Reservation today, speaks of the leadership her people felt from her.

Lozen

Dahteste

Unlike Lozen, Dahteste dressed well and was known for her beauty. She was smart and spoke Apache, Spanish and English well enough to serve as an interpreter. She would have her mother watch her two children while she raided with Lozen, Victorio, Geronimo, her husband Chihuahua and his brother Jolsanny (Ulzana.)

Victorio used Dahteste to negotiate off and on with the Army, but finally gave up. His band was all through with trying to live on reservations. From now on it was war. Victorio gathered three hundred or so Chiricahua and Mescalero raiders and even some Comanches and embarked on one of the most remarkable guerrilla campaigns in American history.

He and his warriors, always travelling with women and children, outran thousands of soldiers and killed hundreds of settlers across New Mexico and west Texas, becoming the epitome of Apache resistance. Juh and Geronimo joined him off and on.

In an early engagement Victorio's men ran into a small patrol from the 9th Cavalry in New Mexico. They killed five Buffalo Soldiers, staking them to the ground and mutilating their bodies. They also took up to sixty army horses and mules. Reservation Apaches quickly heard about it and many jumped the reservation to take up fighting again. By middle September nine American settlers had been killed and the Army had thousands of soldiers and scouts scouring the countryside looking for Victorio and his band.

Victorio headed south along the Animas River with 200 men, women and children. There he encountered miners who had formed themselves into a militia, and killed ten of them, grabbing another 50 horses in the process. Hiding out in the Black Range and positioning his warriors with great cunning, he was ready when two cavalry companies under Captain Byron Dawson came riding along. The soldiers were lured into the canyon by women and shot to pieces by Victorio's men, firing from the canyon walls. Army reinforcements from the 9th Calvary didn't help the Americans. Victorio maneuvered successfully and neutralized them also. Captain Dawson was relieved of his command.

Victorio wasn't done. He was in a killing frenzy and next struck around Alma, New Mexico with raids on settler homes. Today, Alma is scarcely a stop on highway 180 north, with three times as many people represented in the old grave yard as in the village itself. Victorio's band killed 41 people. Driven off by soldiers from Fort

Bayard, Victorio proceeded to Fort Tularosa, about 130 miles and three mountain ranges away, where his men attacked settlers outside the fort and threw arrows and bullets into the fort itself before losing several warriors and heading for Mexico. Victorio students say he was a tough nut and a brilliant tactician. His warriors attacked silver mines in the Mogollon Mountains. They left three dead in the town of Cooney and three more trying to escape. They then killed 35 sheepherders nearby.

CHAPTER 22   Going Separate Ways

San Carlos got a new Indian Agent; Henry Lyman Hart. He didn't appear to be as officious as Clum and got off to a good start at San Carlos when he held a meeting with Geronimo, Naiche, Chihuahua, Chatto and Gordo in which he named Geronimo "Captain" of the 145 Chiricahuas on the reservation. He listened to complaints over the lack of food, disease and general living conditions.

Unfortunately, Hart's attention to the Indians was short-lived. Like other agents before and after him, he succumbed to the prospect of turning a profit. He was soon directing most of his energy towards mining claims on and off the reservation. Off the books, he hired his brother to help. That might not have been so bad, but then he began to divert food supplies intended for the Indians to feed crews developing some of his mining interests. Often-times the Apaches only got half rations. Before long Hart had his fingers into every financial transaction at the agency.

During the winter of 1877, Hart convinced Apaches led by Geronimo, Naiche and Chatto to dig irrigation ditches. But he didn't provide tools. There were three shovels for 100 workers. Men women and children dug with sticks and baskets trying to bring water from the Gila River onto their parched ground. This added significantly to the grumbling.

Naiche and Chatto had the biggest complaint. Their people were dying in great numbers. Clum had located the Chokonens led by Naiche in the Gila lowlands, a stagnant mosquito infested area that soon created a major epidemic. This was years before doctors had made the connection between mosquitoes and malaria. The Chokonens had no immunity and no experience with the disease. Scores died, usually within a few weeks of developing symptoms like fever, chills, and headaches. It's why they called it the shaking sickness. Chatto worried about his three children and another one on the way. Chatto and Nalthchedah had obviously put aside some of their scornfulness for each other and she was now pregnant.

Agent Hart responded by allowing them to get out of the Gila lowlands (black hole) and move into the mountains where fresh air should, and did help. That helped solve one problem, but led to another. Getting away, the Apaches now felt free to brew their tiswin. Drunken parties started taking place. At one of them a drunken Geronimo let fly some verbal abuse at his nephew and the nephew committed suicide. Geronimo knew he could not hide the fact that he had made illegal tiswin and knew he would be put in the guardhouse for it. He left the reservation with his three wives and two children and went back to Mexico.

Geronimo linked up with forty Chokonen already in Mexico who decided to follow him and he took the band to a stronghold in the Sierra Madre which was about one-hundred miles north from Juh's main encampment. There, the two leaders could coordinate raids or act on their own. Geronimo hadn't been in Mexico long before Sonoran troops attacked his camp near Casas Grandes and killed ten of the 44 Apaches there. He would retaliate in Mexico and Arizona for nearly a full year.

Citing security reasons, San Carlos authorities ordered Naiche and his people to come back down from the mountains where they had gone to get healthy again, and to re-occupy the Gila Flats. It resulted in another bout with malaria that took fifty lives. Simultaneously, the army grabbed up any remaining Chihennes from Ojo Caliente and marched them back to San Carlos.

Agent Hart drifted from regular thievery to major corruption. He was making deals with shady contractors and had his hand deep into the cookie jar. At the same time, the Apaches were desperate for basic foods; flour, coffee, sugar. They managed to get word out to Commissioner of Indian Affairs, Ezra Hayt, and he sent Inspector John Hammond to investigate. With investigators closing in around him, Hart resigned in March 1879.

While awaiting the Indian Commission's next appointee, the army's Lt. Adna R. Chaffee took over at the San Carlos reservation.

He was able to clean up most of the corruption at the agency and he listened to the Apache's concerns about food rations and disease. He beefed up the Indian police force with forty men including chiefs Chihuahua, Zele, Chatto and Naiche. At that time working as an Indian policeman or scout was no disgrace because the work generally did not pit the Apaches against members of their own band. Chaffee provided Chatto, Naiche and a few others passes to go into the mountains not to live but to gather natural foods. Naiche and Chatto took their two bands to Eagle Creek near the George Stevens ranch where they breathed easier about disease. There, Nalthchedah delivered her baby, a boy who would be known as Horace. Chatto saw much of himself in the baby; his fat little face, his chubby legs. He was a proud father, even though Nalthchedah gave him limited access to the boy.

    Meantime Geronimo was bringing his raids back into Arizona. During the summer of 1879, he led sixteen warriors into the area south of Tucson. Six of them raided the big and fortified Pete Kitchen ranch and kidnapped a twelve year old boy. Next day warriors took eleven mules and a horse from a barley farmer, O.E. Shaw. Shaw reported this to Fort Huachuca. Troops pursued and shot it out with Geronimo's men a few days later with no losses to either side. But it angered the Apaches enough that they ambushed three more whites. Geronimo was not known for his humanity, but he released the 12-year old boy from the Kitchen ranch.

    Juh also got into the act. This was one of the occasions when he linked up with Victorio. Together they struck an army corral at Ojo Caliente, killed five soldiers and three civilians and grabbed the entire herd of horses belonging to Company E. Within the week they raided the Chavez ranch on Animas Creek. They didn't kill Gregorio Chavez, because Victorio knew him. But they ransacked the inside of his house, stole his wife's wedding ring, roughed up some of his vaqueros, captured most of his horses and cattle and then disappeared. They did the same thing at the McEver ranch near Hillsboro. Only here they killed seven ranch hands. Later the same day they rode down and killed ten Mexicans, men women and children and mutilated the bodies. The death toll was nearly thirty outside the village of Carrizal before the parties split up, each going their separate ways.

Apache scouts chased Victorio on both sides of the Rio Grande. As a reservation policeman, Chatto often rode with them and felt no problems with it. He worried that the killings by Victorio and Geronimo would bring down heavy punishments on any Apaches the white-eyes could get their hands on, namely his family and the other reservation Indians. For one thing, every time there was an outside threat the military required the Chokonens to leave the mountains and go back to the malarial Gila Flats. To Chatto, that amounted to a death sentence for his people.

Riding out under the command of Lt. Charles Gatewood, Chatto and other Apache police from San Carlos tried to trap Victorio in the San Andres Mountains. But Victorio, outnumbered five to one, would not make a stand and escaped. In a second encounter, with Lt. Gatewood reporting to Captain Curwen McLellan, Victorio stood his ground. The scouts assaulted Victorio's positions and drove him from his entrenchments, forcing him to abandon his village. Victorio lost one of his chiefs, the Chiricahua Miguel Tuerto, in that fight and three other warriors. The Apaches wounded eight soldiers before making their escape across the Rio Grande. In his next scrape with the Americans Victorio lost 33 and abandoned a battle site soaked with blood. Weeks later, Apache scouts overtook a small party of Chihennes near Cookes Canyon and killed several, including Victorio's son, Washington. By then, the chief was harboring no illusions about his fate.

Victorio's band, having suffered increasing numbers of casualties in New Mexico, moved south. He was moving along the Rio Grande in the Tres Castillos Mountains of northern Mexico when his band stopped at a good watering hole and, for some reason, did not send out lookouts. They were surrounded by soldiers of the Mexican Army under Colonel Joaquin Terrazas . The Mexicans attacked and a two-day battle ensued. At the end of the second day the Apaches were out of ammunition. Seventy eight of them went down; 61 warriors and the rest women and children. Victorio died in the hail of gunfire. The story would circulate that he took his own life, rather than be captured. Chatto's childhood friend, the warrior Kaetenae, escaped, one of the 17 men to do so. Some of the women and children escaped but 68 of them were captured and sold as slaves after the Mexicans paraded them through the streets of Chihuahua City, waving staffs with Apache scalps attached.

Victorio's war involved a minimum of thirty-nine engagements over the course of a year. Considering only Dan Thrapp's chapter in *Conquest of Apacheria*, his Apaches killed at least 291 people and wounded more than 40, including U.S. and Mexican soldiers, ranchers, sheepherders, and settlers. They stole or killed nearly 350 head of livestock and terrified portions of three states. At the start, they lost one or two warriors to enemy actions but saw more and more of their raiding band die as troops from two countries closed in. Opposing forces killed seventy five or more before the final blow at Tres Castillos.

Nana avoided the massacre because he and a few others were out on a scouting party when the attack took place. Now Nana, at 80 years old, replaced Victorio as chief of the Warm Springs band. Many years later, Juh's son, Daklugie, claimed that Chatto wanted to be named chief of the Warm Springs band, after Victorio's death, and drifted toward the whites when he was not accepted. This seems far fetched. Daklugie was only six years old when Victorio died. And Chatto had no close ties with the Chihenne bands. Daklugie was likely parroting complaints against Chatto voiced by others. It was clear that the young warrior Kaetenae would inherit the leadership after Nana.

Nana had married a daughter of Victorio and a sister of Geronimo. Fighting through partial blindness and misshapen from arthritis, he still "rode like the devil," and led from a position of strength. His band, joined by 15 Chokonen and 12 Mescalero warriors, began raiding Army supply trains and isolated settlers. Writers said Nana's raid was legendary. In fewer than six weeks Nana led up to 40 warriors in eight battles in New Mexico and Arizona, travelling more than one-thousand miles of hostile territory, killing 30-40 soldiers and civilians. His band fled back to Mexico and killed several dozen Mexicans while trailing 200 stolen horses and being pursued by more than 1000 U.S. soldiers.

Chatto was active in the pursuit of Nana too, working within a company of thirty scouts from San Carlos. It was led by Chief Chihuahua, acting as sergeant and including the chief's brother Ulzana, his young son-in-law Beneactiney who would later ride with Chatto's band and Martine, his boyhood friend and fellow scout. The Chokonen scouts probably would not have fired on Nana except in self-defense. It didn't come up. They couldn't lawfully track him into Mexico.

Nana, 1886 Ben Wittick photo, Natl. Archives

By late that year the Indian Commissioner and the army were sending peace feelers out to Geronimo and Juh hoping they could lure the renegades to the safety of the reservation instead of a life of constant strife among the Mexicans. It worked. They sent the Bedonkohe chief, Gordo, to make contact with Juh. Juh stated, "I am not going in. If they get me they kill me." Gordo argued with Juh that it hadn't been true for any of the other leaders and then asked Juh what would happen to the many children in his band when he "was running like a wild man with no sleep, no water."

Juh, Geronimo and other top men sat down in council to discuss this. They were exhausted, hungry and pitiful. The vote to surrender was almost unanimous. One chief voted no. Geronimo shot him. Geronimo brought his family of six and Juh arrived at San Carlos with 103 individuals. They settled next to Naiche's Chokonens.

CHAPTER 23 The Scout

Chatto was unhappy on the reservation. He had not inherited the leadership of the band on the death of Cochise. That went to Taza. With Taza dead Naiche took the title of Chief of the Chokonen Band. Chatto wondered about the promise Cochise had made to him long ago that he would be a chief one day. Eugene Chihuahua, son of the chief, and Asa Daklugie said that Chatto was ambitious. Chihuahua is quoted as saying "Chatto, the liar, was never a chief." But he was, at least, now regarded as a sub-chief. He must have wondered whether it was all meaningless living as a virtual prisoner here at San Carlos. The whites wanted him to farm and he was no farmer. If he were, he still found the ground unsuitable for growing almost anything but cactus. The babies were growing fast. His daughter, Maude was six, Bedisclove was almost four and Naboka, his little princess, was turning two, a handful for Ishchosen. Nalthchedah's child, Horace, was almost one. Chatto, himself, was in his mid 20s, bored, except for his daily play time with Bedisclove, and in need of employment. To make ends meet, and improve his status with the whites, he volunteered to serve as an Apache Scout.

The army had authorized two companies, each containing forty Indians, to serve as scouts in Arizona Territory and now got permission to enlist a third scout company because of increasing raids. In addition, the Arizona Militia paid for an additional 60 scouts who had reported to John Clum. Their mission was to chase renegade Indians in southeastern Arizona wherever the trail would lead. The army paid the scouts at the same rate as an enlisted man; good money for their skill-set.

Chatto, U.S. Army Scout, War Dept.

Under General Crook's regime each Company had a cadre of scouts. The scouts basically determined where the soldiers would go looking for hostiles. They knew the terrain intimately. They knew the weather patterns, the hot spots and shady ones, they knew the favorite routes of Indians moving between New Mexico, Arizona and the Mexican provinces. They knew the hide-outs, the caves and plateaus where natives camped or kept stolen livestock and they read every blade of grass, every scuff mark on the rocks. Each man had these skills. They were the skills that kept entire bands alive, living in the wild and being chased by enemies.

"How did joining the scouts set with some of the other warriors?" asked Welsh

"Many of us joined. Geronimo told me I was a turn-coat. But then he told me to bring him rifles and bullets whenever I could."

"Did you?"

"No, but I know scouts who did. Geronimo and Juh could not see why any Chiricahua would be a scout. But many of us were. We needed the Army pay to get by. I think they did understand that. And they did not have a problem with us scouting against the Yavapai or White Mountain Apaches. If we were not coming after him, Geronimo seemed to be okay with it."

"And if you did come after his band?"

"Well, he would kill you. We knew that."

When Joseph Tiffany came to San Carlos as the latest agent the Chiricahuas seemed to be relatively content. Tiffany went to work to make sure rations were regular, that all the Indians who wanted to work had work; that they had seed and implements to work the ground and their children had a school. He hired Apaches to be teamsters, shepherds and laborers, taught them how to make better adobe bricks, dig canals and build efficient corrals. Most of the leaders, Chatto among them, declined work. It was something a chieftain didn't do. Chatto, however, did continue to serve on the agency police force along with Naiche.

So, Chatto, Naiche, Geronimo, Juh, Bonito, Chihuahua and Loco were all there on the reservation and things were going pretty well when the Army made its next critical mistake.

CHAPTER 24   Cibecue and the Great Breakout

Chatto had been minding his business on the reservation, trying to get along by going along. But an incident in 1881, involving a medicine man and his "ghost dances" inflamed most of the Apache Scouts and made many of them renegades again. It became known as The Battle of Cibecue Creek and it was a sorry affair by the U.S. Army.

Settlers and some of the soldiers were riled up because the Apaches were performing "Ghost Dances" on the Fort Apache Reservation. The natives used it as an escape from the unhealthy and corrupt conditions. After the death of Victorio, the Apaches were terribly demoralized. They were hungry, ill-clothed and hopeless. Chatto, like most others, realized that armed resistance was futile. That's why they sought some escape; why they turned to a prophet; a Western Apache medicine man, Nock-ay-det-klinne for his supernatural power to make life easier. Nock-ay-det-klinne, was a highly regarded shaman often consulted by Coloradas, Cochise and Geronimo. He lived at the Fort Apache reservation north of San Carlos and prescribed local drugs and dancing to let their spirits soar. The dances involved some high degree of drinking tiswin and smoking peyote.

Settlers believed it was a war preparation and wanted it stopped. The Army decided to arrest and remove the medicine man. Indian Agent Tiffany set things off. He decided he had to do something about the Medicine Man and on August 10th, he wrote to Colonel Eugene Asa Carr saying, it "would be well to arrest Nock-ay-det-klinne and send him off or have him killed without arresting him." In other words, he was advocating a murder. The record indicates he also sent messages to the camps of Naiche and Chatto, who were living with Gordo's people, forming a band of about 55 Chokonens and Bedonkohes, to see if they would object if the Medicine Man were neutralized. There is no indication they responded one way or another.

First, the soldiers needed to find Nock-ay-det-klinne and assigned that job to a company of 100 troopers and a cadre of 25 White Mountain Apache scouts under the command of Colonel Carr. Chatto was not among these scouts. They were from Fort Apache, many miles north. But scouts had a way of communicating and Chatto became aware very quickly what happened.

Col. Asa Carr, War Dept.

Many of the scouts were from the same Canon Creek band of the Western Apache tribe as the medicine man. There was some Army discussion about the loyalty of these scouts and whether to allow them to keep their rifles. Some of them had, themselves, attended the ghost dances. Nevertheless, on August 15, 1881, Colonel Carr left Fort Apache with five officers, seventy-nine enlisted soldiers and twenty-three scouts to make the arrest. Carr should not have acted as officious as he did. He was an experienced Civil War Veteran with a Medal of Honor to his credit and numerous wounds suffered at Pea Ridge, Vicksburg, Mobile and elsewhere. He left the war as a Major General.

He told his scouts he was not going to hurt Nock-ay-det-klinne, but wanted the medicine man to come in with him. The Indians didn't understand why a medicine man needed to be arrested for doing good things for the people. The troops rode for two days through mountainous country covered with timber, then deep canyons with rocky sides. An Indian interpreter was allowed to ride ahead to tell the medicine man not to worry or flee. In camp, Carr had a long talk with his scouts trying to reassure them everything would be alright. At a point where the trail divided, Carr thought his scouts were perturbed when he picked the upper trail and they wanted him to go down the lower one. Carr suspected they wanted to lead him into an ambush.

When the command was about two miles from the Apache village, the leader of the Carizzo Creek band of the Cibecue Apaches, a warrior called Sanchez, appeared on a white pony and wearing face paint. He rode with the column for a while, troopers thought he was counting them, and then Sanchez broke off and rode away. Finally the troops arrived at Nock-ay-det-klinne's village and the trail leading up to his wickiup.

Things went well, except the Medicine Man was reluctant to go with the soldiers. He seemed to be stalling. Members of his tribe were gathering around to see what was happening. Colonel Carr explained his mission; that the medicine man would be treated as a friend while an investigation was done and that if he tried to escape he would be killed and if he caused any problems he would be killed and if he didn't come he would be killed. Nock-ay-det-klinne must have enjoyed this conversation.

Carr left the village after introducing the medicine man to his armed guard. Carr would back-track to a wide camping spot near the Verde crossing, with Troop D behind him, followed by the pack train, followed by the medicine man, guards and scouts and finally by Troop E. Nock-ay-det-klinne caused a gap to form in the line of march when he insisted he stop and get more personal belongings, a horse, and a meal. A Lieutenant said "No", and issued orders for him to get a move on.

Colonel Carr wound his way down the mountainside. The guards and their prisoners followed slowly and noticed that more and more Apaches were showing up and that they were armed. Worse, they were only wearing breach-clothes, a thing Apaches did when preparing for battle. They crowded around their medicine man and the talk was lively. Then they attacked.

The scouts joined the Indians. They mutinied, firing at U.S. troops. A brief close range engagement occurred. Nock-ay-det-klinne was wounded in the shooting. His wife and young son were killed. Nock-ay-det-klinne was ultimately delivered to Col Carr and Carr ordered a Lieutenant Byrnes to kill him on the spot. That may have been done with an ax. Soldiers and Apaches fired at each other until the sun went down.

By the end of the fighting, the Apaches had killed seven soldiers and wounded another three. During the next couple of days the Cibecue and White Mountain Apaches ambushed travelers, killed another three soldiers and four civilians, then attacked Fort Apache itself until they were driven off. The Chiricahua at San Carlos didn't get involved in these hostilities except for Bonito. He and twenty of his band skirmished with soldiers during the outbreak. Army patrols went out looking for him. Within a week he promised to turn himself in, but then reneged. By that time the army had arrested 45 Apaches.

One would have expected Chatto, Naiche and especially Geronimo to go crazy when news of the medicine man's fate reached them. But that's not what happened. They remained strangely subdued, that is, until the army over-reacted to the Cibeque outbreak.

The army court-martialed five of the scouts who surrendered, sending two to a military prison. The other three, Sergeant Dandy Jim, Sergeant Dead Shot, and Private Skippy—were hanged at Camp Grant on March 3, 1882.

Dandy Jim: Hanged for scout revolt

But the biggest over-reaction came from Commanding General of the Army, William Tecumseh Sherman. He looked upon the Cibeque revolt as nothing less than the start of another Apache war and he telegraphed Colonel Carr that he wanted the "renegades destroyed." Before long army troops from most of the surrounding camps and forts were converging on Fort Apache and San Carlos. The rumor circulated that the troops were going to wipe out the Apaches or, at the very least, their leadership.

The Chiricahua called together a counsel of all their leaders. Naiche, Geronimo, Gordo, Chatto, Juh, Chihuahua, Bonito and Loco were there. They talked about the betrayal of Cochise and the murder of Mangas Coloradas and vowed they could not fall victim to the white man's concept of justice. Juh and Geronimo dominated the debate. That is to say Geronimo did most of the talking because of Juh's stuttering problem. It was more manly to die on the warpath "than to be killed in prison," he said.

After the conference Geronimo spoke directly to Chatto. "I go. We cannot trust the whites. They are killing the leaders. There will be much trouble for us if we stay. If you would be a strong chief, come with us. If you will be a scout, come get me, and you die."

Chatto noticed the fire in Geronimo's eyes. He was quoted as saying "Geronimo was just like a wild animal," because of the troops swarming the area.

Chatto explained his dilemma to Welsh. "I was very angry at the death of Nock-ay-det-Klinne. There was no reason for the army to arrest him or stop the dances. They were a good way for our people to escape their everyday lives. Geronimo, Juh and Naiche believed the Army wanted to wipe out our leaders. I had my family, my house, and my animals there on the reservation. But what good was that if the Army killed me? Then Geronimo said his warriors had killed the Indian agent. That did it. I had to go or die."

During the night of September 30, 1881, Chatto urged Nalthchedah and Ishchosen to make haste, packing up all their essentials for a quick get-away. Nalthchedah balked.

"I will not go," she said, crossing her arms in front of her. "It is too difficult with the young one and I do not want to live in the Mexico mountains."

"Then we are divorced," said Chatto and he said no more. Chatto took Ishchosen, Maude, Bedisclove and Naboka and joined 375 other Chiricahuas who slit the throats of their dogs and light colored horses and slipped away from San Carlos. The old warrior, Mohtsos, also left his wife and kids, Martine and Helen, on the reservation. 200 of the escapees were Chokonens under Naiche and Chatto. Gordo took 89 Bedonkohes and Juh had 86 of his Nednhis, including the women warriors Lozen and Dahteste. Loco's band which numbered 270 in all remained at the agency. Loco argued that the tribe was at peace and he believed things could return to normal if they just bided their time.

Recalling the incident to Herbert Welsh, Chatto broke a small grin. "We called him Loco because he was crazy enough to trust the whites."

Prior to this Geronimo was certainly a leader, but one of many. With this escape Geronimo began his odyssey of becoming the most notable Apache warrior of the time. He became legendary because he represented an ideal built around fierce independence and the willingness to fight for what he believed. He would be more feared, more vicious, more invisible, and more distrustful than anybody. Coloradas was dead because he trusted the whites and wanted to make peace. Cochise was dead because he sought peace and died in captivity. Victorio was dead because he wanted freedom. Only Geronimo and to a lesser extent Juh, kept the dream alive and he would fight to the end.

Chatto told Welsh, "We were on the trail and moving fast to Mexico when we learned that Geronimo had lied about killing the Indian agent. It was just another thing he said to get us out of there. But it was too late by that time."

Welsh rubbed his chin, thinking about the logistics. "So you and the others had 300 or so people you were leading over the desert and into the mountains?"

"No, no." replied Chatto, "We were not so many miles away from San Carlos when we split into four groups. Juh was our leader because he had fought the Mexicans and Americans to a stand-still so many years. He divided us and told us to meet again in the Santa Terese Mountains. I had one group. Naiche had one, Juh and Bonito had the others. Geronimo split off and got horses for us at many places."

Under the leadership of Juh and Naiche, Geronimo, Chatto and the others who bolted from the reservation staged a brilliant but deadly military campaign getting to Mexico. They traveled almost 220 miles, living off the land and raiding extensively for horses, weapons, ammunition and food. They were pursued by hundreds of troops along the way, with minimum losses. In the process they took about 75 lives. The dead included freighters and ranchers found out on the roads, prospectors, ranch hands, miners and a deputy sheriff, in addition to the soldiers they shot. Only about eight Apachies are documented to have died.

A short time later, and miles away, the White Mountain Apaches under a young chief named Na-tio-tisha retaliated for the killing of their medicine man. They ambushed and killed four San Carlos policemen, including the police chief. This appears to be an incident in which the chief of police tried to stop a young Apache from running away by firing a shot at him and killed a woman by mistake. The Indians didn't wait long before they caught the police chief and killed him. They rode for the Tonto basin, where Lake Roosevelt now sits. Local Arizona settlers were greatly alarmed and demanded protection from the U.S. Army. It sent out fourteen companies of US cavalry from forts across the region.

Na-tio-tisha wasn't the same caliber of tactician as Cochise, Victorio or Geronimo. Within weeks he allowed his warriors to be cut off and surrounded by U.S. troops along the Mogollon Rim of Arizona near General Springs. In the battle named "The Big Dry Wash," from sixteen to twenty-seven warriors were killed, including Na-tio-tisha.

Juh led the Apache escapees to his mountain stronghold east of Casas Grandes and discovered where Nana's forces had crossed not more than two weeks prior. They would link up to bolster their band against mounting Mexican efforts in Chihuahua province. Juh and Geronimo discussed the possibility of going back to get Loco's men at San Carlos because he had forty warriors they needed. Geronimo argued that Loco's people would just wither and die on the reservation. He said Loco should be with them, whether he liked it or not.

Juh decided to send Bonito to San Carlos to scout the situation and perhaps convince Loco to join them in Mexico. Bonito was chosen because he had relatives among the White Mountain Apaches at Fort Apache. Thirty of his own band were still there and maybe he could bring them back. Bonito was trusted as a strong leader. He rode out with a small war party in late December.

Meantime Juh took Naiche and Chatto with 40 warriors south with him, where they raided Mexican mining districts. On January 18th, 1882, Juh, Naiche and Chatto assaulted the mining settlement of Dolores, killing two men and wounding three in a five-hour battle. Next day their warriors captured a thirty-mule train just outside of town, scattering eight teamsters who ran for their lives. These raids prompted the Mexican government to recruit Terahumara Indians to fight the Apaches. For centuries the Tarahumaras had been implacable foes of the Apaches and fierce fighting usually resulted when they met. The Mexican government also offered a new bounty for any Apache, dead or alive.

Separately, Geronimo continued raiding to the north where his band killed fifteen people, wounded five others and captured two children over a period of three days. In early February Geronimo was back with the others when the Apaches assaulted the village of Nacori Chico in the northern Sierra Madre. This time the villagers were ready for them and repulsed the attack, killing at least four of the Chiricahuas.

Then Bonito returned from San Carlos. He had talked to Loco, he said, and the chief said 'no,' he was not interested in joining the renegades. Bonito said he threatened Loco. He told Loco a huge force of warriors would come and get him and his people and they would kill anyone who didn't agree. Loco still said "no." After Bonito left to report to Juh, Loco told U.S. authorities about the threat and assured them he was happy on the reservation.

At the same time several of Chatto's friends, who had remained on the reservation, enlisted in the scouts and would now be pursuing him. They included Dutchy, Jose First, Tsedikizen, Toclanny and Massai. Dutchy and Massai were apparently torn about which side to be on. Sent on a scouting mission, Massai defected and went over to the renegades. Dutchy left his assignment at Fort Stanton and headed toward Mexico. His reputation was tarnished when he and two others killed a Mormon freighter, Jacob Ferrin, and took his horses and guns. That left them with no choice but to join the renegades.

CHAPTER 25   Kidnapping Loco

In mid-April, just a month after General Crook left for the Sioux Wars and Orlando B. Willcox became his replacement as Commander of the Military Department of Arizona, Willcox got his first serious embarrassment. Chatto rode with Geronimo, who led about five-dozen top warriors, including Naiche and Bonito, back across the Mexican border, raiding and killing along the way to San Carlos to convince Loco to join them or kidnap him.

On the way to San Carlos, Chatto had his first serious falling out with Geronimo. Geronimo directed his warriors towards a sheep camp owned by American George Stevens. It was run by a Mexican he knew, Victoriano Mestas.

Outside the Mexican's hut Geronimo yelled "It is me, Mestas. I have many men and we are hungry. We will not harm you for I am Geronimo, your friend."

A hired hand, Richard Bylas, warned Mestas this was not a good idea. "They will kill you. You can't trust Geronimo." Then he yelled out to Geronimo. "You are a liar, Geronimo. You've always been a liar."

But Mestas had lived around Geronimo, had even received gifts from the Apache. He relented and invited Geronimo and his men to stay and eat. His wife put together a whopping meal; tortillas, mutton, even a young pony was prepared because Geronimo didn't like lamb. After the meal Geronimo wiped his mouth with the sleeve of his tunic and ordered his men to tie up six ranch hands with their hands behind their backs. Turning to Mestas he ordered, "Give me your shirt." It was a fancy shirt with impressive embroidery. Geronimo would wear it all the way to San Carlos. Then, he had Mestas and his wife and two children tied up too.

Bylas, who had argued with Mestas earlier that Geronimo was a liar, turned on Geronimo. "Why do you want to kill these people after they have fed you and you promised to harm no one?"

Naiche chimed in, "You ought to pay this woman for the meal."

Chatto agreed, "Why would you kill these people? We would have lost many men if we had attacked this camp."

Geronimo stopped and considered this.

The fierce chief Chihuahua argued the opposite. "These people are Mexicans. Always the Mexicans have lied to us and killed our people."

That was enough for Geronimo. Exercising his considerable power, he ordered his warriors to take a rope and lead Mestes, his wife, their children and the six sheepherders outside, up a hill and he watched as all nine were shot, stabbed and their heads pounded in with rocks. Except Mestas. He was finished off with an axe to the head.

After the massacre, Geronimo walked fast toward Chatto and Naiche, fire in his eyes. They were standing with Richard Bylas and were determined that Bylas would not be murdered also. Naiche made sure Geronimo was within hearing range when he told two of his own men, "If he says anything, kill him." Geronimo didn't say anything.

Things were tense and got worse when the war party discovered that a nine-year old boy, a third son of Victoriano Mestas had been overlooked and Geronimo said, "Kill him too."

That was too much for another warrior who had remained silent while the boy's family was brutally slaughtered. This was Jelikine, a Mexican who had been captured and raised as a warrior by Apaches. He pointed a lance at Geronimo's chest.

"The people you have killed today are my people but something— I think it is their God— has spared the little one's life. Do not harm him or I will kill you, Geronimo." Then he turned to face others. "I will kill any man who harms the little boy."

Geronimo mounted and rode away. The boy was spared.

Naiche looked at Chatto and slowly shook his head. Chatto responded, " I kill," he said, "but I don't do it for fun."

Nearing the Indian agency, Chatto and his men cut the telegraph wires to the west of San Carlos. This was discovered by a telegraph operator who wondered why his messages weren't going through and he repaired the wires then clicked out messages warning that Indians were in the area. One of those messages was delivered to Police Chief Albert Sterling with whom Chatto had worked on the reservation. Sterling quickly recruited one Indian policeman, Sagotol, and they rode out to investigate. Somewhere between San Carlos and Loco's camp, they ran into Chatto, Chihuahua, Naiche and Geronimo. After the Indians killed the Sheriff and his deputy, the story goes that they played football with the Sheriff's head.

A week later, Geronimo's forces stole up outside Loco's camp in the middle of the night. Just before sunrise he lined up fifty warriors outside the village. As they rode in, Geronimo shouted, "Take them all. Shoot anyone who refuses to go with us." Naiche and Chatto rode directly for Loco's wickiup.

The Chihenne chief strode outside and faced them. "I will not go," he said.

Chatto dismounted with his Winchester. He pointed the barrel at Loco's face. "If you don't go, you will die right here," he said.

Within the hour Geronimo's party was marching 300 people, under the very noses of the Americans, away from San Carlos on a torturous journey to Mexico. Along the way, they would slay no fewer than 25 Americans and Mexicans. Chatto, Naiche and Kayitah killed three men near Green's Hill on the first day out.

One of Loco's men was Tzoe, who the whites called "Peaches" because of the color and texture of his skin. He was particularly resentful of being uprooted from the reservation, with his two wives and children and driven into the wilds of Mexico. He would figure prominently when the time was ripe for retaliation.

On April 23, 1882, the Chiricahuas went into camp on a high mountain near Steins Peak, on the Arizona-New Mexico border. Only once had any of the 3,000 U.S. Soldiers sent out to chase them, gotten close enough to exchange gunfire. That morning Chatto ambushed American troopers led by Lt. Col. George Forsyth.

It started when a Lieutenant McDonald was following the trail through a narrow defile with only a few soldiers and scouts who were willing to go into an area ready made for an ambush. Next thing he knew he was looking down the barrels of fifteen rifles in the hands of Chatto's warriors. Almost involuntarily the Lieutenant jerked his head away from a fellow rider who was bumping him and it probably saved him from the bullet that went whizzing by his ear. Three Yuma scouts to his left were shot out of the saddle by a first volley. The soldiers, who had been riding five abreast, turned and galloped for safety, McDonald taking a bullet through his hat. Fifty yards to the rear, the soldiers wheeled about and dismounted to face what they estimated were 150 Apaches. They held on until six more cavalry troops from Colonel Forsyth came to the rescue. The Indians set fire to the grass to cover their retreat.

Forsyth followed Chatto's men into Horseshoe Canyon and found them heavily entrenched. Major Wirt Davis led a frontal charge through the burning vegetation and smoke. Everybody was shooting. After an hour the Apaches fell back again, only to take up another strong position. The Union troops tried to flank them. Chatto responded by ordering his warriors to climb higher into the rock walls of the rugged canyon. There, they fired from twelve hundred feet above the soldiers.

The Americans suffered from the hot, suffocating air in the bottom of the canyon and from the lack of water. At last they could no longer reach the Apaches. Finding a small pool of creek water farther into the canyon, soldiers threw down their rifles and lapped lustily at the water. Chatto's men peppered them with rifle fire, but no one was injured. The crowd at the watering pool scattered for cover as a second volley ripped dirt at their feet. Then there was nothing. The

Battle of Horseshoe Canyon was done. Major Forsyth reported it as a victory. Others said it was far from that. They said the Major had no stomach for combat and failed to perform when he had the Indians trapped. In fact, he had lost seven men. Chatto lost two men and thirteen horses, captured by the soldiers. The main body of Apaches slipped away from that engagement and pushed for thirty-six hours to enter Mexico.

Crossing the border, they thought they were safe and stopped to rest and relax. They made camp, talked and sang. But they did not put out sentinels. They had no idea the Americans, with Chief of Scouts Al Sieber had unlawfully entered Mexico and were edging closer to them.

Sieber was a German immigrant brought to the United States by his widowed mother in time for his entry into the Civil War where he was wounded seriously at Gettysburg. He had prospected in California, Nevada and Arizona Territory when General Crook hired him to be Chief of Scouts. He was in charge of the troops that forced the Yavapai on their long march to San Carlos. Now he developed a careful plan to surround the Apaches and spring a cross-fire trap.

It might have gone that way if some anxious scouts hadn't gone off half-cocked, firing at women who were gathering plants outside the main camp. But those shots alerted the main body of Indians. The army threw together a mad charge toward the village, killing one of Loco's sons and thirteen other Chiricahuas. The Apaches scattered into the rocky outcrops where they blasted away at the troopers. The battle lasted through the morning and into the afternoon.

Chatto had strong warriors with him; Kayitah and Fun, a second cousin of Geronimo among them. A medicine man, She-neah prayed for them and turned to the four directions of the compass, blessing each man. Then they charged the dismounted troopers, firing from the hip, and forced them to withdraw. Chatto believed he killed two soldiers with rifle fire. Soon the Americans ran out of water and ammunition. Chatto again had broken the American attack and his rear guard was able to hold the troops at bay while the band escaped.

Loco, Warm Springs Chief

All in all, the San Carlos raid was a brilliant military maneuver by Geronimo and Juh. They made it into Mexico; 200 miles from San Carlos, within one week after the expedition began. On the trail Chatto confirmed his leadership skills in battle, in helping steal enough sheep to feed everyone, enough horses to provide transportation and food for all and enough rifles to put up a good fight if they were caught. He was now allowed to participate in council where strategies were being discussed. Soon Loco also sat in council. He seemed to have softened his opposition to being uprooted so rudely.

CHAPTER 26   Aliso

Problem was; with 3000 U.S. troops trying to chase down the renegades, Mexican troops were also alerted and positioned themselves to intercept them. And the Mexicans found them in the long valley at Aliso Creek. It was an unmitigated disaster. Loco would lose fully 40 per-cent of his band.

Nearly 200 Mexican army troops, under General Lorenzo Garcia hid themselves along the creek and waited. Near dawn, here came the Apaches with Naiche, Chatto, Kayitah and their bands riding point. Behind them, strung out over a half-mile or so, was Loco's tribe, followed by Geronimo and most of his fighting men, forming a rear guard. The Mexicans allowed Chatto and the other point riders to go on by. They waited for the main body to arrive and then they cut loose with everything they had.

In the indiscriminate firing men women and children went down like bowling pins. Whole families perished in seconds. Some of the Mexicans were within 100 yards of the Apaches. They couldn't miss. Peaches was hit and unable to help his two wives and baby. They buckled from the impact of bullets. Jason Betzinez, one of Geronimo's apprentices at the time, said in his book—*I rode with Geronimo*-- "It was a dreadful, pitiful sight; one I will never forget." Apaches who could run the fastest, or had the best luck, managed to escape. But there was little cover and Mexican infantry overtook many women and children running up the sloping terrain away from the creek bed.

Geronimo and his warriors kicked their ponies and rode directly into the melee and he fought like a wild man. Many of the Mexicans had charged into the Indians with their bayonets fixed, stabbing and ripping at their victims. The battle quickly became hand-to-hand combat and lasted all day. If there was a hero at Aliso it was the fierce teenage warrior Fun, Geronimo's second-cousin. Pinned down in a little creek bed and under orders from Geronimo to retreat, leaving some women and children behind, Fun said, in effect, "Hell no, I won't go." He told his cousin he would shoot him if he insisted on a retreat. Then he jumped over the bank of the creek and charged at the Mexicans, killing several of them with his single-shot rifle and breaking down their line. With Geronimo providing covering fire, the warriors killed more than twenty Mexicans and set fire to grasses along the creek-side to cover an escape.

The Apaches slowly disengaged and started sneaking back into the mountains at dark with many crying because of their wounds and 78 of their number left behind. Loco's son was gone and his beautiful daughter was missing, probably taken hostage with another 32 women. They eventually arrived at Juh's stronghold, where Chatto found that his youthful companion, Kaetenae, from the Warm Springs Band, had also made his way with some of Victorio's men.

There was great blame and recrimination among the Apaches after this ambush. Why, for instance, hadn't Naiche, Chatto and Kayitah ridden to the rescue? They must have heard the gunfire. They knew a huge battle was underway less than a mile away. Years later, Jason Betzinez would say, "Here they were sitting well armed and with plenty of ammunition, yet doing nothing. I felt dreadfully ashamed of them. They never fired a shot, while half a mile away beyond the hill their fellow tribesmen and their women and children were being butchered." It was one of the things Herbert Welsh didn't discuss with Chatto and there is no record of his explanation. And what of Geronimo? Loco's band blamed him as the one who engineered the great kidnapping of the band and brought them here to die, when all they wanted was to live in peace on the reservation. They carried the memory.

CHAPTER 27   Casas Grande

Geronimo shook off the Aliso Creek Massacre as if it were a normal occurrence in the work-a-day world of the Apache renegade. The peace-loving Loco probably wished with all his heart he could just return to the reservation. But if he tried, he knew Geronimo would have him tortured and killed. Chatto may have also longed for the security of San Carlos, but he had cast his lot with Geronimo.

He told Welsh, "I followed Geronimo. He was many years older and wiser than me. He was strong and protected his people. I thought if I would raid with him, I would be the best I could be and my family would be most safe because of his power and knowledge."

Naiche remained the chief of the Chokonens, but he too deferred to Geronimo. In spite of the sheep-camp massacre his relations with Geronimo gradually got better.

Chatto and his family moved along under Geronimo's leadership higher and higher into the Sierra Madres, just below massive snow covered peaks rising to 11-thousand feet and across deep gorges. He and Ishchosen carried Bedisclove and Naboka through some of the snows, always preferring that they walk and build their strength. Over some of this land it was impossible. They followed game trails deeper and deeper into the range until they felt safe. Even today the rugged area is almost roadless. By early May, Juh's camp contained the greatest gathering of Apaches in several years. Chatto helped Ishchosen build a wickiup and provided hides to keep her and the children warm inside. Food and supplies were scarce.

Chatto went with Geronimo and twenty-five Chiricahuas to raid Alma, New Mexico in 1885. On May 16th, the Apaches killed two miners and stole some horses, a routine day's work. Next day Captain Allen Smith set out from Fort Apache with two companies from the 4th Cavalry and some Apache scouts. They were in canyon lands along Devils Creek, in the Mogollon Mountains when the Apaches opened fire from the top of a large cliff. Chatto wounded one scout. Two soldiers were wounded and two of their horses were killed. This type of hit and run attack was typical of Geronimo who was always low on men, ammunition, food, and horses and couldn't afford the losses from pitched battles.

Geronimo, in need of reinforcements, sent his wife She-gah to the Mescalero reservation to ask warriors there to come and join him. Instead, reservation police took her into custody and notified the Army. The Army took her to Fort Apache. Geronimo cursed and said, "I will go get her back." Chatto understood. The Apache band was built around family.

Meantime, the escape from San Carlos and the raiding of American ranches and settlements on the way to sanctuary in Mexico created a sensation in the American press. Perhaps due to exaggerated reports of some of his depravations, complete with bloody descriptions of the victims, particularly if they were young, Geronimo was now the most feared and hated Indian alive. Many publications renewed calls to exterminate all Indians….off the reservations or on.

After Alma, John Clum, now the Mayor of Tombstone, set out once again to capture Geronimo, Chatto and the rest. He put together a posse that contained his friends the Earp brothers, Virgil, Wyatt and Morgan and 25 others. He told his followers since the Army had let Geronimo go before, this time they would send him back in a box. But they were plagued with heavy rains, rider fatigue and the inability to legally cross the Mexican border even though they thought they were on Geronimo's trail. They turned back. Less than a month later the Earps were involved in the gunfight at the OK corral that would signal the beginning of the end for the Earps in Tombstone, and Clum, himself.

Chatto said he wanted no one left alive when he and 10 other warriors attacked a 12-wagon mule train. All of the mule skinners were killed. He felt this was necessary. Chatto's reputation grew as a rough and tough, brutal and cruel enemy. He was proving his leadership to warriors he planned to recruit to his own band. He led other attacks on ranches, wagons and unlucky travelers, where the Apaches provided horses to themselves and herded beef cattle as the body moved forward.

Many of the Apaches wanted peace like they had experienced in the United States, only without being required to live on a reservation. They pressured Juh and Geronimo to work toward a treaty with the Mexicans. Such treaties were often very local in nature, but any respite would be good. The Council asked Chatto his opinion and he said it was a good idea; it would protect the Apache encampments from nearby Mexicans, at least. The two leaders set about to get a treaty so that they could live comfortably just east of Casas Grande. They never seemed to learn about dealing with the Mexicans.

In the late spring, bands headed by Chatto, Naiche, Geronimo, Zele, Sanchez and Juh's group encamped outside the Mexican town of Casas Grande. Geronimo and Juh met with civil authorities, everybody shook hands and they anticipated peace talks. The Mexican army worked out a plan to get all the Indians drunk, surround them and exterminate the lot in one bold attack. Casas Grande civil officialdom was in on the plot and sent two wagonloads of whiskey and corn liquor to the Apache camp outside of town.

It worked just fine; just like it always did. The Apaches never handled their liquor well and Chatto was no exception. He drank the Mexican whiskey. He and most all of the Apaches got very drunk. He danced and howled and stumbled and fell and vomited and drank some more. Three days of this and the Apaches were wasted. Some of the wiser women, Ishchosen among them, knew about this routine and began hustling their kids out of camp. And Geronimo, remembering Janos and a dozen other such traps, got his senses together and started moving his people away while more than 500 Mexicans started getting in place.

As the Indians lay around their camp near dawn, the Mexican troops fell on them, shooting at random. Chatto was awakened, on his end of the encampment, by the sound of rifle and pistol fire. The screams brought him to his feet. His head was spinning. Around him it was less a running battle than a confused panic of escaping Apaches. He took no time to find his horse. He ran. Warriors and women dropped in front of him, behind him. His head throbbed, but he picked up speed and was soon out of the village and heading toward the mountains. Kayitah's wife saved him. She dragged Kayitah into the weeds along the riverbank as soldiers were slitting the throats of drunken warriors. A dozen warriors died that way. The Mexicans captured 30 women and children. Geronimo's second wife, Chee-has-kish the mother of his son, Chappo, was among them. Chatto thanked his lucky stars that Ishchosen had the foresight to be well away from Casas Grande before the Mexicans pounced.

After that, everybody moved to another of Juh's strongholds to the southwest, camping on the brink of the "Great Canyon" where they would be safe. Juh and Geronimo were outraged, out of their heads with anger. They could have blamed themselves for inaugurating the peace initiative and for letting their warriors get so out of control with liquor. Instead, they blamed the Mexicans and vowed to set off on a new round of widespread raiding and killing.

For this purpose, they split up. Geronimo took Chihuahua and Kayitah and 80 warriors with him for raids against Sonora. They would travel three hundred miles, killing everyone in their path; between forty and fifty people. Chatto, Naiche and Bonito went with Juh.

Juh's forces struck Tarachi in late June, 1882, killing four civilians and taking their cattle. Mexicans trying to trail them found two more bodies near the Agua Blanca Mountains. The closest they got to Juh's band was an abandoned camp with fifty wickiups which probably housed 80 warriors. The trail went into the Sierra Madre and divided. In subsequent actions Juh, Chatto and Naiche's men burned a ranch, killed nine women and a child and made off with 200 head of cattle. They killed two vaqueros at Onayas and three out of ten men trying to follow them. Eight Mexican troops died at Rio Chico in July. Almost out of ammunition near Milpias, the innovative Juh had Chatto and other warriors roll boulders down on advancing troops crushing three of them and stopping the assault. The death toll mounted to fifty or more. They raided ranches and fought Mexican troops south of Sahuaripa, 200 miles south of the U.S. border through the summer.

Chatto and Naiche needed a rest. They moved their village south to the Aros River near its junction with the Mulatos River. Loco established his camp nearby. Juh drifted back to Sonora. In the fall, Geronimo rejoined Juh at Guaynopa. Before parting they had all agreed they would retaliate for the attack at Casas Grande, in force, as if they hadn't done so already. The target would be Galeana, deep into Mexico, south of Monterrey.

Mustering nearly 140 fighters, including some teenage boys, the combined bands arrived in place in November, 1882, with a plan. They would raid the huge cattle ranch of Juan Mata Ortiz. They hated him. He had been at Tres Castillos when Victorio fell, he was at Casas Grande when the Mexicans attacked. He was the commander of the town's Mexican garrison. After raiding his ranch, they would be ready to ambush anyone who came after them on ground of their choosing. That ground was the grassy Chocolate Pass in the America Mountains. It took a second raid before the Apaches could get anyone to chase them. When someone did, it was Juan Mata Ortiz, himself, with a posse of vaqueros.

The trap set by Juh and Geronimo didn't quite work out as planned. They expected Ortiz and his men to follow decoy warriors placed out in front of the main body. But with the first gunfire, the Mexicans turned right and dug into the surrounding hills, placing piles of rocks in front of them. Likewise, the Apaches crept closer to the Mexicans placing large rocks in front of their faces as they crawled forward. It was Bonito who really went after them with a handful of warriors. He was so enraged when a Mexican bullet grazed his medicine man across the skull, that he jumped up, gave a war hoot, and ran with his warriors through the middle of the Mexicans and killed a half dozen of them. Chatto fired from rifle-range, along with others, picking off Mexicans one-by-one until almost none were left. Of the twenty three Mexicans engaged, only two survived; a foot soldier and Senor Juan Mata Ortiz, who Juh and Geronimo had ordered to be kept alive.

Juh and Geronimo let the infantryman go. They told Commander Ortiz, "no bala, no cuchillo, no lance, pero lumre" Ortiz must have cringed in fright…it meant "no bullet, no arrow, no lance, but fire." In other words, Ortiz was not going to have a quick death. They built a fire in a pit at the crest of the hill, waited for the coals to glow to a bright orange, and threw Juan Ortiz alive into the flames. Tour groups, some from as far away as Europe, still visit the site, the rocks, the pit. The hill is named for Juan Ortiz.

CHAPTER 28　　　Crook Returns

With the civilized peoples of New Mexico and Arizona screaming bloody murder about Apache depravations, the U.S. Government returned Nantan Lupan, the Tan Wolf, General George Crook, to the Apache wars. He took command on September 4, 1882. For the last seven years he had been fighting the Sioux without unqualified success, considering his column was defeated by Crazy Horse at the Battle of the Rosebud and his young egotist colleague, General George Armstrong Custer, was annihilated at the Little Big Horn. Still, his reputation as an Indian fighter was intact and he was the man to chase down Geronimo and get him in chains or swinging from the end of a rope. Crook issued a report stating that Geronimo and his band "have killed not less than one-thousand persons in this country and in Mexico. They are the worst band of Indians in America."

Again, his actions were documented by his aide, Captain Bourke. John Bourke was a Civil War Medal of Honor winner for gallantry in action at the Battle of Stones River, Tennessee, and later saw action at the Battle of Chickamauga. He had run away from a cultured home in Pennsylvania at sixteen and lied about his age to get into the Fifteenth Pennsylvania Volunteer Cavalry. He was keenly observant as an aide to General Crook and a prolific journalist. The assignment gave him a front row seat in the Apache Wars. It was he who, later, contacted Herbert Welsh, at the urging of General Crook, to investigate Fort Marion, and went along with him.

Joseph Tiffany resigned as San Carlos Indian agent on June 30, 1882, in ill health, leaving behind a legacy of corruption and inattention. He was replaced by another political appointee, Philip Wilcox, who aligned himself with General Crook, forming the first cooperative venture the agents had known with the military.

Crook immediately issued orders that the Indians were to be treated firmly but fairly and he journeyed to Fort Apache and San Carlos to talk to the Apache leaders still on the reservation, listening to their complaints and catching up on the dynamic events that had taken place. Then he appointed Captain Emmet Crawford and Lieutenant Charles Gatewood to take control of the Apache scouts and the Indian police. Both were good choices.

Crawford cut his teeth in the Civil War, during the fierce fighting at Antietam and Fredricksburg, where he was wounded severely enough to miss the rest of the war. Now at 44 years old, he had the Sioux wars behind him. He was in Crook's 3rd Cavalry and fought in the Battle of Rosebud Creek, just before George Custer and the 7th Cavalry was slaughtered at the Little Bighorn. He was in Arizona, at Fort Thomas, by 1882, to deal with the Apache and Crook assigned him as military commandant at the San Carlos reservation.

Captain Emmet Crawford. War Dept.

First Lieutenant Charles B. Gatewood, one year older than Chatto, was a West Point graduate who had been assigned to the frontier from the get-go. He had led some of the first Apache scouts during the wars against the Yavapai and Western bands. He became familiar with Apache ways, learned their language, visited his scouts daily and he didn't talk down to them. The scouts called him Nanton Bse-che: "Big-nosed Captain."

Crook was expected to keep reservation Apaches where they were and to run down, capture or kill all renegades. The Administrations of Grant, Rutherford Hayes, James Garfield and now Chester Arthur were under increasing pressure from their constituents, especially those in the southwest, to end the Indian wars and set the stage for their developments in agriculture, mining, industrialization and growth. The Indian Wars were winding down during Arthur's administration and there was growing public sentiment toward more favorable treatment of Native Americans, except in Arizona. Arthur convinced Congress to provide more money for Indian education and he favored an allotment system that would give individual Indians and not just their tribes, ownership of their land. But two things were throwing a kink into his plans. White settlers and ranchers continued to encroach on Native American lands and the Chiricahua Apache renegades were still violently trying to stop them.

Now and then the Apache renegades would split, then reform for a variety of reasons; disputes, control, safety, familiarity with terrain, resources, personal desires. Juh and his followers decided to go deeper into the Mexican mountains. Geronimo and Chihuahua stayed north. They needed supplies for the winter and raided in Sonora into mid-January 1883, killing great numbers of Mexicans. Again, Chatto, Naiche and Loco went with Juh and were on hand when his leadership ended at a bloody confrontation with the Mexican army.

About December 10, 1882, Mexican militia discovered Juh's substantial trail in the mining country in the south of Chihuahua province. They followed and found where 100 Indians had captured a tobacco train and killed three teamsters near Sahuaripa, on the way to their winter encampment a little north of Guaynopa and Chihuahua City. This is where two detachments of the Chihuahua volunteer troops, augmented by the fierce Tarahumara Indians found them.

The Mexicans attacked from two directions on the morning of January 6, 1883 with 100 men. They ran through the camp, yelling and firing at anything that moved. The Apache warriors scrambled. Chatto had barely enough time to grab his weapon. Ishchosen and the children were huddling in their shelter. The Apaches left possessions and, in the case of Chatto and several others, had to leave their families behind. A battle ensued, but the Apaches had been taken by surprise and had no plan and, in the circumstances, no central leadership. They hit and hid and ran, trying to work out some coordinated response. But it was mayhem.

The ten-year-old Maude looked at her mother with wide fearful eyes. Ishchosen said, "Run!" Maude peeked outside, focused on a rock outcropping and ran for it. She squeezed herself into a crevice and waited, hands over her head, as rifle shots zipped through the air and pinged on rocks and bone. When the Tarahumaras found Ishchosen, Bedicslove and Naboka cowering in their tent they snatched them up and dragged them to the center of the camp where nearly thirty-five others had been herded. Two of Geronimo's wives and their two children were prisoners and several cousins to Naiche. The Mexicans burned the Apache village as reinforcements arrived to seal the victory.

The attack broke the back of Juh's tribe and destroyed his personal power. Twelve Apache warriors were killed and scalped. Juh lost his wife, a son-in-law and a grandchild. Bonito's wife and child were among the dead. All told, the Mexicans reported eighty Apaches killed, wounded or captured.

Hours after the battle, with the Mexicans gone, Maude ventured out of her hiding place in the rocks and stumbled toward the survivors who were still gathering. When she found her devastated father, Chatto picked her up in his arms and held her tight. Then he put her down again and said, "We must go." He and the other survivors now faced the cold of winter with no provisions, no stock and no safe haven. The spirit was gone from Juh. He gathered his own family and a very few others and left for the wilds of the Sierra Madre. Chatto and the others had little choice but to find Geronimo to the north and seek the protection of his band. Geronimo became their single leader.

CHAPTER 29   Chatto's Arizona Raid

In the spring of 1883, Geronimo approached Chatto. "You can ride with me, but we have a greater need."

Chatto folded his arms, "I would go my own way for now. What need do you speak?"

"Ammunition," replied Geronimo. "We have many good Winchester and Marlin rifles from the whites. But we need ammunition. We cannot get it in Sonora or Chihuahua. You take warriors with you to get American ammunition. We will meet in the Sierra Madre in two moons."

Chatto agreed. He would be chief of this new band as Cochise had once predicted. Geronimo was not a chief. He was an important medicine man followed because of his personal power and renowned ability to see the future. But he was no chief. Chatto thought of himself as a natural chief based on his lineage from Mangas Coloradas. Now he would ride at the head of a powerful band of raiders.

The son of Juh, Asa Daklugie told author Eve Ball the Chatto raid was not true. It was Chihuahua's raid. He argued that Chihuahua inspired the raid and Chatto invited himself to the party during the war dance beforehand. While Chihuahua and Nana thought of this as insolence, they also recognized that Chatto was intelligent and brave and would fight, so they allowed him to go along. Author Mark Simmons who wrote a book about this raid suggests Daklugie's remarks were wrong-headed. Chihuahua stayed with Geronimo, raiding in Mexico and there is no record that anyone other than Chatto led the "ammunition raid" into Arizona. Daklugie was very young and very far away when it happened, but, as an adult, appears to have taken pot shots at Chatto at every opportunity, probably based on information from Geronimo after the two became enemies.

A strong handsome warrior walked up to Chatto. It was Bonito. Remembering his rivalry with Bonito in his youth, he wondered whether he should get ready to wrestle with him. Bonito simply said, "I will ride with you." Chatto responded, "And I will council with you." They became the one-two punch in a terrorizing raid.

Bonito

"I was heart sick with grief," Chatto told Welsh. "My wife, my children gone. I only knew that the Terahumara's would not kill them unless they came under attack. They wanted them for slaves or trade. I wanted to track them down and kill the Terahumara, but Geronimo was right, we were running out of ammunition. We would need to get guns and bullets if there was any hope of getting our families back."

Just as the great Cochise had done at Apache Pass, Chatto must now leave his relatives behind for the good of the tribe and hope to recover them later. But as he began his raid into U.S. territory, his heart was heavy. And it was hardened.

Chatto and Bonito, with a handpicked band of marauders, took the trails north toward south-eastern Arizona and western New Mexico looking for supplies. Some women joined their group, along with some youthful Apaches, apprentices, still learning the ways of a warrior. Chatto sent his daughter Maude with a middle-aged woman to the San Carlos reservation where she could stay with his sister Bahnahtsi. The other women and young Apaches would gather firewood, prepare camp, be on look-out for enemies and perform all other tasks the warriors needed.

Among the 26 seasoned fighting men were several warriors of note. Bonito was second in command. The 26 year old White Mountain warrior "Tzoe," (Peaches) who had been so resentful leaving San Carlos, also joined Chatto's raiders. He reportedly wanted to be involved in the raids into Arizona to make contact with his mother and others left on the San Carlos Reservation. Peaches brought with him another young Apache, his only true friend, known as "Beneactiney," one of the bravest men in the band. "Dutchy" joined in. He was so-called because some whites thought he looked German. He was known as a ferocious and cruel fighter. As a scout, Dutchy **had no compunction about stalking and killing other Indians. There was a story that one time Dutchy was sent out to bring in an Apache 'dead or alive' and that Apache happened to be his father. Dutchy brought back his dad's head in a sack.** Naiche, the son of Cochise, was also with the raiders, along with his uncle, and Chatto's cousin, Mangas, the son of the famous chief.

It was an ammunition and supplies campaign, but all knew it would be accompanied by killing for retribution and to leave no one to report their movements. It started before they even left Mexico. **Chatto led his raiders through the mountains near Heachinera, sixty miles south of Douglas, Arizona, and ambushed three men fifteen miles south of the border, killing two Mexicans and an American to capture their nine horses. They took more horses at a nearby ranch. Two more Americans were gunned down at a customs house where the Apaches gained two more horses, a couple of mules and two pistols. They crossed the border into the U.S. on March 20, 1883.**

The speed of the raid was amazing. In seven days they would cover almost 700 miles. Leaving the San Pedro Valley, Chatto turned northwest toward the Huachuca Mountains. At Canelo Hills his band found five men cooking wood into charcoal, which was a key ingredient in pulling gold out of fine ore. His band attacked the charcoal camp. Four men went down in a thick volley of fire. The fifth man ran inside a tent. The impetuous Beneactiney went after him. As he rushed headlong into the tent the miner, P.R. Childs, shot him down. His best friend, Peaches, was right behind Beneactiney. He turned in his tracks and ran away. Childs ran to Fort Huachuca and sounded the warning of a new Apache raid. Citizens from Charleston, near Tombstone and from Tucson came to the charcoal camp and buried the dead, except the body of Beneactiney. They cut his head off and displayed it on a pole on the main street of Charleston. His scalp went to a hotel in Tucson.

Chatto guided his party to the Whetstone Mountains, about 10 miles southwest of Benson. They took at least seven more lives on the way: three men on horseback, a wagon with five men and two miners. There they also cut telegraph lines along the Southern Pacific Railway, then attacked a pack mule train servicing additional charcoal camps, driving 14 mules away and looting a supply wagon. The pack master and three teamsters were hacked to death.

Two miners were killed at the Contention Mine, near Tombstone, and the Apaches turned back toward the upper San Pedro valley to the Winchester range. They attacked two prospectors on the road; one mounted on a mule, the other a horse. One died from gunshots, the Apaches bashed in the other's head with rocks. One turned out to be the brother of Judge Henry C. Dibble, who wrote an angry letter to President Chester Arthur demanding protection from "incorrigible savages." It was published across the country in many papers. The New York Herald wrote, 'These wretches deserve no mercy, and the people of southern Arizona are justified in demanding their extermination."

The U.S. military was strangely quiet. The first information about Apache raiding indicated it might be a few delinquent Indians from San Carlos. General Crook was in Prescott and nobody informed him there was anything amiss going on. Captain Crawford had his Apache Scouts at Cloverdale, New Mexico, in case any Apaches took that route to Mexico, but he was fifty miles away from where Chatto was operating. Chatto had been in Arizona for five days before a count of Apaches at San Carlos confirmed it was not locals out raiding; it was Chiricahuas out of Mexico.

Meantime, to make matters more panicky, Geronimo had come out from his winter doldrums. He and Chihuahua were on a Mexican rampage, killing everyone in their paths. The death toll would go to upwards of 110 people, fully one fourth of them Americans. Arizonans knew it was only a matter of time before he appeared among them too. Mexicans ordered troops to take no prisoners among Apaches.

By noon, March 23, Chatto's band was on the trail toward the Winchester Mountains about 12 miles northwest of the town of Willcox. A couple of hours later they rode to a ranch owned by Jack Howard, who was shoeing horses in his corral with a man named James. When Howard saw a few Apaches riding up, he grabbed his rifle and shot one off his horse. Other Indians picked up the wounded man and took him to safety. The last Howard saw of the Apaches, they were herding 125 horses and some mules across his ranch. He cracked off more shots at them and probably saved his own life. Sweeney wrote that the injured warrior could have been Chatto. If so, it was only a crease that knocked him cold for a while.

Two mountain men on the road to Willcox were surprised to see Apaches. They weren't surprised long. Chatto's raiders dispatched them quickly then passed within two miles of town and took cover in the Peloncillo range within 15 miles of their old stomping grounds in the Dragoons.

Chatto and Bonito talked and decided to send a two man scouting mission to the San Carlos reservation. They chose "Dutchy" and Kautli to make contact with trusted sources and report back on conditions there. They wanted to know if the reservation Indians were howling mad at the renegades. They were curious if there was a chance the raiders could turn themselves in and return to the reservation. They wondered how they would be treated if they surrendered. Dutchy returned with bad news; Chatto and the others were regarded as renegades and would be handled as prisoners of war, if they were not killed first. Dutchy stayed with Chatto for only a few days more and then he rode to the reservation and surrendered.

Tzoe (Peaches), Ben Wittick photo, 1885, National Archives

Next, as the band reached Ash Springs, Peaches wanted to go. He had suffered many losses and was worried about his mother on the reservation. He had seen enough killing and he didn't want blame for any of it. Peaches could endure no more. "Friends," he said to Chatto's warriors, "you know I have been with you all through this hard and dangerous raid. I have suffered when you suffered. I have been hungry when you were without food. Now I have lost my best friend. I cannot go on. I'm going to leave you and return to my old home country."

Bonito was the more benevolent of the two leaders. "Let him go."

Chatto did not want Peaches to desert. "He will tell the white-eyes where we were and where we are going. I don't trust him."

Bonito argued back. "He doesn't know where we are going. He is no good to us now. Best he is out of the way."

Chatto nodded his agreement. The band gave Peaches some travelling food and wished him well.

Peaches may have wanted to turn himself in. Instead, he was captured by Lieutenant Britton Davis and three dozen troops acting on a rumor that Chatto's raiders were camped near San Carlos. Swooping down on the camp, they found only Peaches, who gave up meekly. Davis's report stated, "Peaches seemed little disturbed by his capture and smiled faintly when I took his knife and cartridge belt off of him. My scouts had his rifle."

Peaches pleaded his case with the soldiers: He didn't want to join the Chiricahua renegades. He wanted to stay at San Carlos, but was kidnapped. Worse, he lost two of his wives and their children when Mexicans attacked near Aliso Creek during the great escape. Peaches, himself, had been shot and wounded as 75 others died.

On the current raid, said Peaches, he had not killed anyone. But he lost his best friend at the tent near Fort Huachuca. These losses built up on him. He cooked and carried supplies and did errands for Chatto's raiders. He was not trusted as a member of the band. "I was never allowed to go off anywhere by myself," Peaches said. "Someone was always with me. They made me work for them. I had to cook their food and do things of that kind."

General Crook must have jumped with joy when the telegram arrived telling about the return of Peaches. As he prepared for a major expedition into Mexico, he had no one who knew the trails and camps recently used by the Apache in the Sierra Madres. Peaches would make one hell of a scout if he would cooperate. And he would.

On March 24th, the day before Easter, General Crook was just beginning to receive reports of Chatto's raid. Chatto, himself, led an all-night march from the Willcox area, through the San Simon Valley to a point about half way to Silver City. Moving into the hills, they collapsed and slept.

After Peaches left, Chatto and Bonito split into two war parties probably because they were not attacking large targets and secondly it made it harder for troopers or scouts to trail them. Four companies of cavalry were in the field hoping to head off the raiders as they attempted to escape back to Mexico. Bonito looted a mining camp, shooting down three men. Chatto rustled cattle between Clifton and Lordsburg.

The next morning, Bonito's group killed five more men twenty miles west of Silver City. Then the entire group rejoined and rode into New Mexico, killing seven more people along the way. It was a bloody way of coming home for Chatto, as they camped for the night in the Burro Mountains. He knew the Burros well. He called them Neb-kei-ya-den-de. It meant "Home Place." He lived here, for a time, as a boy with Mangas Coloradas. This brought him near Silver City, New Mexico and the infamous massacre on the Lordsburg Road.

CHAPTER 30   Lordsburg

On New Mexico Route 90, there is a highway marker where Gold Gulch Road intersects between Silver City and Lordsburg which says, "The McComas Incident." The text makes it clear it was Apaches led by Chatto that did the dirty deed. Headlines at the time screamed over the "Lordsburg Massacre," on March 28, 1883.

Local Judge Hamilton C. McComas and his wife, Juniatta left two daughters in Silver City with a baby-sitter and took their six year old son, Charley, along in their carriage to travel the 49 miles to Lordsburg. They went 21.9 miles over and around steep hills and were in Thompson Canyon, about halfway to their destination when the judge pulled the carriage up under a big walnut tree and the three piled out for a picnic lunch. That's where the Apaches found them.

The judge was a prominent lawyer living in Silver City. His wife, Juniatta, was pretty and popular and Charley was the apple of his daddy's eye. Searchers found the judge full of bullet holes and his wife dead from blunt force trauma to the head. They didn't find his son. That's what made national headlines; an upright family, with notable friends and a little white kid in the hands of wild Apaches.

The killing of wagoneers, charcoal makers, ranchers and the like by Chatto's band appeared in the local press, but the McComas incident became a national sensation. You have to understand, these victims were special.

Hamilton C. McComas came from a prominent Virginia Scotch-Irish family. His grandfather, Elisha, was a member of the Virginia Assembly and a Colonel in the war of 1812. His uncle, David, was a brilliant lawyer and Virginia State Senator. His father, William, was a Congressman. Hamilton, also called "Ham" in his youth and H.C. in his adulthood was the eighth child and fourth son in his family. He ran for political office several times, but not very successfully. His brother, Elisha, was a Mexican War Captain and later Lt. Governor of Virginia. Another brother, William Wirt McComas, was a first lieutenant in the Mexican War, while James and H.C. served in the rank and file.

After the War, Hamilton studied the law and migrated to Illinois. Some accounts say he was a federal judge, but as near as I can tell he only worked for a short time as a county judge and tacked the title "Judge" McComas to his name for the rest of his life. In Monticello, he married Louise Pratt in 1859, just two years before the outbreak of the Civil War and had two children by her: David and William. He divorced her when he returned from military service and learned she had been sleeping with his law partner. (Apaches cut the nose off their women for such behavior.) Hamilton rose to the rank of Lt. Colonel in the U.S. Army, but saw no action in the Civil War. Most of his kin-folk fought for the South, brother William Wirt was killed at South Mills.

He moved to bustling Fort Scott, Kansas, in 1868 for business reasons, and probably to escape the scandal of his divorce. There he remarried to 23-year old Juniatta (Jennie) Ware, daughter of a New England Puritan and saddle-maker, Hiram Ware. Her brother, Eugene, became a poet laureate of Kansas and a state senator. Juniatta was a quiet, religious and bookish woman who read everything from fiction to philosophy. She helped raise Hamilton's sons David and William and soon had three children of her own; daughters Ada and Mary and finally, the baby of the family Charles Ware McComas. They moved to St. Louis, "The Gateway to the West" in further pursuit of Hamilton's legal career.

Located on the Mississippi River, St Louis had emerged as a commercial hub, with manufacturing, communications, cotton trading, stockyards and all nature of consumer products that needed to move down the river and thence to the East Coast. McComas became known for his legal expertise, especially in front of juries. There he also became interested in speculating on New Mexico and Arizona gold and silver mines which were opening up like so many daisies in the field. He was hired by his former commanding officer to represent the interests of the Shakespeare Mining and Milling Company in New Mexico Territory. In that capacity, he travelled to Shakespeare, near the Pyramid Mountains of southern New Mexico and soon branched out on his own, investing in his own mine with his younger brother Rufus. Having been ill for sometime in St. Louis, his health improved remarkably in the dry desert air. He loved the open spaces and the general feel of the area. Apaches were one of the last things on his mind.

Judge Hamilton McComas, Mccomas Family Papers

Very soon, Judge McComas was spending most of his time in Silver City, probably the most significant mining district in the territory, where a giant silver strike assayed one hundred ounces of silver per ton. Unlike other boom towns, Silver City soon established a patina of respectability, with effective law enforcement, hotels, banks, newspapers, churches, fraternal organizations, and offices full of doctors, lawyers and surveyors. It never had the raw edge of, say, Tombstone. Today, it remains a bustling city where you can see some of the mining scars on the hillsides near town, where the businesses, most of them franchise outfits, have re-located along the highway through the city, leaving the old historical district to decay amid empty store-fronts.

While still living in St. Louis, McComas recognized the opportunities to not only invest in mines, but put his legal skills to work forming companies, issuing stock, raising capital. He stayed in Silver City and environs for months at a time. He formed at least three mining companies; the Leroy Silver Mining Company, the New Mexico and Arizona Mining and Reduction Company and the Arizona Mine/Victorio District. After two full years of shuttling between St. Louis and Silver City, Judge McComas brought his family with him to New Mexico. He secured a position for his 21 year old son David at the Pyramid Mining Company in nearby Lordsburg and was on his way to visit David, and talk business when his life ended.

In Thompson Canyon, the picnic blanket had scarcely been spread out over the sand when Judge McComas looked up to see a dozen or more Indians watching him from horseback. It wasn't hard for them to sneak up on him; the land is fully covered with scrub pine, white oak, pinon and other trees. The Judge told Juniatta to forget about the picnic food and the blanket; to get Charley into the buckboard muy pronto.

They moved with dispatch and Judge McComas managed to turn the horses around and move the carriage back in the direction of Silver City, when he was hit in the back by a rifle shot that splattered his blood on the dashboard and floor of the carriage.

Seriously wounded, the Judge jumped, or maybe fell, to the ground with his Winchester rifle and started pumping shots at the Apaches as fast as he could. He yelled at Juniatta to get the carriage moving, to get out of there. She moved to the drivers seat.

Judge McComas ran toward the Walnut tree and the Apaches. He continued to fire until his right wrist was smashed by a bullet and another entered his right arm just below the elbow. He switched the rifle to his left hand as another Apache bullet got him through the shoulders, passing from left to right. He staggered and stumbled and more bullets hit him in the thighs, breast, and back. He fell facedown near a patch of bushes.

Juniatta, tried to scream, but nothing came out. With reins in hand, she frantically tried to get the horses on the run but it was like being in a horrible slow-motion nightmare. She only got about 300 yards up the road when an Apache bullet dropped the right horse in his tracks and stopped the carriage. She jumped out and ran toward the back of the buckboard to grab and protect her son. An Apache rode up behind her and laid a blow just above her right ear with a rifle butt that knocked her senseless. The warrior dismounted and hit her twice more with his pistol barrel, spilling her brains onto the dust.

Charley sat stunned and motionless in the back of the carriage. He was snatched up by an Apache and found himself involved in a struggle as two Apaches argued over who would get the child's brightly covered jacket. Bonito settled the dispute by riding up, claiming the boy as his own and swinging him up on the saddle behind him. He tied Charley to his own belt with a piece of rope.

Charles McComas from Harper's Weekly engraving

Locals found the parent's bodies the next day. The Judge and Juniatta had been stripped naked. All of their personal belongs were gone. Perhaps out of respect for his bravery, he had not been mutilated. Investigators found shell casings indicating Judge McComas got off seven shots before he went down. There was a deep woman's heel print where Juniatta had jumped out of the buckboard, but there were no children's footprints near the remains of the carriage, indicating Charley never left the wagon. The buckboard was ransacked, the other horse stolen, its harness shredded by knives. Search teams immediately started scouring the area looking for the trail of the Apaches. But, true to Apache tactics, Chatto's warriors scattered like quail after such an incident, leaving not one trail, but perhaps a dozen.

On March 29th, Chatto took several men and doubled back from the Animas Mountains to see if anyone was on his trail. He saw no troops. But his group did spot a mule and wagon carrying some kind of supplies. They shot and wounded the two Americans who bailed off the wagon. The mules stampeded directly toward the Apaches and they stopped them, finding ammunition, food and nearly a dozen bottles of whiskey.

The newspapers had a field day with this story. The fate of little Charles McComas became "the object of the most widespread and prolonged search in the annals of the Apache Wars."

The citizenry of New Mexico and Arizona was seeing no good Indians. One article said, "In the case of the Apaches there is no room for maudlin sentiment. They are born pillagers and murderers…worse than wild beasts…and enemies of mankind, the defenders of savagery against civilization. There is only one way to deal with these monsters and that is to give them the same treatment they extend to others." Kansas Senator, Eugene Ware, Juniatta's brother and a sometimes business partner with the Judge, travelled to Silver City to help with McComas arrangements and affairs. He spelled out the situation precisely in a letter he wrote to friends at Fort Scott.

"At present is all hostility. No Indian can now leave the reservation without death however found. In fact the feeling is so intense that large bodies of men are organized in the vicinity to move on the reservation and butcher every Indian, big and little. A feeling that seems to be universal is that the entire Apache tribe, quiet and hostile, should be exterminated."

A citizen's militia in Lordsburg went out looking for the Apaches. It could have been successful. Two scouts from the outfit, moving deep into the hills, spotted stolen livestock and a large stack of supplies. But then they counted the warriors. There seemed to be enough of them to outnumber the militia two-to-one. The militia scouts quietly left the area. If they reported the sighting to the leadership, it didn't pursue the matter. The entire group turned back, having done its duty.

In their last attack before re-entering Mexico, fully stocked with ammunition and provisions, Chatto's band killed freighter L.G. Raymond as he drove his wagon towards Deming. His team of horses and empty wagon was left on the road.

During his raid, Chatto's warriors killed 41 people, 37 of them Americans and changed international policy. Driven by this series of incidents Mexico signed an accord with the **United States allowing** military troops from either country to chase Apaches across the border, provided that it was a "hot pursuit." And this was surely that. It opened the door for General Crook to chase the Apaches across the border, through their protective screen.

General Crook was given kudos for organizing the rescue mission for little Charley McComas. Fact is, he had planned to conduct a campaign into Mexico anyway and capture as many Apaches as possible. It was his last crack at Geronimo, now regarded as the fastest, cruelest, most relentless, unforgiving, bad-ass Indian in the world. Four companies of cavalry were mustered to track the Apaches. But if the citizens wanted to think General Crook was setting up this massive expedition just to rescue a poor little white boy that was fine with the General.

CHAPTER 31   Sheridan

On November 1, 1883, Crook got a new boss. General Philip Sheridan succeeded William Tecumseh Sherman as Commanding General, U.S. Army, a post he would hold until shortly before his death. Sheridan was known for the infamous quote attributed to him; "The only good Indian is a dead Indian." He denied he said it, but it stuck and many of his actions argued that if he didn't say it, he still meant it. He had big ideas, a big reputation gained in the Civil War and a big appetite for high living. He was all for going after the Apaches in Mexico or wherever they could be found and he said, "If a village is attacked and women and children killed, the responsibility is not with the soldiers but with the people whose crimes necessitated the attack."

General Philip Sheridan, War Dept. photo

Philip Henry Sheridan's Army career was noted for his rapid rise from Second Lieutenant, coming out of West Point to Major General in the Civil War in about a dozen years. Like General Crook, he had started his career in the Pacific Northwest getting involved in the Yakima War and Rogue River wars, leading small combat teams. There he received his first wound when a bullet grazed his nose. But his star rose more rapidly with the start of the Civil War. He rose from Captain to Major General within six months, fighting at Chickamauga, Chattanooga, The Wilderness, Spotsylvania Court House and the Battle of Cold Harbor.

In the Shenandoah Valley Sheridan employed a scorched earth campaign to deny the enemy any subsistence from the land. He killed cattle, burned crops and buildings and destroyed the economic infrastructure of the Valley. Southerners called it "The Burning." Sheridan would bring these tactics to bear on the Indians.

His finest service of the Civil War and where he received the most accolades was during his stubborn pursuit of Robert E. Lee's Army during the Appomattox Campaign under General Grant. At the Battle of Sayler's Creek, in 1865, he sealed the fate of Lee's army, cutting off Lee's retreat and capturing more than 20 percent of his men. It was the last straw for Lee and the Confederate surrender took place almost immediately. Grant said of Sheridan's performance, "I believe General Sheridan has no superior as a general, either living or dead, and perhaps not an equal."

After service in Louisiana and Texas during the difficult reconstruction period after the war, Sheridan was back in the west charged with conquering the Kiowa and Comanches. He applauded professional hunters who slaughtered 4 million Bison saying, "Let them kill skin and sell until the buffalo is exterminated." Sheridan became known for his brutal approach to Indian tribes and his lack of humanity toward them. His orders to Crook: go after them and bring them in or kill them.

CHAPTER 32   Escape and Surrender

Chatto met up with Geronimo almost immediately after his Arizona raid. They took time to honor the Bedonkohe chief, Gordo, who died from natural causes. Then they gathered up a cadre of warriors for two raids against Sonora and Chihuahua. Chief Chihuahua, with his brother Ulzana would lead the first one—going after stock. And the second one with Geronimo, Chatto, Bonito, Naiche, Kayitah, Zele, Jelikine and 22 others would take captives to exchange for their people. Little did they know that General Crook had already started his expedition into Mexico looking for them.

Crook's Scouts, Office of Chief Signal Officer Photo

Crook made sure he wasn't going to surprise Mexican authorities. He visited Mexican headquarters in Sonora and Chihuahua to lunch and confer with his counterparts and the governors of their provinces. They treated him well. With that done, he was ready.

Crook launched a campaign with 43 cavalrymen, 193 Apache scouts under Chief of Scouts Al Sieber, Captain Emmet Crawford and Lieutenant Charles Gatewood and a 350 mule pack train with 76 handlers towards the wild and rugged Sierra Madres. Crook was extremely fussy with his pack trains, insisting on his scientific way of loading the mules and inspecting them almost daily. On May 1, 1883, led by Peaches, Crook's detachment entered Mexico. To penetrate the Sierra Madre, Crook needed to get through the Sonoran Desert, and then enter a range called "The Mother of Mountains," the home of the Tarahumara Indians. It is a long and deep range of volcanic mountains with snowy peaks rising to 11,000 feet and cut by deep river valleys, in places deeper than the Grand Canyon. Strong oak forests were inhabited by wolves, coyotes, grizzly bears, mountain lions, bobcats, deer, badgers and rodents.

General Crook provided his scouts, most of them Western Apaches, with bright red bandanas to distinguish them from renegade Apaches. They were sent out ahead of the main body with Captain Crawford in command, to ferret out the trails and camps of the hostiles. Finally, after crossing almost impossible terrain, Crawford's advance party came upon a rough, rocky crest, crisscrossed by canyons and grown up with pine trees. It was the camp of Chatto and Bonito. The camps of Naiche and Chihuahua were nearby. Most of the men were out raiding with Geronimo. Chihuahua was the exception.

The army scouts were supposed to report back to General Crook. They were not supposed to attack when they did. But they did and it was pandemonium. Women ran screaming from the camp. Children scattered. Seven Apaches warriors were killed and several women and children captured. One was Bonito's daughter. Another was Naiche's son. Then the soldiers burned all thirty wickiups in camp and rounded up a herd of forty-seven horses and mules.

That turned out to be the only hostile engagement of the entire campaign. The penetration of their territory by US troops was a critical event to the Apaches. Some thought General Crook must have magic to have located it. Before long they were making their way to Crook's camp in the Sierra Madre to surrender on the best terms they could get.

Chihuahua had escaped the melee, but was in the immediate area. Crook sent Bonito's beautiful sixteen year old daughter "Antelopes Approach Her" to tell the chief he wanted to discuss peace. The chief said he would talk, if the general sent him his favorite white horse, captured by the soldiers. Crook sent it to him. Chihuahua rode in the next morning, right up to the General's tent, wearing two pistols in his belt and carrying his lance. He agreed to gather up his people and return to San Carlos. One-by-one other chiefs surrendered; Nana, Loco, Kaetenae and Zele. Zele had been a special friend to Chatto, but on this occasion Zele told General Crook he was in Mexico only because Chatto and Naiche had threatened to kill him when they came for Loco's band at San Carlos.

The Chiricahuas in Crook's camp were skittish because Geronimo, Chatto and Naiche could come back shooting, but it didn't happen that way. Out on his raiding campaign Geronimo had one of those extraordinary visions for which he was so famous among the Apaches. Sitting at a campfire, he suddenly stopped, stared out into space and said, "Our people whom we left at our base camp are now in the hands of U.S. troops!" He ordered everyone to pack up and move toward the camp immediately. Once again his vision was true.

The renegades camped in the hills surrounding Crook's camp; providing an easy escape should they need it. Sending couriers into the army to establish contact, they were assured they would not be shot if they came to talk.

"We had breakfast with General Crook." Chatto told Welsh. "Geronimo was there, me, Naiche and Jelikine. Geronimo thought the General must have supernatural powers to have found our camp. He told us the General might command the sun and the moon; he was so powerful."

"And what did General Crook say?"

"He said he did not come to kill us. He came to bring us back to the reservation where we would be safe. Me and Bonito talked about it," Chatto explained to Welsh. "General Crook being able to get into the Sierra Madre and raid our camp was a bitter blow."

"It meant the soldiers could find you, no matter where you went?" asked the interviewer.

"Yes. And life for the women and children was very hard in the wilderness. Bonito said he would surrender. And he did, along with Nana and Loco. I knew our escape was over. Cochise had seen it many years before. We were not going to be able to fight the white man. He was too many. Too strong."

"Is that when you surrendered?"

"No. I was willing, but my family was still captive and I needed to do all I could to get them back. We had five women captives to exchange with the Mexicans."

That same day Chatto's brother Gonaltsis brought the five Mexican women into Crook's camp. They were thin and haggard. One was nursing a baby. The Americans tried to assure them that they would be protected. That took away the Apache's bargaining power with the Mexicans in Chihuahua, but other hostages would be available.

All the chiefs negotiated their surrender over the next few days. The bargaining went back and forth. Crook realized that he was in no position to insist on complete submission. If he did, the Apaches would scatter into the mountains and the war would drag on for years. Geronimo and Chatto said they needed time to round up all their people and make the trek. Crook therefore accepted promises by Geronimo, Chatto and Naiche to return to San Carlos on their own, within a reasonable time, say, two months. It was a long-long time and many Mexican raids later before Geronimo or Chatto came in. It got General Crook in big trouble with his bosses and the newspapers. Some whites said Geronimo had captured Crook, not the other way around. Nevertheless, Crook led 225 Chiricahuas back to Arizona, arriving at San Carlos on June 23.

Whatever happened to Little Charley McComas? No one really knows. The truth probably lies somewhere within the several scenarios described by various sources. 1. Charley, who was crying and uncontrollable, became a burden and, within a mile or so from his dead parents, was killed by smashing his head with a rock. 2. Two Apaches got into an argument because one of them wanted the child's bright jacket for his own son. In a tug of war, one warrior who had hold of Charley's ankles pulled, swinging the child around so that his head hit a rock which killed him. 3. Charley was taken all the way back to the Mexican hide-out and became a pet of sorts. But when Crawford's scouts attacked and killed a woman, her Apache son, outraged at the attack, retaliated by killing the child. 4. Charley was in the camp when the Crawford attack came and was wounded by bullets. Two Apache women found him lying outside of camp and attempted to pick him up, but then decided to leave him in order to escape with their own children. 5. Charley was in camp but was terrified when the Crawford attack came and ran into the hills, along with an Apache woman, and never returned.

Chatto allegedly told an old scout and hunter, Charles Montgomery, about the jacket tug of war incident, many years later, but many thought old man Montgomery was blowing smoke. Juh's son Asa Daklugie said he had seen the little boy in the Apache camp and that the Indians would never kill a child they hoped to raise as a warrior. General Crook was told on numerous occasions that the boy was still alive and would be exchanged for some favor. Hope never ceased for his whereabouts and welfare, but he never appeared again.

CHAPTER 33   The Interval

While Chatto and Geronimo remained in the wilds of Mexico, the Chiricahuas on the reservation were aware that most Arizona citizens and the regional press were demanding that all Apaches who had been on the warpath ought to be punished. Extermination would be fine. If not that, maybe they could be moved to some other state. Many of the Apaches tried to blunt this hatred by enlisting in the scouts. Toclanny, for instance, enlisted in October 1883 and set the record for the longest serving scout in the U.S. Army; 25 years of service without ever taking up arms against his adopted nation. He was also known as a "splendid man" and the best tracker in the Army. It didn't keep him out of prison however.

General Crook responded to the public criticism in an interview in the Arizona Citizen which said, in part, "As it stands now their spirit is broken, and they are mightily humbled. No one likes to see these red-handed murderers, as nearly all of them are, go back to the reservation. But what are we going to do? To kill them will not bring back the dead and to punish them will only lead to them leaving the reservation. They will take to the mountains only to be exterminated after a long period of time, and then only after they have killed thousands of white people. Now they are willing to go back to the reservation and settle down. They are tired of war and anxious for peace."

That pretty well described the feelings of Chatto. Still, he and the other renegades needed to know things were cool at San Carlos before they went back for what could be the balance of their lives. And there was much to do in order to retrieve their captured relatives.

When Chatto, Naiche and Geronimo failed to turn themselves in after several weeks, Captain Crawford sent Bonito and a small party out looking for them. Bonito was considered the closest to the renegades. He set out in late August, working his way to the Sierra Madres. We need to understand the importance of family to the Apache and why retrieving them was paramount. Family is the baseline grouping. First, the family, then a small grouping of families, then a larger grouping of families, forming a band; all of them immensely interdependent and intensely loyal.

Newspapers carried dramatic reports of raids in Mexico, and made virulent attacks on General Crook for what he had been unable to do. This, as Geronimo, Chatto and the rest tried to replenish the horses taken by Crooks scouts. Chatto led raiding parties through Bavispe, Nacori Chico and other Sierra Madre villages, stealing stock. His men shot and killed a Mexican farmer, kidnapped his wife and before long killed her too. Chatto then linked up again with Geronimo and soon Juh joined them forming a war party with nearly 200 men.

Even Juh said he would return to the San Carlos reservation, but everybody wanted to make one last attempt to recover their people. Before doing that they also agreed they needed more supplies and cattle. That meant more raids and death. They staged a series of raids into Sonora killing fourteen people and stealing 150 head of stock. Sub-chief Jelikine was shot down during one of these raids. A Mexican marksman, firing from long range, put a bullet through his head. The Indians took the loss hard. Jelikine had been an outstanding warrior. Now, with revenge added to their agenda, Chatto, Geronimo and Juh continued raiding among the Mexicans and attempting to set up a negotiation with the Mexicans for a hostage exchange deal. If that were successful, they would have no need to return to an American reservation. Geronimo and Chatto each where thinking primarily about wives and children in captivity.

Chatto learned more about his wife Ishchosen and the children when Geronimo's wife Taayzslath turned up in camp after escaping from Chihuahua City where she had been detained in a large cell with others, surviving on corn tortillas and soup made from cattle heads. She trudged through dry washes west to the Sierra Madre Mountains without shoes. It took her a month to find Geronimo's camp, living all the time on herbs, berries, and roots. By that time her legs and feet were swollen and she was emaciated. She reported that thirty five Apaches were alive and being held by the Mexicans. Chatto's family, one of Chief Chihuahua's brothers and two other wives of Geronimo were among them. This spurred Chatto, Geronimo and Juh to do even more to seek the return of their people, through negotiations.

They met Lieutenant Colonel Miguel Gonzales outside Casas Grandes in mid-September.

Geronimo spoke for himself and Juh. "We have heard many of our people are being held captive in Chihuahua City. We want them back. If you can bring our people back, we will not raid in the territory surrounding your city and we will turn over our hostages."

The Colonel twisted the tip of his luxurious mustache with his fingers. "I do not know that this is true. If you give me time I will send riders to learn if they are there and if we can have them released to my custody."

"How much time?" asked Chatto.

"No more than one, maybe two weeks," replied the Mexican officer. "Make your camp here, outside the city." He looked around to the other delegates. "We will send food and whiskey to you and when we receive word, we will know how to go forward."

This was music to the ears of Juh and he nudged Geronimo to agree. They camped. The Mexicans delivered the food and whiskey and Juh stayed drunk long enough to lose his effectiveness as a leader. In fact, Chatto got drunk with him the night before he died.

Geronimo, who did most of the talking, Chatto, Juh, Naiche, Kayitah and others held a second conference with Gonzales a couple of days later and it became apparent to them that the Mexican officer was stalling them. He was waiting for 200 cavalry troops to arrive to help wipe out the Apaches. He promised to produce three of the Chihuahua City captives as a sign of good faith. Naiche was skeptical of the whole set up. Chatto was desperate to see his family, as were Juh and Geronimo. Unfortunately Juh was so intoxicated he was barely able to mount his horse when the meeting ended.

The following day the Nednhi chief had been sipping whiskey again when he mounted a wild horse which bucked him head-first into a creek. He was found dead, his face under water. This was devastating news to Geronimo. His life-long friend and brother-in-law was gone. It delayed the talks over hostages.

Returning to their camp, the Chiricahua found that Bonito had arrived. They welcomed him heartily. Late in the day, when the sun moved toward the western horizon and cool shade was available, the leadership sat in a circle to hear Bonito and talk of the future.

"Things are good at San Carlos," said Bonito. "It is a good time to return. The people are being fed and are safe."

Geronimo scowled. "If we go back, we will be killed."

"No," protested Bonito, "General Crook says there will be no punishment for people who come back now. We know the word of Nantan Lupan can be trusted. He wonders why you are delaying what you promised to do."

Geronimo said, "We have gathered cattle and rounded up our people, but our wives and children are still captives of the Mexicans or the Terahumara. We need to get them back."

Chatto argued, "We have many guns and ammunition, but we have big problems getting our families back by fighting. If they are held by the Terahumara, they will be killed if we attack. If they are held by Mexicans in Chihuahua City, we will lose many warriors attacking a big city. The Mexicans must agree to return them to us."

"Don't trust the Mexicans," Bonito warned. "Do I need to mention this to you who have seen how the Mexicans work? Your best hope is to get General Crook to bargain with the Mexicans for your families."

"I, and my people," said Naiche "are ready to return to the reservation and try to get the United States Army to negotiate for my family or fight the Mexicans. I will go, with my followers in two days." Kaetenae and Chihuahua nodded in agreement.

"Take my son Chappo with you," said Geronimo. "I will tell him to look closely at the reservation and ride back to me. I do not want to lose my life by returning to a death camp"

Chatto joined his idea. "I will send Gonaltsis, my sister and my cousin with Naiche. Tell General Crook this is my gesture that I intend to keep my word and surrender soon."

They smoked and drank mescal and talked into the starlight.

Days later, Chatto and Geronimo continued their bargaining with the Casas Grande Mexicans, but they became convinced they were getting sucked into another Mexican ambush. They pulled out of the talks and moved away from Casas Grande. Chatto later told a writer, "The way the Mexicans make a treaty is to get us all together and then kill us." It was clear the time had come to return to San Carlos.

Meantime at San Carlos, another turf battle was underway between Department of Interior agents and the army. This time it featured Indian Agent Philip Wilcox and Captain Crawford. Wilcox had official responsibility for feeding and administrating the Indians on the reservation, but had gone the way of other agents; hiring relatives, creating a monopoly on supplies, spending more time in Denver than on the reservation and still trying to take control of Indian affairs. Worse, he didn't want the renegade Chiricahuas to return to San Carlos and tried to get the Interior Department to back him up. This would have been a crisis for Crook and Crawford. So they ignored Wilcox, directed the returning warriors to San Carlos anyway and arranged for the War Department to feed the Indians if Wilcox refused to do so.

Later, on December 11, 1883, Captain Crawford sent out Geronimo's son, Chappo, along with Chief Chihuahua and Dutchy, to convince Geronimo to come on in. He was convinced Chappo would make a favorable report to his father about conditions on the reservation. Chihuahua, who was very trusted, if not feared, by Geronimo, left two soldier escorts at the Mexican border and said he and his group would return in twelve days. When they returned, they did so with news that Chatto, with a party of a dozen or more, was on his way to San Carlos and Geronimo would be in some time later.

Chatto suffered a slight delay when his herd of horses was stolen by Mexican soldiers and he had to steal them back again. His party arrived at the U.S. border at San Bernardino on February 7, 1884, and linked up with a U.S. military escort. He had 20 Apaches in tow; ten men, ten women and children, a large herd of horses and cattle and a promise that he would be good from now on. There is no evidence he did otherwise.

"At that time, I realized it was not fruitful to fight against the white people." Chatto looked straight into the eyes of Mr. Welsh. "And I had seen and felt the difference between the way we had to live and the way the white-eyes lived. I knew the world was going their way and I thought I must live successfully in this system for the benefit of my tribe and my family if I could get them back. I changed the way I looked at it all."

Admitting to Captain Crawford that he had formerly been "on a crooked trail," Chatto made a deal that he and his people could live in the camp of Naiche and that he wanted the agreement to "last as long as the sun." He volunteered to help straighten out the bad men of the tribe. Crawford took him to see General Crook

"I will serve with the Scouts," Chatto told the General.

"You're a good scout, Chatto," said General Crook. "No more running off with the renegades. I'll make you a chief...a Sergeant. You'll have about 40 scouts reporting to you."

"That is good, Mr. General, but please, If I will be a good scout, please help me to get back my wife Ishchosen and my two children. I need to see them safe."

General Crook leaned in to Chatto to enhance his sincerity. "I'll make you two promises, Chatto. One, I promise I will do everything I can to get your wife and children back, working between my government and that of the Mexican government. And secondly, if you work with us to bring peace to your people, I promise you and your people will live better, more fulfilling and prosperous lives than you have known. Do I have your promise?

"Yes," said Chatto, "I want peace for us."

General Crook tried. Crook told his troops to be on the constant lookout for this trio, a young mother and her two children. He wrote letters to Mexican authorities, alerting them to the captives, asking for their return. Crook asked the War Department to intervene, to work out some deal with the Mexicans to get Apache captives back. Unfortunately Mexican authorities didn't think renegade Indians should be rewarded in any way.

Following Chatto's lead, nearly all of the Chiricahuas with whom he had grown up enlisted in the scouts. His brother, Gonaltsis was assigned to Company A, under Lt. Britton Davis. Most were in Chatto's Company B: Bonito, Naiche, Chihuahua, Mangas, Chappo, Fun, Colle, Noche, Ahnandia, Dutchy, Ashadodilges, Kaydahzinne, Jose Frist, Martine, Kayitah and eventually even the testy and independent Kaetenae joined the army. Captain Crawford had his doubts about Kaetenae's sincerity. Kaetenae had been a constant thorn in the Captain's side ever since he came in from the wilds. He was the youngest of the chiefs and the most irascible, claiming he had never been whipped by the soldiers and had never lived on a reservation. He spent considerable time whipping up the ire of other Apaches. But it didn't make them want to go on the warpath again. Not yet anyway.

As Grover Cleveland was becoming President, Lieutenant Davis hurried back to the border to try and find Geronimo. Taking his sweet time, Geronimo came in on a white pony and trailing a large herd of cattle and stolen Mexican horses. He demanded a three day rest to graze the animals on the way to the reservation. Davis explained to him that the U.S. Army could not be in the position of escorting stolen cattle near the border and urged the Apache to keep moving. Reluctantly, Geronimo went along. He arrived at San Carlos in March, 1884, where the Army took the cattle and horses away from him, sold them and sent the proceeds to the Mexican government. Geronimo was outraged.

After talking to Chatto, Geronimo also negotiated for the Army to help retrieve his captured wives as a condition of his return. He also insisted on separation from the other Indian tribes which he mistrusted and suitable land for farming and hunting. Crook agreed the Chiricahua should live apart. He gave them their choice of locations, as long as the land was on the reservation. They chose Turkey Creek about 40 miles northeast of San Carlos, on the Fort Apache reservation; a land of pines, streams, deer and patches of arable land. Geronimo wanted even more favorable land, but it was a concession for General Crook to approve all the Chiricahuas living together, and not scattered around the reservation for security reasons. Geronimo could not have his way and he griped about it.

On their way to Turkey Creek, the Chiricahuas were joined by General Crook, himself, making a two month tour of Fort Apache and San Carlos. The General basically reminded them to settle down and go to work and things would be fine. Both Bonito and Chatto made little speeches to the General. Bonito recalled the Mexican attack on Juh's camp which cost him his only relatives. He told the General "I am alone in the world." Chatto plugged for the General's intervention with the Mexicans to return their captives. Again he gave the General the names of his wife and children: Ishchosen, Bedisclove and Naboka, plus a niece and other kinfolk. Crook again promised to do what he could. Chatto was grateful and became fiercely loyal to Crook and Captain Crawford.

The Chiricahua reached Turkey Creek in early May, 1884. They were glad to be away from the San Carlos agency in the lowlands. Turkey Creek was more like their mountain homes in the Dragoon and Chiricahua Mountains. It sat at 8,000 feet altitude and was covered with pine and meadows with many streams. There were many edible plants, berries and nuts and wild game. It was the first time all the Chiricahua bands were together in one place.

Things looked pretty good to Captain Crawford for once. In spite of the ongoing battle with the corrupt and lazy Indian Agent, Philip Wilcox, he had hopes that the Apache wars were over, once and for all, and that the natives could spend their considerable energies raising crops and stock instead of stealing and killing. To his satisfaction, the Interior Department relieved agent Wilcox of his duties.

At Turkey Creek, Geronimo and Chatto both became proficient farmers, harvesting corn, wheat, beans, potatoes and pumpkins. Brief references in the histories to "Chatto's wife" suggest that he linked up again with Nalthchedah and her son Horace. The Turkey Creek Chiricahuas cultivated nearly 5,000 acres and the transition seemed to be going nicely. A report signed by Captain Crawford for the fiscal year said the Apaches were going-Jessie with their farming. Their corn crop was two-million 625 thousand pounds, 180,000 lbs of beans, 135,000 of potatoes, and 200,000 of barley. They raised 100,000 pumpkins, 20,000 watermelons and scores of musk-melons, cantelopes, cabbage, onions, cucumbers and lettuce. Captain Crawford was a happy camper. If it hadn't been for the endemic corruption on and around the reservation, the Apaches could have concluded that they were involved in a richly rewarding enterprise.

One source of agitation for them was; they knew they were being spied upon. Lt. Britton Davis, who had ridden out to find them, set up camp near Turkey Creek along a nearby stream. Davis was a Texan who graduated from West Point in 1881, just as the Apaches were rounded up for the most part. General Crook now put him in charge of his Chiricahua scouts and Davis, following General Crook's orders, appointed Chatto his first sergeant. Company B had an authorized strength of thirty scouts. Chatto delivered daily reports to Lt. Davis and gained his trust. Concurrently, he lost the trust of Geronimo. Forty years later as Lt. Davis was fading, he said Chatto was "one of the finest men, red or white, I have ever known." Chatto shared his loyalty to General Crook with Captain Crawford and Lieutenant Davis. That friendship further alienated Chatto from Geronimo, Kaetenae and other hot heads who called Chatto "a spy."

In addition to Chatto, Lt. Davis used Peaches as a messenger, riding dispatches between San Carlos and Fort Apache, and Mickey Free, the kidnapped stepson of John Ward was one of Chatto's scouts. Geronimo regarded Mickey Free with deep suspicion and would never forgive Peaches for leading Crook to the Apache stronghold. Davis, Geronimo suspected, had two or three spies inside his camp. So when Chappo enlisted, it was because his father wanted counter-intelligence from the soldiers. Chappo served as Lt. Davis's "Striker," a sort of aide-de-camp.

Mr. Welsh shifted on his bench and asked, "How did Geronimo react to this spying for the Army?"

"He came to me and said I was a traitor. He said I had given up my people and was becoming a white man. I tried to explain to him about my family. But he spit at me and said, 'you can forget your family. We should be your family, but you have chosen another.' He was very angry."

CHAPTER 34 Tiswin Trouble

For more than a year Geronimo, as restless as he could be, appeared to be a good reservation Indian and Chatto went about his farming and scouting work without incident. Kaetanae was also placed with them at Turkey Creek, but Lieutenant Davis often considered whether this was a mistake. Kaetenae in his new leadership role after the death of Victorio was young and something of a wild man. Captain Crawford said he was unreconstructed, moody, surly, suspicious, and generally a bad man. Recently he had been beating his wife, secretly making tiswin, holding drunken parties and telling people that they were fools to surrender. Geronimo liked him a lot.

The Chiricahua raised crops and continued to forage for wild berries and herbs; they killed many deer. Chatto kept his ex-wife, Nalthchedah, busy jerking the meat and tanning the hides for their clothing. They ground corn and acorns for meal. Often they, as did others, saved one-half of their corn, whether grown by them or supplied by the government, for brewing tiswin.

But the army couldn't leave things alone. Maybe it was pressure from above, but General Crook started tightening the regulations for the reservation Indians. He forbad warriors from beating their wives or worse, cutting the tip of their noses off for infidelity. Then the worst of all, the Army clamped down on its ban on making or drinking tiswin. The Apaches liked their own tiswin only slightly less than American whiskey. These restrictions came at the same time that food rations were drying up because Army men and civilian agents were continuing to pilfer supplies. The beef provided by the government, some of it bought from the Clanton Gang rustlers near Tombstone, got more stringy and less digestible.

When not making tiswin, the Chiricahuas were buying whiskey from what Bourke called "white vultures" swarming around them. Bourke said, "All the troubles of the Chiricahuas can be traced to this sale of intoxicating fluids to them by worthless white men."

It's incredible that the Army would make such a big deal out of tiswin. It's corn beer. The Pueblos and Papagos made it for centuries by grinding up corn, boiling it in water and sugar if it was available, then letting it ferment for a few days before it was ready to strain and enjoy. The Apaches made it from corn or the pulp of the Saguaro cactus or, in a pinch, from Prickly Pear. It wasn't just an alcoholic drink. It was part of Apache culture and ceremony. This was serious. The Apaches ignored the ban.

Lt. Britton Davis, War Dept. Photo

Geronimo and others argued with Lt. Davis about it. They pointed out that Davis himself loved his whiskey, so it wasn't fair that they should be told what to do regarding tiswin. So the peace on Turkey Creek started to break down.

It was becoming clear that two factions were choosing sides; the ones like Chatto, Bonito, Zele and Loco who seemed satisfied with conditions on the reservation, who were glad they came in and were generally amiable and joking around. On the other side were

Geronimo, Kaetenae, Naiche and Chihuahua who were more often morose, quarrelsome, suspicious and restless.

Things started coming to a head when Davis arrested Kaetenae for being drunk and stirring up trouble. The biggest trouble was when Kaetenae plotted to assassinate Lieutenant Davis and Davis got wind of it the night before the arrest. Davis summoned Kaetenae to his tent and the warrior came with some of his angry friends. They raised pistols; some were even cocked and ready to fire. Chatto was there and raised his rifle. He meant for others to notice his thumb going to the hammer. He is credited with saving Davis' life. Zele, Askadodilges and Dutchy also prepared to go into action to support Davis. The Lieutenant took his life in his hands when he walked up to Kaetenae and disarmed him, taking his revolver and his cartridge belt. It was a tense moment. The Lieutenant then had the warrior shackled by Chatto and the scouts, and removed to San Carlos. Kaetenae was convicted of inciting the tribe to warfare and sentenced to three years hard labor at Alcatraz. The Apaches were very angry and it didn't help that General Crook reduced the sentence to one month in irons. The hostile camp, led by Geronimo and Kaetenae, Chihuahua and others heaped vitriolic attacks on Chatto maligning him as the Devil incarnate, blaming him for the Kaetenae arrest.

The army was worried that the arrest and conviction of Kaetenae might result in an insurrection, but it didn't. Kaetenae, himself, once out of prison became a model reservation Indian. Bourke reported he was changed, "he had become a white man, and was an apostle of peace." Maybe, but not before the tiswin trouble had played itself out. The soldiers didn't feel the resentment building up over the tiswin ban. About this time Chatto's enlistment expired, documented by the papers he handed to Herbert Welsh.

"But I re-enlisted very soon after I was discharged," he told the Indian Rights representative. "I thought that it was the best thing I could be doing to bring peace to the reservation. We still had to bring in some people who were making trouble, and it gave me access to any information about our captives in Mexico."

Though tiswin consumption was unlawful and Chatto scrupulously followed the rules, he was not above drinking the "gray water" on occasion. A story came down from one celebration in which Chatto, about two sheets to the wind, challenged other warriors to a bet. He had been training his sixteen year old nephew in the ways of a warrior and claimed the boy could ride any horse bareback with only a rope on it. The bet was five gallons of tiswin, worth about as much as a horse. The warriors gave the boy a wild stallion with a rope around its nose. And they challenged him to ride it down a steep hill. Chatto knew what he was talking about. The kid did it. Chatto took home five gallons of tiswin.

As it turned fall it was clear that it could be a harsh winter at higher elevations of Turkey Creek. The Chiricahua began their move to the lowlands near Fort Apache for the winter, before the first snows. Among the goods they packed up was 45,000 pounds of corn. The tiswin parties in the mountains had caused no huge problems, but they would surface as a major distraction nearer Fort Apache.

Lt. Davis chose a site for the Chiricahuas along the White River, only about three miles from the fort. The Indians camped there and in secluded canyons in the foothills of the White Mountains. Soon the weather prevented Lt. Davis from making regular inspections. He relied on Chatto and his scouts for information on how things were going. At one point Eugene Chihuahua claimed he overheard Chatto and Mickey Free reporting to Lt. Davis that his father, Chihuahua, planned to kill the lieutenant. Maybe. The two scouts surely reported regular tiswin parties going on during the winter doldrums. As other Indians were arrested for being drunk on tiswin, Geronimo told Chatto, "You are coyote dung." The coyote was a lowly term to Apaches. To be called this meant, at best, half-breed status. Meantime Davis telegraphed Captain Crawford saying this tiswin thing was an activity he really was unable to stop.

Davis wasn't surprised when Chief Chihuahua complained about the arrests; he complained about practically everything. But he was surprised when Mangas protested. Mangas had been a steady supporter of Davis. Chatto set him straight. "Mangas' wife, Huera, is the most skillful tiswin maker in the tribe," he said. "Everybody wants her tiswin and they pay top prices."

The Apaches felt even more justified in ignoring the tiswin ban when no word came about their captive relatives in Mexico. They grumbled that General Crook had gone back on his word. Another source of agitation was annuities, the distribution of supplies, including winter clothing and blankets. They didn't care that the tug of war between the Indian Agency and the military was holding up distribution. They only knew they needed the supplies and they were not coming. So while Crawford, Davis and General Crook assumed they had things under control on a reservation full of happy Indians, they would soon learn differently.

That winter of 1885, General Crook had some of his first communication with Herbert Welsh, with the Indian Rights Association. We can presume Welsh had asked questions about the Apache reservation and Crook wrote back a detailed letter largely discussing the disenfranchisement of the Indians. True, said Crook the Indians are abused by white men selling liquor, who then con them, rob them, take advantage of them. The General didn't believe the Apaches needed all that much guardianship if they had some of the rights white people did; protection under the law, reasonable wages, the right to sue in the courts, an equal shake from the government. He said the Apache is the intellectual equivalent of any people and is willing and able to work within the system, if the system stops screwing him over. "To sum up," said Crook, "my panacea for the Indian trouble is to make the Indian self-supporting, a condition which can never be attained, in my opinion, so long as the privileges which have made labor honorable, respectable, and able to defend itself, be withheld from him."

The good news, if there was any, was the appointment of Charles D. Ford as the new Indian Agent. Like his predecessors, Ford was a political appointee, but unlike them he was forward-looking, pleasant and cooperative. He sought to end the rift with the Army and particularly Captain Crawford.

Unfortunately, Captain Crawford was having none of it. Maybe he saw Ford as another know-nothing or corrupted agent, perhaps another Department of Interior pest who would challenge his authority over the Apaches. Whatever was going though his head, Crawford was singularly rude to Ford and snubbed the agent for a minimum of two weeks when he came on duty. He didn't want Ford to come anywhere near the Indians. Crawford intervened when Ford was trying to direct farming operations, which were under Ford's jurisdiction. He refused to have Ford present when supplies were handed out. Ford said it was his duty to be present when supplies were distributed. Crawford turned a deaf ear. So Ford did the only thing he could. He withheld the supplies. The only ones to really suffer from this were the Apaches.

With two months of this treatment under his belt, Ford issued a formal complaint to the top. This looked like a potential face off between the Department of Interior and the War Department, but General Crook's record was strong. Not one Apache raid had happened in Arizona for a full year; 1884, and he was backing his Captain, even though he knew Crawford was wrong and acting irrational. Also, the Department of Interior didn't really want full control at the reservation. In case of any flare-up it would make the department look bad.

Maybe it didn't matter. Crawford had had it up to here. He was done. He asked to go with his Third Cavalry being transferred to Texas. Crook approved, providing he could lay his hands on the captain in case of need. The general put Captain F.E. Pierce in charge of the police at the San Carlos reservation. The Civil War veteran from New York City proved to be a good choice. One of the first things he did was establish cordial relations with Agent Ford.

Lt. Gatewood, at Fort Apache and Lt. Davis at San Carlos wanted out too, but General Crook was not going to allow all his best "Indian men" to fly the coop. They remained in place.

Chatto took it all in with composure. His mind-set at the time was into his scout duties and showing the whites that he was a progressive leader. He welcomed Captain Pierce and continued to report directly to Lieutenant Davis. He was instrumental in helping Lieutenant Gatewood arrest an outlaw Apache, named Gar, at a dance-feast scheduled just before the Indians were set to move back to their summer camps at Turkey Creek. Chatto and another scout spotted Gar there and informed Lt. Gatewood. Circling around behind him, they tackled Gar and Gatewood placed him under arrest. This, according to some, fatally broke the relationship between Chatto and Geronimo, especially after Gar escaped from incarceration, but was later found and killed by unnamed Apaches.

Meantime, General Crook was making some progress on the Mexican hostage situation. Chatto worked with Lt. Davis to produce a detailed list of known captives; names, ages, details of their capture. This list went to the State Department and to General Crook, both negotiating with Mexican authorities. Crook learned that most of the adult male captives were dead. Many of the children had been adopted by Mexican families and six or more of them were dead. Mexico released sixteen women but, rather than escorting them to the border, left it to the women to make their way north. It took the ones who made it several months. Chatto's wife was not among them.

In May, 1885 the Chiricahuas held their next and biggest tiswin blow-out at Turkey Creek in the camp of Geronimo and Mangas . It would lead to a split among the Chiricahuas and murderous consequences. No-one saw it coming.

"We had about 125 warriors there and ninety of them were drunk as lords," Chatto reported."

"And you?" asked Herbert Welsh.

"I was the only chief not invited," replied Chatto, "But I heard them hootin' and howlin. I heard Geronimo and Chihuahua were yelling that the white-eyes couldn't tell them how to treat their women, what to eat and drink; that it was none of their business. They all decided to go to Lieutenant Davis's tent the next morning and have it out."

Friday morning, May 15th, Davis awoke to a commotion outside his tent. He stepped out into a crowd of thirty prominent Chiricahua warriors. Geronimo, Chihuahua, Naiche, Mangas, Nana, Loco and Bonito were all there, armed with knives and revolvers. They were all in foul moods.

"I got there early." Chatto told Welsh, "Lt. Davis had me and some of the other scouts stand guard with our Springfield rifles and he invited the chiefs into his tent. Geronimo, Chihuahua, and Naiche were still drunk. They told Davis they had all been drinking and asked 'What are you going to do about it?' We could hear them arguing. Nana started, but he was cut-off by Chihuahua. Then Nana got mad and walked out. They told Lieutenant Davis they agreed to be peaceful…agreed to be farmers, but they never agreed to stop using tiswin. They said, 'Our ancestors drank tiswin…we should drink tiswin.' It wasn't a good meeting."

Davis stayed cool. He said he couldn't decide this issue; he would need to telegram General Crook. By happenstance General Crook was away and the telegram got filed away and the General never received it.

"There was a report," said Mr. Welsh, "that you had started making the sign of throat slitting by running your finger across your neck at other Chiricahuas?"

"I don't remember that. I know they did not like me standing guard over them. They called me a traitor. And maybe I was….to them. Geronimo told me I had sold out and had become an enemy. I told him, "I am not hurting my people. If you continue to resist and drink and raid and kill, the white-eyes will see no good Apache or bad Apache. They will only see bad Apache. I had to choose between these chiefs and my people."

"Yes," said Welch, "And that's eventually what happened. It's why Arizona wants no Chiricahua ever in its territory again."

Chatto was still on his previous wave-length. He said, "I thought if I was to be chief, I must look out for my people and it was too hard on them to go against the whites. It was time for us to have real peace. Geronimo said, 'We are all doomed. We all know that. The choice is whether we die in captivity or we die as free men. "

"It is a strong argument," suggested Welsh.

"Yes, if you believe we are doomed. I didn't believe that. Conditions on the reservations were often bad, sometimes very bad, but they were worse living on the warpath. I didn't believe it was a choice of how we died, but how we lived."

Within a few days, a rumor spread that General Crook had ordered scouts to come and arrest Geronimo and Mangas for violating the tiswin laws. Mangas's wife Huera, told her husband and Geronimo, "If you are warriors, you will take to the warpath and then the Tan Wolf must catch you before you are punished."

Geronimo conferred with his young cousins, Fun and Tisna. "We are leaving the reservation. You must help us to confuse and delay the blue-coats so that we can get away."

Fun responded. "We follow you. What can we do to help?"

Geronimo drew close to the pair, "You are in the scouts, only you can get close enough to kill Lieutenant Davis. Kill him. And kill Chatto too. Do it now and then ride to Eagle Creek to meet us."

Next morning, on May 17, 1885, many hours before the sun broke the horizon, Geronimo, Mangas, Chihuahua, Naiche, Nana and Lozen with a total of 124 Chiricahuas, including 40 warriors and the rest women and children, stole away from Turkey Creek. Geronimo told Chihuahua and Naiche, "You must come. You will be hanged if you are caught here."

"Why? Asked Chihuahua.

"Because, we have killed Lieutenant Davis and Chatto," said Geronimo.

Knowing this would bring death down on them or, at the minimum, great punishment, they left with Geronimo. It was the fourth time Geronimo escaped a reservation.

Fun and Tisna entered the ranks around Davis' tent at morning call. Chatto felt his muscles twitching. Something was amiss. He had eleven scouts with him and ordered each one to "ground your weapons," that is, hold them with the rifle butts touching the ground. Then, loud enough to be heard by all, he ordered Dutchy and Askadodilges to "Shoot the first man who raises his rifle away from the ground."

"I had a premonition that morning," said Chatto. "I had known Geronimo all my life and I couldn't think of anything good about him."

Fun and Tisna looked at their odds of getting away with murder and quickly determined they were not good. Without acting against Chatto or Davis and as soon as possible, they simply slipped away and re-joined the renegades. The escaping Apaches would kill thirty-four white people in Arizona and thirty-nine in New Mexico on their way to Sonora.

The white population took little note that only 124 or so Apaches took off and started raiding again, while three times that number of the Chiricahuas stayed in place on the reservation under the leadership of Chatto, Bonito, and Loco. Captain Bourke said in his book *On the Border with Crook,* that "The work done by Chatto and the Chiricahuas who had remained on the reservation was of an inestimable value, and was fittingly recognized by General Crook." Hardly anyone else did.

"Me and Bonito were very bitter about them leaving." Chatto told Welsh. "It was the coward's way and not good for the people leaving or the people staying behind. It set all the white people against all of us and ruined much of what we had done."

After morning call, Lieutenant Davis went to the agency to umpire a baseball game. It was there Chatto and Mickey Free found him and reported that a large group of Indians had bolted the reservation. Chatto knew that Geronimo would head for the most difficult terrain he could find and it was imperative to get on that trail fast, or lose it.

"How did you feel about riding out to kill other Apaches?" Herbert Welsh asked Chatto.

"I felt very bad. But that is wrong. We did not ride to kill anybody. I thought we could be a go-between for the Army. It was best to convince Geronimo and others like him that we could live in peace. But if they fought, we would fight. If they killed, we killed."

The escapees didn't fare particularly well. White Mountain Apaches quickly found one warrior, killed him and cut off his head. It was an omen, within a few weeks 33 percent of the renegades would be dead or out of action.

When the newspapers got wind of the escape they were off and running with blazing headlines again. Any dead cow was attributed to Geronimo and his renegades. The threat of the "Red Menace" put everyone on edge. Editorialists wondered why General Crook could run so lenient an operation that hostile Apaches could just leave at will to imperil civilization.

CHAPTER 35   Chasing Geronimo

The Army had two companies of cavalry on the trail within two hours after they heard of the escape. Captain Allen Smith took charge and had Lieutenants Davis and Gatewood reporting to him with their 21 scouts. Chatto took the lead with ten scouts and led the detachment southeast pointing out horse tracks and moccasin prints heading toward the old encampments along Bonito Creek, in the Chiricahua Mountains.

At one point, Chatto dismounted to study the horse tracks. They showed that the renegades had split up, probably to re-unite at some pre-determined spot. There were signs that their trails had been broomed with mesquite branches to wipe out the traces. At Bonito Creek, Chatto's scouts found that the telegraph wires to Fort Apache had been cut, then reattached to appear normal. It looked to Chatto as if Mangas was leading the group. Geronimo would have taken a different route. Whoever was giving the orders, the trail led over terribly bad terrain, through canyons, down creek beds, over mesas. His scouts were making good headway, but the white soldiers were struggling through this territory. Before long they were reporting injuries to their horses and even a broken leg for one trooper.

Chatto's group reached Black River, to the southeast of Fort Apache about three in the morning. Captain Smith ordered everyone to dismount and rest up for a couple of hours. By five, they were on the trail again, crossing the river and following the trail as it turned eastward toward Eagle Creek. Chatto pointed to a dust cloud ahead and with his binoculars, Lt. Gatewood could see the Chiricahuas about six miles ahead. Chatto told the troopers to hurry. But Captain Smith, who had no idea how fast Apaches can travel, nixed the idea of making a run for the renegades. In fact, Geronimo, Mangas and the others travelled 95 miles their first day.

In mid-afternoon Smith's men reached Eagle Creek and settled in for the balance of the day. The horses were tired and the pack train had fallen behind. They had covered nearly 70 miles in the last 20 hours. While Smith's party bivouacked, the renegade Apaches kept going and were soon out of reach. Frustrated, Lt. Davis and Chatto left Smith's detachment with ten other scouts and rode back to Fort Apache.

Back at the fort, Lt. Davis and Chatto figured they had a long campaign ahead of them and they better prepare for it. Chatto wanted to hand pick the scouts he would take with him to hunt down the renegades. Lt. Davis talked to him about it.

"You and your scouts are best suited to find and contact these people. General Crook wants you to talk to them. Tell them nothing bad will happen to the ones who return."

Chatto nodded, "We will follow them. I think Geronimo will not meet with me. He will try to kill me. But I can talk to Naiche, Chihuahua, and maybe Mangas"

"Please understand," said Davis, "General Crook has tried for one year to bring back your relatives. If we can't return most of these people to the reservation, General Crook will not continue to try to get back their relatives from the Mexicans…or yours."

At headquarters, Crook looked at the maps and contemplated a number of possible routes Geronimo might take into Mexico. He stationed cavalry at all posts on the way to the border. He called on troops and cavalry from almost every military post in New Mexico and Arizona to cut off the fugitives or hunt them down at all costs. Before long, he had more than twenty troops of cavalry and a total of two thousand men chasing Geronimo. But he had really handed ownership of the renegade roundup to Chatto and his scouts, challenging them to come through, or else give up any thoughts of getting their relatives back.

The reservation Chiricahuas held a war dance the evening of May 21, 1885. They danced over the prospect of tracking down their own people, perhaps killing them. And they were divided. Although 400 had stayed on the reservation, many revered Geronimo as their true leader, a man who would not buckle under to the white man and kept their hope for freedom alive. Still others thought that Geronimo had outlived his time and was responsible for many Apache deaths like the fiasco at Aliso. They put their faith in Chatto and Bonito who urged them to follow the ways of the Americans with hope that it would be a better way of life than they had known in peace or war. Many Chiricahuas believed Chatto had "great medicine," revealed to him in dreams. He believed it too. It came to him accompanied by his muscle tremors. All were united in wanting relatives or friends held captive in Mexico to be returned to their families.

     A war shaman sang and the men danced to demonstrate their bravery. And the shaman praised Chatto singing, "Chatto you are a man and a great warrior. You have fought your enemies hand-to-hand. Come dance with us." Chatto sprang to the center of the circle, carrying his rifle and shooting it into the air. He, in turn, sang the names of other warriors who would join him hunting the renegades; Bonito, Gonaltsis, Cooney, Charlie, Mickey Free, Tuzzone, Feliz, Dutchy, Kayitah, Martine, Jose First. Fifteen of the twenty-two scouts were Chokonens, and seven were Chihennes who hated Geronimo for kidnapping Loco . As he sang and twirled it seemed to Chatto that the fate of his family would rest on whether he captured or killed Geronimo. He knew Geronimo would kill him on sight. He needed all the strength the tribe could give him on this night. His peaceful Apaches were now at war with the hostile ones; a fact never considered by the highest levels of the U.S. Government when it came time for punishments.

     With morning light on May 22, 1885, Chatto led fifty-eight scouts under Lt. Davis out of Fort Apache and headed for the Mogollon Rim. They travelled light. Chatto later told a writer, "I carried a double cartridge belt with forty-five to fifty rounds of ammunition. The belt was as rough as cowhide. It rubbed the skin from my back as I led men over the small ridges and in different parts of the country. My gun was loaded and my hand was on the trigger, following fresh trails of the hostiles, not knowing what moment a bullet might go through my forehead or breast if we were ambushed." All the scouts had army-issue Springfield rifles and were given a blanket, a tent, a hunting knife and clothing consisting of a blue shirt and pants, which they hardly ever wore. They said they didn't need their daily ration of soap. They traded it for tobacco.

Davis's Apache Scouts

At almost the same hour that Davis left Fort Apache, the renegades with Geronimo, Mangas and Naiche, ambushed a troop of cavalry at Devils Creek. They pounced on troopers leading their horses, single file, through a deep ravine. Geronimo set off the ambush with a shot that seriously wounded one trooper. The others cut loose in a thunderous volley, forcing the soldiers to dive for cover. Wounding another trooper and one of the scouts, the Chiricahuas withdrew. The renegades paired off with Naiche joining Chihuahua and Geronimo and Mangas forming a second band, all of them making their way toward Mexico.

Lieutenant Davis and Chatto's scouts picked up Chihuahua's trail on their eleventh day on the trail and followed it to the Gila River. Early the next morning they spotted where the Apaches had camped. Chatto led the command north along Sheep Spring Canyon. They found the bodies of two newborn Indian babies which their mothers had been forced to abandon. At mid-day Chatto's scouts and Chihuahua's outriders spotted each other and opened fire, exchanging almost one-hundred rounds before the renegades took flight. They left behind seventeen horses and a couple of mules.

After that skirmish, Chatto took several scouts who were members of Naiche's band and tried to open talks with the hostiles. However, neither Chihuahua nor Naiche was still in the area. They rendezvoused in the foothills of the Pinos Altos Mountains, attacking a sawmill, killing the operator and stealing eight horses. Davis, Chatto and the scouts were more than a day behind them.

Nearing Mexico, the escaping Apaches split up again. This time it was not to elude the cavalry. Warriors bringing up the rear reported to Naiche and Chihuahua that Lt. Davis and Chatto were alive. Geronimo had lied to them. Chihuahua was outraged; so angry at Geronimo that he vowed to kill him and rode toward Geronimo's camp to do so. Geronimo wasn't there. He got out while the getting was good. Geronimo and Mangas made it safely to the Sierra Madre, near Casas Grandes. Naiche and Chihuahua crossed the border near Bisbee, after Chihuahua's warriors killed three soldiers at an undermanned army supply camp near San Bernadino.

After the four-way split up over Geronimo lying to them, Naiche and Chihuahua stayed pretty close to each other, going their separate ways but most often linking up again between raids. The same can be said of Geronimo and Mangas. Wherever they went there were reports of hideous deaths and stolen stock.

As General Crook prepared for a column to enter Mexico, he sent for Captain Emmet Crawford to rejoin him. Crawford arrived on June 6th, 1885 and called on Chatto to be his main advisor in going after the renegades. Moving into Mexico, Crawford linked up with Lt. Davis and took command of their combined forces. Chief of Scouts Al Sieber arrived with pack trains, but it was clear that Chatto would be in charge of his own 22 Chiricahua scouts, if not the entire contingent of 92.

Chatto had a pretty good idea where the renegades would be. He told Captain Crawford, "All I have to do is think where I would go if I were on the run." He thought he might head for the Teres

Mountains near the town of Oputo, about 80 miles south of Douglas, Arizona. He had been there often in the old days. He told Captain Crawford, "We should approach it from the west, to not be seen." It was a grueling route through San Louis Pass into Chihuahua, but it gave the best chance of surprise. They began a series of 16 hour-a-day marches, often through temperatures of 120 degrees, starting three of the most difficult months in their lives.

About that time, June 14th, Naiche moved into the heart of the Sierra Madre, putting aside his anger to join Geronimo and Mangas. Chihuahua, still angry with Geronimo, stayed to the east and out of the mountains.

The next day Chatto ordered his men to stop for the day just east of the Bavispe River, a long drainage that runs north and south and meanders back and forth creating deep canyons. He just happened to come to a halt at a mescal camp and that evening he and all 92 of his party got drunk. Some of the Mexicans recognized Chatto and asked him where his friend Geronimo was. Geronimo had been a good customer. "I have not seen Geronimo," he responded. "Have you seen him?"

At the same time Lieutenant Gatewood was leaving Fort Apache with Kaydahzinne and his scouts to patrol along the headwaters of the Gila River in New Mexico. He needn't have bothered. The escaped Apaches were long gone.

Following the Bavispe River, as Chatto had predicted, the trail became very rough and the men had to dismount because the deep canyons were impractical for their horses. Finally reaching Huasabas, about 15 miles east of Moctezuma, they entered the Teras Mountains where Chatto expected to find some of the Chiricahaus, if not all of them. At mid-day two scouts rushed in with news that Mexicans had shot two of their scouts, killing one of them. Chatto's scouts stripped for action yelling that they would kill any Mexicans they could find. It took considerable leadership and persuasion for Chatto to calm them down. A day later Chatto and Lt. Davis rode to the site of the ambush and buried the dead scout.

At the same time, Chief Chihuahua was near Moctezuma stealing stock and headed for Oputo June 22nd. Chatto's scouts found the trail of eight or ten of Chihuahua's warriors and reported the fact to the Lieutenant. Chatto took control and with 30 scouts, went out to track the Apaches. They rode through moonlight for nearly three hours when a heavy rain fell, wiping out the tracks. Chatto told his men to hunker down and wait it out.

Next morning he, his sergeant Big Dave and the scouts, resumed the hunt. Chatto knew he was on the right track when they ran across eight butchered cattle. By nine-o'clock the rain had stopped and as the mist cleared, Chatto spotted Chihauhau's camp through his binoculars, not five-hundred yards away near a peak called "El Tigre."

Chatto took five scouts and laboriously worked his way around the Peak. Big Dave directed the remainder forward, remaining in hiding until Chatto could open the attack. Davis had told Chatto to spot the Apaches and send word back so the main body could move into position. Chatto could have followed those orders, but the risk was too high. He needed to strike now.

Chatto fired the first shot into camp. It hit Cathay (Colle) in the leg. Colle went down cursing Chatto and vowing his revenge. Chatto's five scouts followed up with a volley that threw Chihuahua's camp into a panic. Hearing this, Big Dave's scouts opened up from below the camp. Chihuahua's nephew, his brother Ulzana's son, went down in the first shooting…and his mother-in-law. Several Indians led women and children to a cave. Then the warriors, who felt they were no match for the scouts, fled. They tried to get Chatto's men to chase them, but Chatto knew that would come to a sorry end. He entered the camp, picked up weapons, ammunition, saddles, and very soon found the 15 women and children Chihuahua had left behind. Chatto had scored a significant victory and his men were unharmed, except Big Dave had a bullet hole in his elbow.

Chihuahua's entire family was among the captured. The wife of his brother Ulzana had two leg wounds, received as she protected her two small children. Now Chihuahua wanted vengeance not only on

Geronimo, but on Chatto. In his anger, he rebuffed an offer Chatto sent to him through one of the captured women; either surrender, or go kill Geronimo.

Chatto and his scouts returned to Captain Crawford's camp and an escort, led by Lt. Hanna was quickly on its way to San Carlos with the captives. Big Dave was sent back for medical attention and Chatto's old raiding buddy, Dutchy was sent back, under arrest, because he had been on a drinking binge and was disruptive. On the way, they crossed the trail of Geronimo's group heading toward Sonora with nearly 100 men, but the two parties remained out of touch with each other. Geronimo, Mangas and Naiche were raiding and getting pressure from Mexican troops.

Back in the states, General Crook assigned Captain Wirt Davis to lead a second expedition into the Sierra Madre and ordered Lt. Gatewood to turn over a new group of 100 Apache scouts, authorized by the War Department, to Davis. The idea was to have troops both east and west of the Sierra Madres. Meantime Crook assigned troops to every known border crossing in Arizona and had others standing by near train stations, ready for quick transport wherever needed.

Captain Wirt Davis, of the 4th Cavalry, filed an after-action report saying Chatto and 86 of his scouts ran into renegade Chiricahuas in March, 1886 in the La Howa mountains. They ambushed a small party and killed two "hostiles," capturing their horses and saddles. When the Apaches fled over the mountains, Chatto and his men went right after them, killing one and wounding two more. One of Chatto's men was wounded in the leg, but overall, said the Captain, the scouts "behaved very gallantly and others worked zealously and did well through the campaign." This was nice to hear at the time, but became important in later years when the scouts were trying to get out of prison.

On the reservation, Bonito and Loco had held another knock-down-drag-out tiswin party and Bonito's wife had killed another woman over a minor insult. Lt. Brit Davis had been right all along; you can't stop Apaches from drinking tiswin. General Crook called on the

White Mountain Apaches to put pressure on the Chiricahuas over this drinking, suggesting they would suffer too if it didn't get under control.

On July 10, Captain Wirt Davis led his Fourth Cavalry troopers toward Mexico. Another Civil War veteran, Davis was renowned for his dead-eye shooting ability and his drinking. He wasn't known to drink out in the field. He followed Captain Crawford's route into Mexico. Among the men leading his scouts was Buckskin Frank Leslie, who had reputedly killed eleven men in Tombstone and was known as a cohort of the Earp brothers. As Davis arrived about half-way to Oputo, the Chiricahuas, being tracked by Mexicans, split into three groups. Geronimo, with most of the women and children went northeast, Mangas went east and Naiche, with 35 in his band went north to hook up with Chihuahua again. Those two chiefs raided in Arizona on July 17th, killing one man.

Captain Davis got close to Geronimo on July 20th when a rider from Moctezuma reported Indians at Oputo, in the Teras Mountains and Davis' scouts got close enough to camp to see individuals moving about. But as Davis moved his troops stealthily up the mountain, Geronimo received a vision from an old squaw and, although skeptical at first, followed her warning to flee the area.

If "the power" worked for Geronimo, Captain Davis thought it might work for him too. He called his Apaches together and requested they hold a drum and song ceremony designed to tell him where Geronimo was. During the dancing a shaman came to Davis and told him where Geronimo would be, providing an oral road map.

By August 7th Davis' scouts, accompanied by only one white man, Lt. Day, found Geronimo's camp at Bugatseka, almost the exact location where Crawford had found Chatto and Bonito's camp two years previous. This time the army found Geronimo at home. Their surprise attack was marred by a braying mule which alerted the Chiricahuas, but effective nonetheless.

The scouts killed two women and one boy with their first volley. They captured 16 women and children including Geronimo's wife Taayzslath, five of his children and the tiswin maker, Huera, who had urged the breakout from San Carlos. They wounded Geronimo's daughter Dohn-say. Geronimo, himself, grabbed one of his young sons and ran for cover with bullets splattering all around him; the only time he was seen. In brief, everything the Shaman told Captain Davis, turned out to be true.

      The attack scattered Geronimo's group. He headed southeast towards Chihuahua City, but not before replacing his captured wife by marrying a young girl his band had captured from the Mescaleros, Ihtedda, who was only three years older than Chatto. Mangas fled south to Juh's old stronghold at Guaynopa, almost 200 miles south of El Paso, never to rejoin Geronimo. To stay low profile, Mangas and his small group gave up raiding.

      When Lt. Day and his captives arrived back at Captain Davis' camp, Captain Crawford and Chatto were there. Chatto interrogated Geronimo's wife but she had no idea where her husband was going. Captain Crawford tried his hand and got so frustrated that he pulled a gun on the women, scaring the wits out of them and probably damaging his credibility.

      Captain Crawford agreed with Captain Davis that he would follow Geronimo's trail and Wirt would go after Chihuahua and Naiche by working his way west of the Sierra Madres. On the same day, those two renegades were responsible for one of the bloodiest days of their run.

      Operating in concert, if not always together, Naiche and Chihuahua were raiding to survive and it was turning into a blood-bath. At Cananea, only about 20 miles below the Arizona border, they killed two of four miners working their grubstake. They killed a sheepherder and wounded another at a nearby ranch. They killed two Mexican soldiers from a patrol that was following them. They killed two Mexican cowboys who were rounding up cattle. On July 23, Chihuahua entered Arizona, killing a Mexican in the Whetstone Mountains and a mail carrier near the border. Rejoining near Cananea, they raided a ranch and killed eight people, including two women and a child. Chihuahua, probably the strongest and most intelligent of the chiefs, was on a rampage.

Captain Wirt Davis kept his troops on the move and was getting ever closer to Chihuahua. On the 27th of August he met up with a Mexican General commanding 336 troops who reported that he lost two men two days ago fighting with Apaches. Wirt's scouts picked up Chihuahua's trail southeast of Tepache and they found his deserted camp three days later. In early September they came upon a man and his wife who were travelling with three miners when the Chiricahuas hit. The woman, Belle Davis, had stripped a shotgun and shells from a dead companion and blasted away at the Indians, who soon thought better of it and left the scene.

Only two days later Chihuahua's sentries opened fire on Captain Davis' advance scouts and set off a long-range rifle skirmish that killed men on both sides. Scouts yelled out to Chihuahua to stop fighting and to talk. Chihuahua agreed. But then, Captain Davis lost an opportunity to bring in roughly half of the Apaches when he forbad his scouts from holding a parlay with Chihuahua, assuming they would be killed. Next day, when Chihuahua and his people were gone, Davis and his officers went to where Chihuahua had last been seen and found one of his scouts with a knife driven through his face. Davis cursed and vowed that these Indians would not be returning to the reservation under any circumstances.

CHAPTER 36   On the Trail

"Take off your boots." Chatto told Lt. Marion Maus

"What for?" Asked the irritated Lieutenant.

"You make too much noise. Apache hear you coming."

So the boots came off and Maus's patrol marched all night in their bare feet and it was hell; 18 hours of tripping over rocks and plants. In addition, it was slow and they were trying to catch up with a dozen Apaches herding stolen cattle. It was also slow because some of the scouts had gotten drunk at the little town of Hussavas, Mexico. A couple of them ended up being shot and wounded by Mexican guards. One, called "The Apache Kid," was slated for a Mexican firing squad, but Chief of Scouts Al Sieber was able to get him off with a twenty dollar fine and sent him back to the reservation.

Toward dawn, they heard the lowing of the cattle, and peeking over a rise, saw them. The Apaches were snoozing. The barefoot troopers opened up with their carbines firing more into the air than at the Apaches, who were quickly up and on the run. The cattle were recaptured and Chatto's boys cut another notch in their rifle-butts.

Chatto's work as a scout was appreciated. Chatto tracked down renegade Apaches with great skill. On one occasion his scouts came upon an abandoned camp. From the signs left, Chatto told officers about the Apache party as if they had left written instructions. He felt the ground under their campfires, counted the number of fires, looked at tent peg holes to learn the size of the dwellings and the number of Indians. He found moccasin prints and identified the tribal branch from the stitching patterns. The Chiricahuas almost always had a flap over the toes of their moccasins that left a distinctive print. From examining crushed grasses and the dryness of horse dung he knew how long ago the party had passed. Horse tracks determined that the party was not in a big hurry. Comparing urine puddles to hoof prints, he knew most of the horses were male and that it was a war party because warriors seldom rode mares. He counted the different footprints for the number of horses and riders. By the end, he knew a great deal about the renegades. He saw that the hostiles were travelling, as much as possible on rocky ground that wouldn't show tracks, they jumped from rock to rock. They broomed their tracks. It took super skill to follow them.

There was a joke going around. A Cavalry officer rode up to an old Indian who was lying on his stomach with his ear to the ground. "What's up Chief?" said the officer. "Heap big party on seven horses and leading two, riding fast from the west and heading for the mountains," said the Indian. "Wow, you can tell all that by listening to the ground?" said the soldier. "No," said the chief, "Sons a bitches ran over me an hour ago."

Word of Geronimo's escape and later depravations terrified the frontier and again he was headline news. The headlines howled about "Bloodthirsty Red Devils on the Warpath" There was justification for the alarm because the depravations were often horrendous. One of the worst reported was when the Apaches massacred a family near Silver City and took one girl and strung her up alive with a meat hook through the base of her skull.

Captain Crawford considered he had his best team going after Geronimo. It included 42 scouts, headed by Al Sieber, Chatto, Mickey Free, and a young Apache Sieber had befriended on the reservation, Haskay-bay-nay-natyl, whose Apache name meant "The tall man destined to come to a mysterious end." People called him "The Apache Kid" because his name was so hard to pronounce. He was the scout who had been in trouble at Hussavas and, in fact, he did come to a mysterious end, but that comes later. They formed up under the command of Lt. Britton Davis.

But Geronimo's feat remains one of the most impressive ever accomplished. For 24 days Geronimo led his small band more than 500 miles over some of the steepest, roughest terrain in the world, zigzagging, dropping down into deep caverns and ascending massive peaks, always changing directions to confuse his pursuers.

On August 13, 1885, Chatto picked up Geronimo's trail. He told Lt. Brit Davis, "Look, it is Geronimo. Look at these tracks. He has been traveling with one shod mule."

"How do you know it was Geronimo?" asked the Lieutenant.

"See," said Chatto, "here is his footprint. It is this long and this wide. He carries double-stitching on the heels of his moccasins, and his right leg is bowed so that the outside of his footprint is deeper in the dirt than the inside. That is Geronimo."

Trouble was, they were 36 hours behind the rebel and it started raining cats and dogs. Captain Crawford sent his "A-team" to the front to track him. It would be a grueling chase, sometimes over and around mountain peaks that stood 9,000 feet. They had no idea what was Geronimo's destination. In fact, the renegade leader had hatched a daring plan to break his family out of Fort Apache.

Then, there was a critical delay. Captain Crawford sent Lt. Charles Elliott forward with supplies for Lt. Davis and he ran into big trouble with Mexican soldiers. Elliot's men shot two cows for food. Next thing they knew they were fronted by fifty short, dark-skinned Mexicans, many from the Terahumara tribe, who introduced themselves by firing on Elliot's party. White flags were waved, explanations were yelled out, but the Mexicans continued to shoot. One hundred shots later, Elliott was able to get them to stop, only to be surrounded, disarmed and hustled to San Buenaventura, paraded through the town and thrown into the city jail. Fortunately, two of Elliott's scouts escaped to ride forward and tell Lt. Davis what had happened.

Davis cursed under his breath as Chatto's scouts started stripping down for war and loading their rifles. Chatto convinced them not to go off half-cocked and accompanied Davis to the site of the confrontation. They found no bodies. The Mexicans would have left bodies lying in the field if there had been a massacre. The two breathed a little easier.

Davis announced he would go alone to the Mexican city and try to unravel this situation. Chatto counted one-thousand-one, one-thousand-two, and then, without notifying Sieber, went after Davis with ten of his scouts. Davis made his way to the Commander in town and was able to convince the Mexicans that the U.S. troops were no threat...and more, that their mission was identical; running down the Apaches who had been killing their countrymen.

Chatto had stationed himself outside the jail and did considerable pacing back and forth before the order came to release Elliott's men. By mid-morning August 24th Davis, Chatto and the Geronimo-hunters were underway again, but seriously behind schedule. Elliott returned to Captain Crawford who congratulated him for coming through unscathed, but was so angry with the Mexicans that he rode his men directly into San Buenaventura as a show of force. When a Mexican officer told him he should get out of Mexico "now," Crawford said, "If they want a fight, tell them to come on."

In Lt. Davis' group, Chatto picked up Geronimo's trail again...but, after riding 125 miles, the closest they got was spotting tiny dots, through their binoculars, disappearing into the flat plains ahead. They ran into a strong Mexican force while still about 100 miles south of El Paso. The Mexicans said they had the situation in hand and the best thing the Yankees could do was go home. They did, and it was a tough march. Chatto was given high praise for getting the group across the desert while their water gave out, their horses failed, their boots and moccasins became threadbare and the men believed they could not take another step. They arrived at Fort Bliss, at El Paso, a spent mess. Lt. Davis was so fatigued that his troops didn't see him for two days.

Nana, who had ridden to Janos with Geronimo, split off to hide and rest while Geronimo continued into New Mexico with five men and five women. He chose a widely circuitous route to avoid soldiers at all the known border routes.

In seventeen days, between September 7th and 24th, Geronimo moved from the Mexican border, past Deming, New Mexico and Silver

City, into the Gila Mountains of Arizona and to the mountains north of Fort Apache. During his trek he stole more than 20 horses and mules. Why trail so many horses? They served triple duty. The Indians could ride them, use them as pack animals, or eat them. He and his men killed six people on their way to Fort Apache and one on the way out; a rancher, a herder, a woodchopper, a miner and a 16 year old boy, whose brother, Santiago McGinn, was kidnapped. The Army put up a $100 reward for any of his men dead or alive. The death toll could have gone higher if a farm-house dog, belonging to a Mrs. Allen, had not attacked Geronimo, allowing her and her two young children to bolt for safety and hide-out.

On September 22nd, Geronimo arrived on the east fork of the White River, where he expected to find a Chiricahua camp. He only found an old Apache woman tending a small camp. She told him his wife She-gah and her child had been moved closer to Fort Apache. Stealing several horses from the White Mountain Apaches, Geronimo galloped off toward the agency. Two days later, he literally walked into camp, took his wife She-gah, her child and one or two other Chiricahuas, and left again, under the nose of the U.S. Government.

His men spotted a delivery wagon and killed the driver, A. L. Sanborne on the way back to New Mexico. They found the wagon loaded with candy. They spent the rest of the day laying around and eating candy. They got sick as dogs from the sugar high. On October 3rd, they headed back toward Mexico. The boy, Santiago McGinn, reported he owed his life to Apache gambling. The ones who wanted to let him live won at a game of chance and though he would remain in Geronimo's custody for many months, he lived to tell the story.

Almost immediately after arriving back at Fort Bowie, the exhausted Lieutenant Britt Davis resigned. He had had enough. In El Paso with Chatto he had, by chance, met a friend of his father who offered him a nice job in Chihuahua, managing a mining and farming operation. General Crook tried to talk him out of leaving. Davis was down in the mouth and wouldn't hear of staying. He would later make a fortune in Mexico, but lose it during the revolution. He moved to

California in 1924, wrote a book about chasing Geronimo and died there six years later.

Mickey Free, War Dept. Photo

Coming out of that campaign, in a June 15, 1887 report, Captain Allen Smith told how Chatto and his scouts chased Apaches out of the high mountains and hit them from the rear, capturing 17 ponies, two mules and six saddles. He said Chatto and his boys "behaved remarkably well" and probably saved the settlers on Eagle Creek. Herbert Welsh copied the report to use in his arguments with the government.

In Washington D.C. Secretary of War William Endicott called on the new Commander-in-chief General Philip Sheridan to discuss sending all Chiricahuas—not only Geronimo, but the reservation

Apaches and the scouts, as well, to Florida prisons because the administration was getting so much pressure from the public. Of course, Indians didn't vote.

President Grover Cleveland had been in office since March of 1884 and he was too busy with the economy, eastern railway strikes and other impedimentia to allow wild Indians to whip up agitation among his constituents in Arizona. He had seemed to be liberal in his Indian policy, advocating for the Dawes Act, which provided for giving individual Indians land, rather than holding it in trust. He viewed Indians as wards of the state, kind of like children under a benevolent but firm adult. He encouraged cultural assimilation. That meant the Indians were expected to assimilate into white society, not retain any of their own culture or behaviors. He stuck up for the Winnebagos and Crows in Dakota Territory when he reversed an executive order by his predecessor, Chester Arthur, opening up four million acres of Indian Territory to miners and settlers. He sent troops in and kicked the white men out. But it angered him when Natives stepped outside the arbitrary bounds set by the government. So, he had no tolerance for the renegades in the southwest, and eventually no tolerance for any of the Chiricahua. This was because of the tribe's history of violent independence, represented by Victorio, Nana, Naiche and, most of all, Geronimo.

On September 26, 1885, Naiche and Chihuahua were reported moving north in Mexico toward the U.S. Border. Chatto's scouts were worried. They assumed the two chieftains were planning another rescue of relatives from Fort Apache, and they believed the renegades would also want revenge against the scouts and their families. Chatto knew he was a target because he had led the raid on Chihuahua's camp back in June. General Crook agreed to send three Fort Bowie scouts to Fort Apache to provide additional protection and to watch closely for Naiche to make contact with his mother and sister, who had remained on the reservation when Naiche bolted. His mother, Dos-the-seh was Mangas Coloradas's daughter and Chatto's first cousin. She claimed she had dis-owned Naiche because he was a bad boy. She was obviously not going to get involved in bringing him in.

Naiche and Chihuahua separated their forces after crossing the border. Naiche skirted the western side of the Chiricahua Mountains, moving north. Chihuahua, with 12 warriors travelled the east side. Naiche and his men raided for horses near Turkey Creek and shot a cowboy. They ran off dozens of horses from ranches near Sulphur Springs, spared the life one rancher, but killed another, before re-uniting with Chihuahua in the lower portion of the mountains.

Moving the opposite direction to re-enter Mexico, Geronimo killed three more men on October 9th.

In the Chiricahua Mountains, Author's photo

General Crook sent Chatto out on a patrol to the west side of the Chiricahua Mountains. It was a wonder that Chatto found Naiche's trail. The Chiricahau Mountains are one of nature's wonders; a high and rugged wilderness with thousands of tall columns of eroded rhyolite, standing side-by-side surrounding deep canyons full of Mexican Pinon, Allegator Juniper, Arizona Sycamore, Oak, Ponderosa Pine, Agave, Yucca, Cypress, Mesquite and Douglas Fir. It had been the home of the Chiricahua since the 1400's and the tribe knew every nook and cranny, every stream and valley. I thought to myself as I hiked along the Echo Canyon Trail in what is now the Chiricahua National Monument, "No white man could find a Chiricahua in here." It's why General Crook said it takes an Apache to find an Apache.

Chatto found the trail and followed it exhaustively. From reading the signs, checking the moccasin prints, inspecting the horse tracks, probing the campfires, Chatto reported that Naiche and the rest of the band were headed back into Sonora. In appreciation, General Crook sent another dispatch to the War Department saying that Chatto had done "everything in his power" to assist the army and asking, again, for the federal government to bring its considerable power to bear in bringing Chatto's wife and children out of Mexico and back to him.

While meeting with the Governor of Arizona and in dispatches to his superiors, Crook outlined a new strategy. First, he would discharge most of his current scouts because they were worn out and needed a period of rest to be with their families. Chatto's discharge was dated October 23, 1885. His performance rating on the documents said "Excellent." Crook would recruit new scouts during the remaining days of October and November and have them ready for a winter campaign into the Sierra Madre. He hoped the four separate groups of renegade Apaches under Naiche, Chihuahua, Geronimo and Nana, and Mangas, would come together into a winter camp where his troops could get a crack at them rather than continued forays all over the wilds of Mexico.

In fact, all of the chiefs, except Mangas, did get together in Mexico, but they developed no plan to stay together. Geronimo wanted to go deeper into Chihuahua province, Naiche would stay with him. Chihuahua and his brother, Jolsanny, also called Ulzana, wanted to rescue relatives and tribesmen at Fort Apache. Ulzana's raid was violent enough to become the subject of a motion picture starring Burt Lancaster in later years. More important to our narrative, it would aim directly at Chatto and target him in two ways. First, Ulzana had vowed he would kill Chatto for raiding his brother's camp. Secondly, the violence of the raid would create such a stir in the territorial press that it would change Chatto's life and that of every other peaceful Chiricahua.

CHAPTER 37   Ulzana's Raid

The plan called for Chihuahua to stage a diversionary raid into New Mexico, hopefully drawing troops away from Ulzana's main raid with a dozen warriors, aimed at Fort Apache. Starting with an assault at the Sabrinal Mines in Mexico to gather horses, Ulzana entered New Mexico on October 17, 1885, and rode to the Animas Mountains, only about 12 miles north of the border. There, his warriors holed up for a few days, sending scouts forward to check for the presence of troops. Cathay (Colle) was along and reminded other warriors in camp that he had been shot in the leg by Chatto and wanted to be in on the kill. Moving to the Florida Mountains, just south of Deming, Ulzana's men ambushed two army couriers, killing a scout, wounding a trooper and capturing their weapons and ammunition.

On November 7, the band approached two adjoining ranch houses. John Shy was home with his wife and son. The owner of the other house, Andy Yeater, was gone with his wife to Deming to buy supplies. The Indians yelled for Shy to come out. Suspicious, Shy got up from his breakfast table and grabbed his Winchester. Just then a window was shattered by Apache bullets. Shy fired back and a standoff was underway. The Apaches set fire to the Yeater home next door and as the fire got out of control, it set fire to Shy's house too. John Shy, his wife and son ran through the front door and through the smoke to a gully near the front of the house, Shy firing as he ran. Single-handedly he held off Ulzana's warriors. Fearing the attention the smoky fire would generate, the Indians rode off. Shy became a local hero.

Andrew Yeater wasn't so lucky. By chance, Ulzana's group intercepted Yeater and his wife, in their wagon, returning from Deming. It was not a significantly different episode from Chatto's killing of Judge McComas. Yeater got off a dozen shots before the Apaches cut him down. His wife died from a hatchet wound to the head. When the press learned of this tragedy they went bonkers, accusing General Crook of being a liar and coward and calling for the removal of all Indians from Arizona. It became a drum beat. It sealed in concrete the government's determination to rid Arizona of all Chiricahuas.

Ulzana (Jolsennay)

Ulzana continued to feed the newspapers ammunition, killing 32 people in a rampage that lasted all month. General Crook ordered families of the hostile Indians moved from Fort Apache to San Carlos where Ulzana would have more difficulty getting to them.

Around November 8th Ulzana went underground, dropping off the map for a time as soldiers scoured the territory trying to pick up his trail. Under Lieutenant Charles Eben Nordstrom, Chatto led a group of ten soldiers and eighteen scouts trying to track down Ulzana, but the renegade was lying low. Ulzana resurfaced again about nine days later, stealing 50 head of stock near the Arizona state line and butchering at least eight of them.

Six days later, Chatto and his ex-wife Nalthchedah were working crops in the field near Bonito Creek when he had one of those "power" moments and experienced a twitching of his muscles which had always told him something was wrong. He yelled to Nalthchedah to grab her 6-year old son, Horace, and mount up. The three of them rode hard for Fort Apache, unaware that Ulzana had been watching the two of them from a distant hill, planning his attack. It saved their lives.

Ulzana captured four Chiricahuas the next day and gunned down two ranchers before moving on to Turkey Creek where an incident took place that stirred Ulzana's hatred of the White Mountain Apaches and led to a massacre. Ulzana had posted a teenage boy as a sentry at Turkey Creek. A Cibeque Apache named Sanchez sneaked up on the boy and shot him with an arrow. To receive a one-hundred dollar reward, Sanchez then cut the boy's head off, stuffed it into a sack and delivered it to the Army. Ulzana went crazy.

Leading his raiders to the home of Sanchez, Ulzana found not Sanchez, but his family, a wife and two children, at home. He butchered them. The next day he attacked White Mountain encampments and slaughtered 21 men, women and children. He then rode for the Gila, twenty miles east of San Carlos where another White Mountain boy was killed and a herd of horses stolen.

This massacre could easily have turned into a war between White Mountain Apaches and Chiricahuas. Unable to run down Ulzana, Sanchez was furious enough to take out his pound of flesh from the peaceful Chiricahuas on the reservation. Chatto got wind of this and jumped in to avoid it. Recruiting 17 scouts to help him, Chatto rode to make contact with Sanchez and other White Mountain Apaches. They held a pow-wow.

Chatto said, "We are on the same side. Your people have been killed and kidnapped by Ulzana. My people have been killed and kidnapped by Ulzana. To the whites it does not matter if they are White Mountain or Chiricahua. They only know that their ranches and cattle and their families are being killed by Apaches and they will make revenge on all of us. We must join together to get rid of Ulzana. We must not fight one another. Kill Ulzana and we return to peace."

Meantime Commanding General Phil Sheridan arrived at Fort Bowie to get a firsthand look at the situation and to respond to General Nelson Mile's criticism of General Crook. A letter from the ever ambitious Miles had stated that the situation in the southwest "is not satisfactory." This naturally implied that he was still the right individual to make it right. Sheridan had already decided to remove all

Chiricahuas from Arizona. At Fort Bowie General Crook and Captain Crawford argued strongly against doing it at all and certainly not now. The removal of peaceful Indians would send an irrevocable message to the renegades to never surrender. That would mean continued years of raiding, killing, and chasing shadows. Sheridan stuck by General Crook, for now, and gave him more time.

Chatto stayed at Fort Apache and away from his farm while Ulzana was raiding in the region. He went again to the White Mountain Apaches after General Crook had recruited them strongly to find and kill all of Ulzana's band. Leaving the bedside of Nalthchedah, who had come down with malaria, Chatto rode to the White Mountain Apaches and gave them a pep-talk

"I told them if we want peace, we must fight for it. We must kill Ulzana and join the war against the hostiles. We are living well compared to the old days. But Ulzana and Geronimo will ruin this life for everybody." Chatto looked at Herbert Welsh and nodded his head affirmatively, as he had done in front of the White Mountain Apaches.

Ulzana was not finished with his campaign. Operating from the Mogollon mountains, he killed three Americans in late November, he stole ten horses at the Mule Springs Ranch on December 5, killed two farmers in a wagon the next day, burned the cabin at Lillies Ranch near Clear Creek on December 9th, killing the owner and a ranch-hand and engaged in a fire-fight with Lt. Sam Fountain and his troopers who were riding to the rescue.

On December 19th Ulzana attacked the Siggins Ranch at Dry Creek where Lt. Fountain chased the Indians up a narrow valley, only to be ambushed with the loss of five killed and three wounded. December 24th Ulzana surfaced again at Steeple Rock where his band stole 40 horses, killed three men and wounded another three. Navajo Scouts under Lt. John McDonald refused to cross the Gila River in pursuit. The chase was taken up by Arizona Rangers down through the San Simon Valley into the Chiricahua Mountains, where they found that Ulzana had killed a local sheriff and his deputy. Then the Ranger's horses gave out and they turned back in a snowstorm.

By December 29th, Ulzana was making his way back to Mexico, killing two wagon drivers in the Sulphur Springs Valley and stealing 15 horses. He had been in the U.S. for two months, had taken 38 lives and stolen more that 250 horses and mules, but had failed to accomplish his dual missions. He hadn't rescued any relatives from the reservation and he hadn't killed Chatto. What he had done is guarantee a tougher federal policy toward all Chiricahua Apaches, one that would cost Chatto 27 years of his life.

Chatto went back to his homestead and nursed Nalthchedah back to health, but she was very weak for a long time. Chatto gathered his strength and started to prepare for the planting season which was three to four months away. He had much to do to be ready.

Meantime, as 1885 waned, Captain Crawford's command continued its torturous tracking of the hostiles in Mexico. They spent Christmas Day near Nicoro Chico where locals reported seeing many Apaches in the area, setting off a pursuit, including an all-night march that located Geronimo's camp about January 9th on a high ridge called Espinosa Del Diablo.

Attempting to surround the camp, Crawford's soldiers and scouts stirred up some of Geronimo's stolen burros. They started braying and it alerted the Indian camp that something was up. Then, White Mountain scouts, over-anxious to destroy Geronimo, fired prematurely and the Apaches scattered, abandoning most of their stock and equipment.

Next day Geronimo and Naiche sent a woman to Crawford's camp saying they wanted to talk. They asked to meet with Crawford the next morning.

CHAPTER 38   The Crawford Affair

Early on the morning of January 10, 1886, Captain Crawford was prepared to meet with the renegade Apaches but the day was interrupted by Mexican Troops marching under the command of Major Mauricio Corredor. The Mexicans had one motive; take Apache scalps and collect the bounty on them. They didn't care which Apaches they scalped and Crawford's scouts, including Chatto's brother Gonaltsis and his fellow warrior Dutchy, looked like good candidates.

The Mexicans, many of them Terahumara Inidians, approached Crawford's troops and started firing. Apache scouts started firing back. Crawford, his second in command Lt. Marion Maus and Chief Scout Tom Horn, yelled out and tried to communicate with the Mexicans. Crawford waved a white handkerchief. He shouted "Soldados Americanos." They were able to get the Mexicans to stop advancing and to send Colonel Corredor and ten soldiers to neutral ground for a parlay. Corredor apologized to Crawford, saying he thought his men were firing at hostile Apaches. It really didn't matter to the Mexicans, but Crawford didn't know that. They were prepared to destroy Crawford's unit. Corredor had set up a sniper before the conference with instructions to take out the U.S. Commander on his signal.

Corredor's Terahumera troops, meantime, were hurling insults at Crawford's Chiricahua scouts and getting an earful in return; this was part of the historical hatred the two tribes had for each other. As Crawford heard rifles being loaded and cocked, he told Lt. Maus, "For God's sake don't let them fire." Then he jumped up on a big rock and waved his handkerchief again in a "hey calm down, we're friendly" gesture. Corredor's sniper fired. The bullet hit Captain Crawford in the temple and he went down like a deer, brains spilling out.

Now Crawford's Apache scouts opened up, killing nine of the ten Mexicans who were in the parlay. Dutchy ran up and shot the

Mexican commander, Corredor, through the heart. The firing then became general and continued for almost two hours until the leaderless Terahumara's broke off the engagement and retreated. Some of Geronimo and Naiche's warriors watched the action from a nearby high point and rushed to tell their chiefs that Crawford, who they trusted, was dead.

Lt. Maus took charge. Crawford was not dead, but there was little anybody could do for him. They packed him onto a wagon and Maus gave the order to pull back several miles. Next day a messenger from Geronimo arrived, saying the hostiles still wanted to talk. They arranged a meeting.

Maus sat on the ground in a semi-circle with Geronimo, Naiche, Chihuahua and old Nana. He nodded to each one of them and met their gaze.

Geronimo spoke first. "Why have you come here?" he asked.

Maus turned to him without flinching and said, "We have come to capture or destroy you and your band."

With the interpretation, the Apache leaders let out a series of laughs and murmurs between themselves. After some discussion among themselves, Geronimo continued.

"We want to meet and talk with Nantan Lupan…General Crook. We might want to come to the reservation, but we want to hear his word."

Maus told the Apaches that could be arranged and they discussed a place and time. Then he said, "How can General Crook know you are being truthful?"

Nana piped up. "I will come with you now and bring my wife, who is the sister of Geronimo. Geronimo's wife Ihtedda and her child will also go with you now.

"And I will send my wife, Haozonne and our son," said Naiche, "as a token of good faith for the General. And we have seven others who wish to return to the reservation with you."

They all agreed and parted company.

After only one moment of semi-consciousness, Captain Crawford died two days later. As Maus arrived back on the reservation with his group of Indians in tow, Chatto took news of Crawford's death hard. General Crook took it even harder. Crawford had been his very best Indian man and a close confidant. A report by Captain Wirt Davis said, "The death of Captain Crawford was a sad one, and will cause profound sorrow and regret in the United States." Crawford's remains were moved from Mexico later for burial at Arlington National Cemetery.

CHAPTER 39   Geronimo Meets Crook

When the general and the hostile Apaches sat down in a cottonwood-shaded ravine called Canon de los Embudos on March 25, 1886, the negotiations were doomed from the start. Geronimo complained about the treatment he had received from Chatto, Mickey Free and other turn-coats. But the real subject was surrender conditions. Geronimo wanted absolution for past crimes and a return to Turkey Creek. That was not possible. Under directions from the President, General Sheridan sent General Crook into the meeting with no negotiating room. The Indians had to surrender unconditionally and would be regarded as prisoners of war.

Crook wasn't gentle with Geronimo. He asked why should 40 of your men be afraid of Chatto or Mickey Free? And if that's the reason you left, why did you have to go and kill innocent people? What did they do to you? Crook told him if he fled because of rumors, that too was a phony excuse. "There are foolish rumors every week," said Crook, "but you are no child, you don't have to believe them." Crook told Geronimo he was a liar for promising in the Sierra Madre that the peace would last. Now, "I can't believe you," he said. And he chastised Geronimo for sending his cousins to murder Chatto and Lieutenant Davis. Now he gave Geronimo the choice; "You can surrender and face your punishment, or you can stay on the war path. If you chose the war path, I will stay after you and kill your whole band if it takes fifty years."

One other pawn played by General Crook in these talks was bringing along Kaetenae to prove two things, one; terrible things did not happen to Kaetenae when he went to prison and two; he was now a good white Indian and was doing okay.

Crook thought his orders allowed him to offer two years of prison time, then a return to the reservation. On that basis Chihuahua surrendered with 75 people, Naiche said he would give up as did Nana and finally Geronimo. That being settled, General Crook assigned Lt. Maus to escort the Apaches back to Fort Bowie and left the canyon to return and telegraph General Sheridan that he had a deal with the renegades. Chatto warned General Crook this was not going to work towards an agreement. No sooner did General Crook start his return trip than things started going wrong among the Apaches.

First, a trader named Charles Tribolet appeared near Geronimo's encampment and sold them nearly 15 gallons of whiskey....enough fuel to blow the deal sky-high. The Apaches were drunk for three days, yelling and shooting and talking tough. During this time Naiche shot his wife Eclaheh in the leg, reportedly in a fit of jealousy. It could have been the liquor. It was certainly an indication he was edgy.

Lt. Maus got everybody on the road, but it was slow going. Another thing; the Indians were sure that General Crook was going to appoint Chatto as the Chiricahua chief and they would be taking orders from Chatto. Geronimo, in particular, hated that idea. He had come to despise Chatto. In general, they felt that there was something phony about the surrender terms from General Crook. He had been too stern and it scared them.

On the trail to the border, Lt. Maus failed to notice that Chief Chihuahua camped separately from Naiche and Geronimo. He didn't see it as a sign that they planned to split up. And in the middle of the night Geronimo and Naiche sneaked away and disappeared with about 40 people, 18 of them men.

Lt. Maus sent a detachment of soldiers to destroy all the alcohol supplies of the trader, Charles Tribolet. One sergeant said the trader ought to be hanged on the spot.

Chihuahua, his brother Ulzana and his 50 followers remained in place and continued to Ft. Bowie with Lieutenant Maus. They would very soon find themselves being herded aboard freight trains headed for Florida where they spent two months camped in the rain at Anastasia Island near St. Augustine, while a well was dug at the uninhabitable old Fort Marion and it underwent just enough repairs to house the Indians. A second-lieutenant wrote to his family saying the

Anastasia camp was the pits; poor water, no shade, a generally bad location.

Chihuahua's wife and children shipped to Florida

They were unaware that government policy toward them had changed twice recently. In September, 1885, after Geronimo's raid to Fort Apache, the government decided that no hostile Apache could remain in Arizona. In November, after Ulzana's raid, it decided that no Chiricahua, hostile or peaceful, could remain in Arizona. Chatto naturally assumed this did not apply to him.

When General Crook cabled Sheridan that Geronimo and Naiche had flown the coup, the Commander-in-chief was beside himself with anger. He telegraphed Crook, in return, telling him to go back and tell the hostiles that the government would spare their lives, nothing else, and if they didn't agree, then they would be destroyed, period. It was impractical, if not stupid, and General Crook told his superiors so. He said if he could communicate with the renegades at all and told them that, they would never surrender and the southwest would be in for more years of depravations. Worse, it required Crook to go back on his word to the Apaches and he just couldn't do that.

In his final telegram to General Sheridan, Crook finished by saying, "I believe that the plan upon which I have conducted operations is the one most likely to prove successful in the end. It may be, however, that I am too much wedded to my own views in this matter, and as I have spent nearly eight years of the hardest work of my life in this department, I respectfully request that I may now be relieved from its command."

That was fine with Sheridan. He cut the orders relieving Crook and replaced him with General Nelson Miles. Under Sheridan and Miles the policy changed from trying to negotiate with the Apaches to whipping them with military power and reducing the role of the Apache scouts.

Before General Crook left, he used his influence to get Captain John Bourke an important posting in the Inspector General's office in Washington D.C. He wanted someone near headquarters and would be calling on Bourke in the future. And Crook had praise for Chatto in official reports. He recounted the raid in which Chatto, with a picked body of scouts found an Apache camp and opened a fight, "scattering Apaches through deep canyons with their women and children." He said Chatto had been made a sergeant of the scouts and was held in high esteem by the soldiers. He continued to urge the War Department to bargain for Chatto's wife and children.

CHAPTER 40   General Miles

General Nelson Miles had been thoroughly agitated when the Arizona Department went to George Crook, back in '71. Miles thought the post and the promotion should have gone to him. Miles was eleven years younger than Crook. Unlike the older man, he did not attend West Point. Like him, he made a name and future for himself in the Civil War.

He started out as a First Lieutenant in a Massachusetts infantry regiment, and quickly rose to Lt. Colonel when his commanding officer lost an arm at the Battle of Seven Pines. After recovering from his own wounds, Miles was given the 61st New York Regiment. Here again, his commander was wounded at Antietam, one the bloodiest battles of the war, and Miles led the unit for the rest of the battle. This got him promoted to full colonel.

General Nelson Miles

He was in command of the 61st at Fredericksburg and Chancellorsville, both Confederate victories, where Miles was badly wounded. Later he received the Medal of Honor for his actions. Missing Gettysburg due to his recovery, he was back in action by the time of the Battles of the Wilderness and Spotsylvania Courthouse. Coming out of those battles he was promoted to Brigadier General and reported to General Grant as he pursued Robert E. Lee through Virginia's Cold Harbor and the Siege of Petersburg. He was there, at the surrender at Appomattox. He was still 26 when he became a Major General and was given the job of imprisoning the captured President of the Confederacy, Jefferson Davis.

It was here that the first public criticism of Miles surfaced. People said it was cruel the way he kept Jeff Davis in chains and mistreated him in other ways. Other officers already knew he was ambitious. Now he showed a vain streak in replying to his critics, telling them to piss-off. As the war time army was disbanded, Miles asked high ranking acquaintances to go to bat for him to keep his general's stars. It didn't work and he was offered a colonels commission in the post-war Army.

If his rank went down, his social status went up when he married the daughter of Major General William Sherman, the engineer of total war during his push through Georgia. **In fact, the marriage probably slowed down his career as Sherman tried to avoid the appearance of favoritism. Notwithstanding,** soon enough Miles was on the frontier leading a new regiment. He took part in several campaigns trying to round up Indian tribes and herd them onto reservations, including the Red River War against Comanche, Kiowa, Southern Cheyenne and Arapaho. **He drove his men so hard that, during one dry overland campaign, his troopers actually cut their arms to moisten their lips with their own blood.**

He was then ordered north to operate against the Lakota Sioux after Gen. George Custer had gotten the 7th Cavalry annihilated at the Little Big Horn. He campaigned relentlessly and forced many of the Sioux and Cheyenne to surrender or flee to Canada. **He employed the**

"Total War" strategy against Indian camps, attacking with unbridled ferocity and with little concern for humanity.

Miles took credit for the surrender of Chief Joseph and the Nez Perce after General Howard's historic campaign from Idaho to Alberta. Thereafter he spent five years in command of the Department of the Columbia.

Miles had written to Sherman trying to get Crook's job. For this and other reasons Crook hated Miles and Miles hated him in return. Miles thought Crook went too easy on the Indians, what with digging ditches, setting them up in business, relying on scouts and the like, and Crook thought Miles, and his boss Phil Sheridan were too hard on the natives.

So now, replacing George Crook, who would never forgive him, he was expected to capture Geronimo and whatever other renegade Apaches were still raiding Arizona, New and Old Mexico. For this purpose Miles was given 5,000 soldiers—one fourth of the entire U.S. Army, to capture or kill Geronimo's little band. Maybe it was his vanity. He didn't think he needed Apache scouts. And he definitely did not want anyone else taking credit for the capture.

For his part Crook would continue to advocate for the Indians and Miles would try to annihilate them.

CHAPTER 41 Bear Valley

Geronimo was pretty much alone in the wilderness by this time. At most he had 36 warriors, one of them the woman, Lozen, Victorio's younger sister. After the breakdown in negotiations with General Crook and under the more militant regime of General Miles, Geronimo and Naiche were raising hell.

Operating in the wide area south of Nogales, Mexico and Douglas, Arizona, Naiche and Geronimo moved fast, hitting ranches and killing people almost every day. During the first six weeks of General Miles command they raided no fewer than a dozen ranches, stealing an estimated 226 horses, mules and livestock. On one occasion they made off with 50 head of horses in one foray.

They killed Mexicans and Americans indiscriminately, mostly ranchers but including campers, wagoneers, army troopers and anyone with whom they came in contact including one baby. Some they kidnapped. A woman named Trinidad Verdin was snatched at a ranch in Sonora and a 6 year old boy was taken from an Arizona ranch. The boy was left behind when the Apaches were surprised by an Arizona posse. The woman remained captive. On one occasion Geronimo let a rancher go free because he said he was unarmed and appeared to be "a good man." There was no accounting for his vicious acts or those of his mercy. Between April 3rd and May 22, the death toll reached in excess of 52 people, most of whom had not seen it coming. On two occasions the Apaches had traded shots in firefights with both Mexican and American troops, suffering no heavy losses before breaking off and vanishing into thin-air again.

In April, riding out of their stronghold in the Sierra Madres of Northern Mexico, Geronimo, Naiche and his Chiricahuas raided four cattle ranches in or around Bear Valley, just north of the border, one of the last actions in their campaign. Geronimo would later deny his involvement, probably to get better treatment, because the attacks were vicious.

Though not officially a scout any more, Chatto kept himself available to the army, but did not have a personal relationship with General Miles as he had enjoyed with General Crook. Miles conferred with Chatto off and on, trying to get his bearings on Apache behaviors. Chatto told him about the normal routes of travel into and out of Mexico, where the general could expect trouble and locations his soldiers should avoid. On each occasion he pestered the general to do more to bring Ishchosen and the children back. There is no record that Miles pursued this in any way. And Chatto told him that he wished for Geronimo and Naiche to be captured and the Apache Wars to end, for the good of his people.

When the renegade Apaches entered Bear Valley, they first attacked two men who were traveling through the desert near Oro Blanco. The men were A. L. Peck and his assistant, Charles Owen. They were ambushed about two miles from Peck's ranch in Agua Fria Canyon. Owen was shot and killed instantly but Peck was taken prisoner. The hostiles tied Peck to a tree and kept him under guard for about an hour before setting him free without his shoes. Peck then ran barefoot back to his home where he found that the house was destroyed and that his wife and eleven month old baby had been murdered. Peck also found that his twelve-year-old niece had been captured. The girl's body was found two weeks later, near the ranch, by some cowboys. Apparently the Apaches had crushed her head with rocks.

After the attack on Peck's ranch the Apaches continued on towards Sycamore Canyon homesteads south of Tucson. One such homestead was the cattle ranch of John "Yank" Bartlett and his partner Henry Hewitt, located at the head of the canyon.

That day a local farmer, Phil Shanahan was visiting the Bartlett ranch and his ten-year-old son, Little Phil Shanahan, was staying with Yank's son Johnny Bartlett. Shanahan left Little Phil at the Bartlett's while he rode back to his own ranch, only a few miles away. Before very long, Shanahan stumbled back into view of the ranch house saying he had been shot by Indians. Yank sent his son Johnny for a doctor and to alarm the townspeople. He told Little Phil to go home and warn his mom and sisters. This was not very good advice considering Phil's dad had just been shot along the same route. But Little Phil took off and made it home. His family hid in the hills.

Sure enough, Apaches attacked their house, stealing everything they could get their hands on, and killing cattle. On his way to town, Johnny got spooked by men in the distance and went back home. But Apaches were there too, firing into the house. He rode right through the firing. His horse was shot out from under him and died at the front door. Johnny made it into the house. There he saw that Mr. Shanahan had died from his wounds. His dad was shooting back at the Apaches and took a bullet to the shoulder. He yelled at Johnny to ride to Oro Blanco again.

Johnny sneaked out late, leading a horse and walking barefoot for the first two miles to avoid making too much noise. He reached the E.W. Smith ranch several miles away and found that somebody had broken in. Mr. Smith was hiding. He yelled at Johnny and together they rode to Oro Blanco, arriving in the middle of the night. Johnny returned with help by dawn's early light, worried all the way what he would find. He found his father okay. Yank had fended off the Indians and they were gone.

For their bravery, both Little Phil Shanahan and Johnny Bartlett each received a commemorative rifle from the citizens of Santa Cruz County. When the army learned of the raid, it sent a troop of Buffalo Soldiers out chasing the Apaches for more than 200 miles. They found more than two dozen horses the Apaches had ridden to death.

Catching up with the marauders in Mexico on May 3rd, the troopers traded shots at Indians on a hilltop and took some casualties. After several hours of fighting, the hostiles retreated further into the Mexican wilderness, having lost two killed and one wounded. Geronimo's band was slowly, but surely, being whittled down. Other army units came up to help and eventually found the Apaches encamped on May 15, near the village of Santa Cruz. Another skirmish ensued and the cavalry routed the Apaches, killing or wounding at least one man and capturing their horses and camping equipment. The Apaches retaliated at a watering hole five miles from the town of Santa Cruz, killing two Americans and wounding two. Again the Apaches went on the run and disappeared.

Things went differently for Geronimo on June 18th when a Mexican rancher pulled together 29 men and found Geronimo's small group at a watering hole and charged them, rifles firing. Geronimo grabbed the hostage Trinidad Verdi and threw her onto his horse. One of his wives stood her ground, firing a pistol until she was out of bullets and cut down by Mexican fire. Geronimo's horse stumbled on a rock and threw him and Miss Verdi to the ground. He yelled for her to follow him into the box canyon ahead and scrambled that direction. But she turned and ran to the Mexicans and safety.

Geronimo holed up in the mouth of a cave and the Mexicans came after him. They were unaware that Geronimo was a crack shot and that he carried an 1873 Springfield .45 caliber rifle that could fire 15 rounds per minute in the hands of an expert. The Mexicans broke off the assault when three of their number went down killed and one wounded. The three dead men had bullet holes through their foreheads.

Upwards of 5,000 U.S. Troops were searching for Geronimo and couldn't touch him. On the other side of the coin, his band was dwindling down to the hardest of the hard. His small band kept moving over wastelands with little food or rest. He was in the wilds for more than a year, becoming the most famous Native American of the time and earning him the title of the "worst Indian who ever lived" among white settlers.

CHAPTER 42   Gatewood

One of the ways General Miles and Crook differed was; Miles didn't trust scouts and thought regular troops could catch Chiricahuas. Crook said Chiricahuas were impossible to catch without Indian scouts. Miles kept only a small contingent of Indian scouts and none of them were Chiricahuas and they were not to be used as fighters. He ran his regular troopers over thousands of miles of desert and mountains trying to capture Geronimo and was singularly unsuccessful at it. Finally, General Miles asked around Fort Apache and at San Carlos if there was an Apache willing and able to get a message to Geronimo and Naiche. Nobody stepped forward. Miles consulted with Chatto and Noche, who had taken over Bonito's band when Bonito married a White Mountain woman and went to live with her people. Chatto recommended Martine, one of his scouts. Noche recommended Kayitah who was probably trusted by Geronimo. Then Miles enlisted Lieutenant, Charles Gatewood, who he always considered "a Crook man" to go out along with his scouts and find Geronimo.

Lt. Charles Gatewood

Gatewood had ridden in the attempts to capture Victorio and he was reporting to Colonel Asa Carr when the Cibique medicine man fiasco happened.

General Miles chose Captain Henry Lawton from Troop B, 4th Cavalry, at Fort Huachuca, to lead the expedition, with Gatewood as his second in command. **Miles knew that Gatewood was well known to Geronimo, spoke some Apache, and was familiar with their traditions and values; having spent nearly 10 years in the field with them and against them.**

Even though he was sick and getting worse, Gatewood was sent out by General Miles to see if Geronimo would talk peace. On the trail, he linked up with Lt. James Parker who guided him 150 miles into Mexico to find Captain Henry Lawton, also in the field with a mission to find and kill Geronimo.

Lawton wasn't happy to see Gatewood. Their missions were quite different. One was a kill mission; the other was a peace mission.

Gatewood was feeling so bad from his rheumatism that he asked a surgeon to medically discharge him. The surgeon, Leonard Wood, refused. Gatewood sucked it up and kept going.

In late August, Geronimo and Naiche had just returned from a series of raids on ranches in which they had stolen 60 horses and killed more than six men. They were feeling celebratory but very tired when Crawford's scouts located Geronimo's camp. Gatewood sent the two scouts, Kayitah and Martine, into the camp to make first contact and tell Geronimo this was not a war party. Kayitah told Geronimo frankly, "You have no friends in the world." He told Geronimo the army would track down and kill everyone in his band "if it takes 50 years." Geronimo scoffed at that, but nevertheless sent Martine back to Gatewood to say they could have a sit-down. He sent a sample of cooked mescal as a gesture. Naiche told Martine to pass the word that Gatewood would be safe in coming. They held Kayitah in their camp.

Kayitah

Gatewood rode to Geronimo's camp with only two soldiers and two interpreters, one of which was the well-known Tom Horn. He also brought 15 pounds of tobacco as a gift and ice-breaker.

Geronimo, who was recovering from a gunshot wound during a shoot-out with six Americans at Santa Rosa, Mexico, on August 11th, told Gatewood. "You are very thin and you look sick. But you are always welcome in my camp and it was always safe for you to come."

Gatewood urged Geronimo to abandon his fight. He said Geronimo could accept General Mile's terms or fight it out to the end. The renegade was down to about 20 warriors and 14 women. The Apache wars had taken the lives of nearly 60 percent of the Chiricahua tribe in the ten years since their reservation had been closed. Geronimo's people looked tired and worn out. Still, when Gatewood was unable to bargain favorable terms Geronimo told him, "Take us to the reservation or fight."

Gatewood astonished Geronimo when he told him his family and the other Chiricahuas were no longer on the reservation, they were in Florida. It wasn't yet true, but Gatewood believed it was. Geronimo took the news like a punch to the gut.

The next day, as Gatewood was leaving camp, Geronimo came to him and said, "Forget that you are a white man. Think like an Apache and tell me what you would do."

Gatewood replied, "Put your trust in General Miles."

Geronimo agreed to meet with General Miles. His band rode with Gatewood to Lawton's camp in Guadalupe Canyon. Lawton greeted Geronimo and agreed the Apaches could keep their weapons for continued security against marauding Mexicans.

When Lawton left to get to a telegraph station and inform General Miles, he left Lieutenant Abiel Smith in command. Smith wanted to disarm the Apaches. Gatewood figured he wanted to murder them. Gunning down Geronimo would make him an instant star.

Gatewood told Smith, "We are not disarming anybody. That would reverse everything we've accomplished so far."

"They are prisoners of war," responded Smith

"We have promised them their weapons for protection against the Mexicans," said Gatewood.

"I'm not comfortable with armed Apaches in our camp," said Smith.

"Let's put it this way," said Gatewood. "I will blow the head off the first soldier in line (who tries to disarm them)."

That ended the debate. The troops and the Apaches travelled to Skeleton Canyon, Arizona, and arrived one day ahead of General Miles, on September 2, 1886.

CHAPTER 43   Going to Washington

Relieved of his duties as a scout, Chatto set about to make the best of life on the reservation. For many it was a struggle and everyone complained. But Chatto had started a small house, constructing a hard mud floor, making the adobe bricks by hand near where the front door would be, laying the bricks in a neat rectangular shape and using mesquite trees for window sills, door frames and roof beams. Outside, mesquite also formed his corral.

He got up every morning at the crack of dawn and would do nothing until he had his first cup of coffee. He laced it heavily with sugar, if he had any, or with syrup. Then he would step out into the sunshine and face the east, saying a brief prayer to Ussen, stretching his arms out and upward, letting his palms catch the rays of light. After his prayer he would stretch himself according to his routine. He would turn his head to left and right, then up and down, then windmill each of his arms, loosening up the shoulders. He would clench and unclench his fists and work his forearms. He would arch his back backward, holding it in position that way, then bend far forward touching his fingertips to his toes. Then he would squat with his legs three or four times and he was ready to inspect the garden. Near the corral were rows of squash, corn and peppers requiring him to pack water from the creek bed no more than 50 paces away. His work was accompanied by the frequent sounds of mules braying and horses whinnying. He liked the work.

In the late afternoon and into the evening, at least once a week, he and other former warriors would sit around swapping war stories and latest rumors. They had no direct knowledge of the depravations of Geronimo and Naiche, but they had been there and done that and they knew the story. They talked about Chihuahua and his 77 people being shipped off to Florida. Chatto and Kaetenae had pleaded with the Army to let those Chiricahuas remain on their part of the reservation, but by the time they heard what was happening the machinery was in motion. They had no idea the deportation plan went to the highest levels of the U.S. Government. They had no strong suspicion it would happen to them. After all, Chihuahua had been a renegade and a pretty powerful one. He must have known he would be punished in some way. For the rest of them, several hundred Chiricahuas who had been living in peace, life was pretty good.

General Miles had proposed shipping the Indians to Fort Leavenworth, Kansas or developing new reservations in Oklahoma that would get them well away from Arizona population centers. He argued that if these places were a bit more livable the Apaches wouldn't want to escape all the time. General Sheridan fired back a telegram that said, "The proposition to remove the Chiricahua and Warm Springs Indians to any reservation or military post west of the Missouri River cannot be entertained." He said President Grover Cleveland was in favor of forcibly arresting all reservation Indians and sending them to Fort Marion where the Army had previously stashed Indians of other tribes

Separate correspondence had asked the Commander at Fort Marion how many Indians he could handle. The answer came back; 75. Before the government was finished, it would ship more than 500 Apaches to the Florida fort.

General Miles wrote to the War Department again saying, "I presume it is not the purpose of the Government to keep permanently the seventy-seven Apaches, (Chihuahua's band) mostly women and children, in Florida, where they were recently sent. They are a mountain race, accustomed to high latitudes, and would in a short time, most likely die if kept in the lowlands of Florida. Should the Apaches in Arizona and Florida be permanently located in some place healthful and suited to their natural requirements, I believe the hostile element would surrender."

The War Department was having none of it. General Sheridan had no place in his thoughts for Indians and Secretary of War William Endicott seemed to be on the same page. Both sent orders down the chain of command to plan on moving all the Chiricahuas out of the state of Arizona. Miles approached Chatto, to arrange for him to meet a representative from the Interior Department to talk about relocating. Secretary Lucius Lamar agreed to send his son, Lucius Jr. Soon Lamar Jr. had convinced Chatto to head a ten-man delegation, that would include Noche, Loco and at least one of his wives, Kaetenae, Charley, Askadodilges, Gonaltsis and Mickey Free as interpreter to come to Washington D.C. to discuss how much better life might be in a new location.

"I told them I didn't want to move," said Chatto. "I had my house, my garden, my mules and cattle. Besides, I needed to be there if the Army could locate my wife and children. I still held hope that could happen."

"Did the others feel the same way?" asked Herbert Welch.

"Yes, this was now our home. It was not good, but we made it better and we did not know how another land would be. It might be worse. We would have to start all over."

"But you and the others went to Washington?"

"Yes, we met with the high man in the War Department and the Indian (Interior) Department and with the President."

"Tell me, as best you remember, what was said to you."

"The man in the War Department, his name was Endicott. He said he wished the wars to be over and we said they were. He said if we did not raid or steal we would be good. Most of us had not raided for a long time."

"And the Secretary of the Interior, Mr. Lamar?"

"Mr. Lamar gave me this silver medal. On the back it says, 'To Chatto from Secretary Lamar.' He said the white leaders wanted to give us a new reservation with 60 square miles of land and the land would be better than where we lived. I said 'No.' I told him we did not want to move. He asked if I needed farm tools or implements and said they would be given to me when I returned home. He said I would return to Fort Apache.

Lucius Quintus Cincinnatus Lamar II, Sec. of Interior

And you saw the President, Grover Cleveland?"

"Yes. He was a big man with much hair on his face. And he smelled funny. He asked us to go back and tell our people we must move to Florida. I said we did not want to leave our homes. He said for me to go home, to work and to behave myself. I said I would. I asked him for a paper that would say we could stay at our homes in Arizona."

Welsh sat forward and asked, "And did you get such a document?"

"Yes," said Chatto. "But he knew I could not read his language and later I was told the paper only said that I had visited the White House on a certain day."

"Do you remember getting a similar paper from Secretary Lamar?" When Chatto hesitated, Welch shuffled through a stack of papers and read from a certificate. "Department of the Interior, Washington, July 1st, 1886. 'This is to certify that I know personally,

Chatto, Chief of the Chiricahua Apache Indians, and that since his return to the reservation in 1883, he has lived peacefully with mankind, exerting at all times a good influence over his people. He has made the reputation of being a reliable and brave man. L. Q. C. Lamar, Jr."

Chatto shook his head, "That has done me and my people a lot of good, hasn't it."

While this was taking place, General Miles was trying to implement his plan for neutralizing the reservation Apaches without sending them to a Florida prison, apparently notwithstanding his standing orders from Army Chief Sheridan. In a letter to the War Department on August 27, 1886, Miles wrote if the Apaches get word that they will be banished to Florida, their removal "over mountainous and timbered country" will very difficult. Miles said he could get them to agree if we (the government) can move them at least 1200 miles, disarm them, send their stock along, scatter the grown children through industrial schools and then provide them with permanent residence and means of self-support. He said they would be under control and satisfied and the people relieved of their presence without loss of life. He was starting to sound like Crook.

In another dispatch General Miles didn't think moving Apaches to prisons in Florida was a good idea, in light of Chatto's invitation to Washington. He knew that Chatto was going to Washington D.C. to be convinced, one way or another, to leave Arizona with his tribe. Miles wrote to the War Department telling his superiors they could move the Indians and it might make Arizonans happy, but it would be viewed as an "act of bad faith," by the Indians. He asked how the government could invite more Indians to Washington if they didn't do right by Chatto's group. And if that happens, he said, "I think it would necessitate a war of extermination against those that are down in Old Mexico, for if banishment were the fate of those that have been peaceable they would expect theirs to be much worse, and I think all would have to be killed before any more would surrender." Speaking of Chatto, he said, "The charge that Chatto, the leading spirit and bravest of the tribes, has committed serious crimes, is undoubtedly true, as it is of every other representative of the wild Indians that has appeared in Washington from the days of Red Jacket (Revolutionary War Seneca Chief) to the present time. That he was present or concerned in the murder of Judge McComas and family is a matter of some doubt, He is said to have been in another place at that time."

If there is credence to that statement by Miles, it would be from reports that Chihuahua, and not Chatto, staged the Arizona ammunition raid. This is what Juh's son, Daklugie reported years after the fact.

Acting Secretary of War, R.C. Drum responded that "some deference" should be paid to General Miles, but the Indians should be treated like prisoners of war and sent to Fort Marion immediately. And, he said, Geronimo should be hanged.

In an emergency meeting in President Cleveland's oval office, a majority, including Secretary of War Endicott, Secretary of Interior Lamar, his son Lamar Jr., and Captain Dorst who was escorting Chatto's party, voted to betray their promises to the peaceful Chiricahuas. Captain John Bourke, now assigned to prestigious duty in the War Department, argued strongly against treating all of the Indians the same. He said it was a gross violation of General Crook's agreement with them. It mattered not. They voted in favor of a double-cross. Sweeney called it an "egregious disgrace unworthy of a country founded on the democratic ideals of liberty, equality and justice for all."

Within days, the Chiricahua at Fort Apache were called in to be issued rations on the normal day when that occurred. They were summarily rounded up, including about 40 scouts who had served with the Army and put in a corral under guard. Their women and children were then summoned and the lot of them were herded toward the train station. Chatto knew nothing of this. Neither did Geronimo or Naiche. Chihuahua's son Eugene said of the scouts, "the only good thing we got from those terrible twenty seven years as prisoners of war is that the scouts, too, were prisoners. And we made it miserable for them. "

CHAPTER 44   Geronimo Surrenders

At Skeleton Canyon, Lt. Gatewood promised Geronimo that he and the 16 warriors, 12 women and six children with him would not be killed on the spot but, he later claimed, that was about all he promised. After General Miles arrived with his entourage, greetings were exchanged, photographs were taken and then the meeting got down to the serious business at hand. Who told what to whom is still debated. The bargainers worked through the obstacles of language, interpretation, attitude and mistrust. The word "unconditional" didn't come up and Geronimo wouldn't have understood it anyway. But later, when the surrender terms were examined, a great debate broke out about what the Army promised Geronimo and what the United States delivered. Would Geronimo have surrendered if he had known he would be immediately shipped to a prison in Florida and his wives and children shipped to a different prison?

Based on his understanding of the promises made, Geronimo handed over his Winchester lever-action rifle, his Colt single-action army revolver and a Sheffield Bowie Knife, all of which now reside in museums, and he handed over his freedom.

As Geronimo and his band were being herded across the plains to Fort Bowie, the scouts who found him, Kayitah and Martine were also under arrest and being regarded as POWs. Similarly, Dahteste, who had interpreted for General Miles was also a prisoner. On the desert trail to the remote fort, the wife of Geronimo's son, Chappo, had a baby. At Bowie they would wander among the buildings at the fort and await their fate while news headlines all over America said the last of the wild Apaches had been captured. Immediately Geronimo and his band were ticketed for Fort Sam Houston, near San Antonio; final destination, Florida. Many of the Indians were convinced they would be killed along the way and they were nervous. Seven warriors slipped away and went back to the mountains of Mexico. For the others, the conditions on the train were deplorable. They had to sleep on the floor. Worse, they had to defecate inside the rail cars because no toilets were provided. It was hot and sweaty and cramped. At least two Apache warriors, Massai and Gray Lizard, escaped from their prison car and made their way back to Arizona in a 1,200-mile journey to their ancestral lands.

The Apaches stayed in San Antonio nearly six weeks while the military decided where to put them. Naiche was given a tour of the city. President Cleveland was all for hanging them, but knew better. He declined to let civil authorities intervene because they would have found the Chiricahua guilty of various outrages and hanged them too. The President figured the politically correct thing to do was put them in prison and that's what the administration did.

People in Pensacola, Florida, quickly petitioned the government to send Geronimo to Fort Pickens, instead of Fort Marion. Geronimo would be a tremendous tourist attraction for the Florida folks. Geronimo's family was separated from him when everyone reached San Antonio. The women, children and two scouts were placed in a different railroad car. Geronimo went to Fort Pickens. His family went to Fort Marion.

Photo by J. McDonald, 1886, National Archives

Right after the separation in San Antonio, Geronimo and Naiche formally complained they were being double-crossed; this was not what the Great White Father had promised. They appealed for a meeting with General David Stanley, the Commander of the Department of Texas.

He listened to their story and fired off a lengthy letter to the War Department on Oct. 27, 1886. First, he confirmed that Geronimo and 19 Apaches, including the two scouts Martine and Kayitah were shipped to Florida on the previous Friday. Under his orders "the women, children and the two scouts were placed in a separate car before they left." He had informed Geronimo just before the train left the station where they were going. Geronimo and Naiche protested to Stanley that the "separation of themselves from their families was a violation of the terms of their surrender." They went back over their negotiations with General Miles in great detail, explaining how General Miles had used stones and lines in the dirt to explain where they were, where they were going and making promises that their families would be with them within five days and that, while Fort Marion was small, they would be moved to larger facilities within months.

General Stanley said he was reporting this at the request of Geronimo and Naiche. Then he said, "While not desiring to comment on the matter, I feel compelled to say that my knowledge of the Indian character and experience I have had with Indians of all kinds, and the corroborating circumstances and facts that have been brought to my notice in this particular case convinces me that the foregoing statement of Natchez and Geronimo is substantially correct."

Geronimo and warriors at Fort Pickens

The government required 45 days to sort out the Geronimo surrender. It found itself burning up the telegraph and mailing reams of correspondence trying to cover its tracks and figure out what was really promised to Geronimo at Skeleton Canyon and whether the Apache leader understood it and agreed to it.

Writing his own life story years later, Geronimo said General Miles promised him he would be protected by the government and it would build him a house, fence his land which would have plenty of trees, water and grass, provide cattle, horses, mules and farming implements. He would be provided men to work his land so that he, as a chief, wouldn't be required to work. He was promised blankets and warm clothing for the winter under government protection. He was to live with his tribe and family and finally, he said, General Miles took his hand and swept it across the ground saying Geronimo's past deeds would be swept away like this. Geronimo was prone to bending the facts. If that was his understanding, he had another thought coming.

General Miles told the War Department that Geronimo asked for surrender conditions and he said "No," they must surrender as prisoners of war. He said "I promised not to kill them." And he asked the Indians to rely on "the justice of the Government and trust their future to the President of the United States." Miles said the Indians understood explicitly they would have to leave Arizona for all time. But Miles didn't put any of this down on paper as General Crook always did. It contributed to the "I said, he said" problem with the whole business.

Mangas, who had not seen Geronimo or Naiche since the past May, rode into Fort Bowie to surrender. His tiny group, which had not raided in the interim, arrived at Fort Pickens in the fall of 1886.

CHAPTER 45   The Stab-in-the-Back Letters

The day was drawing to a close at Fort Marion, as the last rays of sunlight filtered through the windows of the chapel. Herbert Welsh adjusted his glasses and shuffled through his old leather briefcase, pulling out a thick sheaf of papers. He had not yet interviewed others on his list, Dutchy, Noche, Martine, Kayitah and more, but that would have to wait until tomorrow.

"I have a number of letters that I intend to bring to bear on your situation. We can go over some of them if you like." Welsh had accumulated them over a long period of time from sources within public agencies.

Chatto nodded his approval. He had learned well never to trust white men and did not know about this one when he arrived. But something about him said that Mr. Welsh could be trusted; that maybe he would help. He had few other options. Chatto found himself opening up to Herbert Welsh.

Welsh continued, "I'll take these in order. Here's one in July, 1886, in which General Miles says he agrees the Apaches can be moved away from Arizona and New Mexico and says that your trip to Washington was for the purpose of learning what the Government would do for you."

"Yes they did say what they would do for me. Then they didn't do it."

"That's what Geronimo and Naiche are telling people at Ft. Pickens. And there is a great debate happening about exactly what General Miles promised them to get them to surrender.

"Well, They lied to me and I was no threat. "

"Here's a letter, when you were still a scout, where the Acting Secretary of War, R.C. Drum, says the Apaches should be treated as prisoners of war and shipped to Fort Marion and that Geronimo should be hanged."

"I think that is much different than they were telling Geronimo."

"Yes. In fact, the next day, Secretary Drum wrote another letter indicating he knew Fort Marion could only hold about 75 prisoners and the commander at the fort recommended no more Indians be sent there, but he wanted to put 400 to 500 Indians there.'

"That's why we have lost many people, many children. They get sick and die. New babies have no chance."

Welsh remembered a newspaper clipping from the New York World from 1886 that said, "Their transfer to the confinement in the warm climate of Florida will simply result in their dying off like so many sheep. Experienced army officers do not think that there will be one of them alive in the next five years." But Welsh held up his forefinger to make a point, "I thought the government packed all the school-age children off to Carlisle School in Pennsylvania? Didn't they send the first batch off in November, shortly after you arrived?"

"Yes. We called it the "Stealing of the Children." They didn't ask us. They just stole our children. Mothers tried to hide their children under blankets, under their skirts. But the white soldiers found all of them. My son, Horace was taken and he is there now. He's only eight. We saw Indian children when we went to the Carlisle School. They were dying there. One-hundred children were sent to Carlisle and twenty-nine of them died. At Carlisle we saw all of their hair cut short. They were not allowed to speak Apache, they had them dressed in uniforms and they had renamed all of them with white-man names and they were forcing them to accept a new God."

In fact, Welsh had visited the Carlisle Indian School before he came to Fort Marion. He disagreed with Chatto's assessment of it and would give the school high marks in his report. Welsh learned that Chatto had married Bay-gis-cley-aihn (Helen), the 15 year old sister of Martine, here at Fort Marion and part of the reason was to prevent her from being taken away to Carlisle. He also knew that earlier, Commandant Loomis Langdon had recommended that the children should be trained at Carlisle, but that their parents should accompany them and live there. Disregarding Langdon and the Apache parents, the government swept into Fort Marion in three raids snatching children and hauling them off to Pennsylvania. Colonel Langdon would have little more to say about it. He was slated to be transferred to Fort Pickens to take control of Geronimo and his group.

But Chatto, he thought, was correct about the diseases at Carlisle. It got worse. Seventy-six (43%) of the 177 Apache youth sent there died in the first three years. Most died from Tuberculosis, an infectious disease affecting the lungs and other parts of the body. Carlisle was perfectly situated to produce Tuberculosis in its population. The youngsters lived in close quarters in daily contact with others who might be coughing, sneezing or spreading the disease through talking, laughing or singing.

If there was a good side to the Carlisle experience, Welsh believed it was the valuable knowledge Indian kids picked up about the culture that ran their country. They mastered the English language and learned practical skills. The boys were taught carpentry, blacksmithing, printing and farming. Girls learned cooking, sewing and nursing skills. And most of the students were sent out on work assignments in the community that often evolved into full apprenticeships and wage-earning power.

"Getting back to the letters affecting you," Welsh opened and read from another page, "Here's a letter from War Secretary Drum to General Miles, on August 29, 1886. It's about your group that had visited the President. He says "Since you recommend that none of the Indians at Fort Leavenworth should be permitted to return to Arizona, they will remain at Leavenworth until further orders."

Chatto's ears perked up. "After we visited in Washington D.C. they said we would return home, but they wanted us to visit the Indian school at Carlisle, where we could see what schooling and manners were being taught to Indian children. We were there several days and then got on the train to go home. We were three days and three nights on the train, and stopped at Fort Leavenworth in Kansas. I was very happy to be going home. We did not know about this letter. So

General Miles did not want us back." Chatto shifted in his chair and brought out his large silver medallion. "The President said when I returned home, to keep up the good work. As long as I am good no harm would come to me. He wished me luck."

"Same day, August 29th," said Welsh. "Let me read a part of it to you: Secretary Drum to General Sheridan: 'You will cause the Apache Indians now at Fort Leavenworth to be sent under charge of Captain Dorst, Fourth Cavalry, by the most direct and expeditious route to Saint Augustine, Florida, and upon arrival to be turned over to the commanding officer at that post for confinement with other Indian prisoners now there."

Chatto shook his head sadly, "Captain Dorst was with us all the way. That's the order to send me and our peaceful delegation to prison here. Nothing was said to us. We only knew that the train started up to take us home but then when it stopped again and when we got out, we were not at home but here at Fort Marion in Florida. And we were prisoners. I do not think this place looks as though it contained sixty square miles. In not many days the rest of our band came to Fort Marion. Nalthchedah and Horace came, Maude, Gonaltsis, Bahnatsi, Gotsi and all my friends from the reservation. Then they sent the women and children from Naiche's band."

"Well," said Welsh, "the government said it was necessary…for the public service. You understand, they were looking at your activities with Juh and Geronimo, not your service as a scout. How many people did you kill?"

"I don't know. Not as many as the ones killed around me."

"But, said Welsh," They assume if you had the chance, you would kill again without regret."

Chatto scowled, "We were at war. Our men, our families were being shot down from every direction. It was kill or be killed. There was nothing else. But we have been at peace for a long time."

"But," ventured Welsh, "even in our army, when a man is taken prisoner of war, he is expected to continue to resist and to try to escape. Geronimo and Naiche and Juh did that, but you didn't. I need to understand why."

"This is not hard." Chatto stopped for a moment, putting his thoughts together, trying to explain to this small man. "I have said this to you. I wanted peace for my people. I respect Geronimo and Naiche for their courage and bravery. But I do not respect them for the death they brought to the Chiricahua. They looked out for their people, but it was on the warpath. I looked out for my people, but it was in seeking peace and a normal, no, a better way of life for them. Maybe each of us was wrong. Look where we are today."

"What about Chief Chihuahua and his band here at Fort Marion?' asked Welsh, "Do you think he would go back on the war path if he were released?"

"Chihuahua, his son Eugene and his brother Ulzana, talk to me very little. They tell everyone I am a traitor and a coyote and they are glad I am also in prison along with them. I think they talk tough, but would not take to war again for the same reasons they surrendered."

Welsh went back to his stack of letters. "Actually, you are mentioned, specifically in his letter of September 11th when the Secretary of the Interior says, I'll read it to you, "I think that Chatto and those with him should be sent on to Fort Marion."

Chatto held up his hands, palms up, "I don't know August, September. I guess it was about then. They knew before we came to Washington that they would not take us back home. It is the most dishonorable thing. Apaches hate liars."

"Yes," said Welsh, "and in that same letter the Secretary mentions the possibility of turning Geronimo over the civil authorities. You know what that means? It means they would put him on trial for murder and hang him. Apparently Mr. Drum really wanted to have Geronimo hanged."

"And probably me too." Chatto's mouth curled into a scowl. "I have been watching over Geronimo's family here. They wonder if they will ever see him again. He has three wives. One of them gave birth here. The baby was the first Indian born here. They named her Marion, you know, after the fort. Family was always very important to Geronimo. And to me."

Herbert Welsh held up a wad of letters relating to the surrender of Geronimo. "It is clear that a lot of angry letters went back and forth in the War Department to find out exactly what was promised to Geronimo and why he surrendered," he said. "We don't have to go through them, but General Miles and his witnesses repeated that Geronimo wasn't promised anything except he wouldn't be killed and he would never return to Arizona and he would be with his family."

"Read to me what General Miles said."

Welsh dug through his letters, produced one and read to Chatto. "Geronimo's Apaches wanted surrender terms and privileges. I informed Captain Lawton that their request could not be granted. I could only accept their surrender as prisoners of war. I informed them that I was removing all the Chiricahua and Warm Spring Indians from Arizona, and that they would all be removed from this country at once and for all time, and this they understood. Geronimo replied that he would obey any order I might give and go to any place, and that he would bring in his camp, which he did. Natchez subsequently surrendered his camp in the same way. Their status is the same as that of Chief Joseph, Sitting Bull, and hundreds of others; they are strictly prisoners of war, the result of the skill and fortitude of our troops."

Chatto responded, "Well, in every talk before that, the Apache had been able to work out things they needed; land, time to gather up people, where they would be on the reservation, food and supplies. I wasn't there; I don't know what was said. But I know Geronimo. I don't think he just laid down and took what the General gave."

"By the way, one letter said that Geronimo and Naiche didn't surrender earlier because you, Chatto, were trusted by General Crook and you might end up as their chief."

"Yes, I told you Geronimo was plenty hot about me, ever since the tiswin thing and he knew I had something to do with finding him in

Mexico. And he was right, I recommended Kayitah and Martine as the best scouts to go and see Geronimo if they found him."

"This letter also says that General Miles told Geronimo, 'Lay down your arms and come with me to Fort Bowie, and in five days you will see your families, now in Florida with Chihuahua, and no harm will be done you"

"And, of course, it was the last time Geronimo saw his family."

"I don't know if you are aware that General Stanley, in Texas, tried to go to bat for Martine and Kayitah. He sent a telegram saying both of them were men of good character and suggesting they ought not to be going to prison with Geronimo's people."

Chatto asked, "Did you find a answer to that telegram"

"Yes, I have General Sheridan's response right here. It says, 'The Indian women and children at San Antonio, and two Indian scouts, nineteen in all, are ordered to Fort Marion, to be held under the same conditions as the other prisoners there. The two scouts will be discharged from the service, but remain with their tribes.' He's saying we don't want them in the Army and we don't want them free."

"He's saying 'the scouts can go to hell.' Why do they act so angry with the scouts?" asked Chatto. "Why do they fear us?"

"That's one of the important things I am trying to find out," said Welsh.

So now, virtually all the Chiricahua leadership was dead or in prison. Whereas some had been regarded as good Indians and some as bad Indians, they were all lumped together as bad Indians, presumably for the rest of their lives.

Infuriated by the mistreatment of his scouts, General Crook roared: "The surrender of Geronimo could not have been affected except for the assistance of Chatto and his scouts. For their allegiance, they have been rewarded by captivity in a strange land." He was the one who wrote to John Bourke asking him to contact the Indian Rights Association requesting this investigation.

CHAPTER 46   Welsh Goes Public

In March, 1887, Herbert Welsh published his report. It was scathing. Chatto was his prime example of injustices. He wrote, "This man was at one time hostile and doubtless committed such acts of violence as Indians on the war-path indulge in. But in 1883 Chatto surrendered to General Crook in the Sierra Madre Mountains, at which time he made a promise of good behavior for the future, which he has never violated."

Welsh pointed out the correspondence in which General Sheridan, Secretary Endicott and Secretary Lamar had conspired to stop Chatto's return trip and divert him to the Florida prison along with his entire tribe. He said, "No hint was given to Chatto that he was under suspicion of wrong-doing, or that his proposed journey to the Capital was to terminate within prison walls."

Welsh was incensed by the detaining of reservation Apaches who had lived peacefully and more so by the imprisonment of Apache scouts who, he said, had served the country at the risk of their lives. To him Chatto's story was an outstanding injustice. He said, "It is an interesting fact, and one to which I desire to call especial attention, and upon which I desire to lay the strongest possible emphasis, that of the 82 men (at the fort) not more than 30 have been guilty of any recent misdoing,"

He said, "That these men should have been imprisoned on the same footing with those Indians who were at war with the United States, and that their fidelity, and, in some instances, their invaluable service rendered to our arms should have been rewarded by incarceration, is a fact well calculated to attract attention and to elicit the condemnation of the public. Such is the case." This paragraph was an obvious threat to go to the press if the Government didn't move on the plight of the Apaches.

Later, Welsh stated, "It really seems, then, that the time has come to consider the question, what is to be done with these prisoners? In the nature of things they cannot remain prisoners here until they all die." Regarding Geronimo, he reported, "Geronimo and 16 of his men are confined in Fort Pickens, on the West Coast of Florida. The wives and children of these men are in Fort Marion. This separation is a direct violation of the terms on which Geronimo surrendered to General Miles."

Geronimo at Ft. Pickens

In light of Chatto's imprisonment, Welsh also used the words of the Secretary of War against him. Secretary Endicott had issued a press release near the end of July which stated: "Chatto, Chief of the Chiricahua Apaches, has-been on a visit to Washington to see the President. He has made known his intention to refrain from war and to work for his living. President Cleveland has assured him that so long as he shall keep faith with the Government his interest shall be looked after. In a more prolonged interview with 'Chatto,' I have endeavored to impress upon his mind that his future prosperity depended upon his following the path of peace and civilization. (Signed) Wm. C. Endicott, Secretary of War."

Welch's report responds, "I hold that in this case a fundamental principle of just and wise policy in the treatment of Indians, has been violated, for not only have the innocent been condemned unheard, but the meritorious have received the punishment of the guilty."

Senator Henry Dawes, (R) Massachusetts

Welch's report set off a wave of debate and indignation. Welsh immediately had the support of Massachusetts Senator Henry Dawes, Chairman of the Committee on Indian Affairs, and from General Crook who wrote, "I assert, moreover, without reserve or qualification of any nature, that these Chiricahua scouts, under Chiefs Chatto, Noche and others, did most excellent service, and were of more value in hunting down and compelling the surrender of the renegades than all other troops engaged in operations against them combined." This was not just an appeal on behalf of the Apache scouts, but also a statement that Generals Sherman, Sheridan and Miles were full of crap. Crook was getting old, but during his final years, he continued his lifelong campaign in favor of his former enemies, speaking out against white encroachments, unfair treatment, broken treaties and failed federal policies.

Having distributed his report for the Indian Rights Association and waiting only briefly to see if the government would respond, Herbert Welsh, true to his threat, went to the press in March, 1887.

The New York Times printed an eleven-hundred word article about Welsh's report and the Apaches at Fort Marion. In it, the

Department of Interior called Welsh a liar. A department spokesman said, "Chatto was induced to come here to talk about a removal from Fort Apache, and that, according to the Interior Department officers, is about the only fact correctly stated in Mr. Welsh's report." The Government justified imprisoning the Apaches because "There was an imperative demand from the people of Arizona that the Apaches should be removed, as they were bad Indians, likely to go on the warpath at any time, and their presence was a constant menace to the lives and security of the people." According to the Government, Chatto actually requested to be sent to Fort Marion, when he learned that Arizona civil authorities wanted to arrest him. It smacked of a classic bureaucratic cover-up. Just to seal its argument, the Interior Department source added, "Chatto is known to be a blood-thirsty murderer, and no injustice would have been done to him if he had been hanged or shot, in either of which events the people of Arizona would have properly rejoiced."

Herbert Welsh couldn't believe his eyes. He published a response; "I am at loss to understand why such apparent evidences of good will were given to a man who was judged by the Interior Department to be a blood-thirsty murderer worthy of death. Does it not savor somewhat of sentimentality for high officials to confer silver medals and their photographs on 'bloodthirsty murderers,' whom they afterwards declare worthy of death?"

In April, the Philadelphia Recorder picked up the story and ran it under the headline, "The Imprisoned Apache Indians," It was not the most sympathetic approach, but indicated some government movement toward improving the lives of the Fort Marion prisoners.

It said, "The agitation set on foot by Senator Dawes and Mr. Herbert Welsh relative to the 'imprisonment' of the Apache Indians who are at Fort Marion, Florida, has had its effect upon the President, who brought the matter up in Cabinet meeting this week, and has caused the Secretary of War to prepare an order for the removal of the Indians to a more secluded reservation. The Indians are comfortable enough where they are, but they are hemmed in by sightseers and are made a show of. It is thought that it will be better for them to be in a quieter place, where they can have a better chance to move about, and also a better chance to do work, if any of them can be made to work. Geronimo and his fellow cutthroats will be retained at Fort Pickens, where they now are."

John Bourke had to be careful what he said about his bosses while still in office. His book, published in 1891 undoubtedly represented his feelings at the time of the Welch report. He said, "The incarceration of Chatto and the three-fourths of the band who had remained faithful for three years....can never meet with the approval of honorable soldiers and gentlemen." He complained about some Indians who were not Chiricahua at all, but had just recently married into the band, but were imprisoned just the same. He finished with a flourish, "There is no more disgraceful page in the history of our relations with the American Indians than that which conceals the treachery visited upon the Chiricahuas who remained faithful in their allegiance to our people."

With the brouhaha set off by Herbert Welsh still reverberating in newspapers, Lt. Charles Gatewood felt called upon to put in his two cents because he was present when Geronimo was located and the subsequent surrender. His letter to the editor of the Army and Navy Register is less than complimentary to Chatto. "Indian camps on the reservation have been the source and rendezvous of the hostile element, and from them have been made the bloody raids that devastated Arizona and New Mexico for years. Not less than five hundred citizens have been murdered in the last ten years. There is not a Chiricahua Indian man that has not been engaged in some of their outbreaks, and Chatto, Dutchy, Kaetenae and many others are now under indictment in the civil courts for their crimes. It is true that some of them have been in the service as scouts, both before the outbreak and afterwards, and there can be no doubt that much of the ammunition issued to them went into the belts of the hostiles. As far as my observation went in the earlier part of the campaign, Chatto and the other Chiricahua scouts could scarcely be considered faithful; they hindered rather than aided the operations of the troops." It was strange, perhaps, that Gatewood would side with the Army. General Miles never gave him a dimes worth of credit for the capture of Geronimo. In fact he made Gatewood an aide-de-camp to keep an eye on him, refused to allow Gatewood to attend a gala in Tucson where he was the guest of honor, and then had the seriously ailing Lieutenant shipped to an outpost in South Dakota. Years later, General Miles reversed himself and recommended Gatewood for the Medal of Honor, which was denied because the danger of entering Geronimo's camp was not considered "hostile action." By this time Gatewood was hospitalized in Virginia and died within a short time of stomach cancer.

But other professional soldiers sided with Welsh. General James Stanley wrote in the Grenville Advocate December 22nd 1886, edition "Is the Government capable of an act which in the individual is a crime? Placing it mildly, is indifference to (the Apaches) fate worthy of a Republic which claims to be land of refuge to the oppressed of all nations? We deprecate the light manner in which the sure death of these Indians is spoken of, and if death is merely a question of time, as we are told, it should be brought before the Government. If these Indians have committed crimes worthy of death, let the sentence of the law be executed and not in the refinement of cruelty, by inches or atoms."

Lieutenant Britton Davis came out in defense of the peaceful Apaches and the scouts who served directly under him in thoughts that later appeared in his book: *The Truth About Geronimo.* "In my talks with the Indians they showed no resentment of the way they had been treated only wonderment at the why of it. Why had they been shifted from reservation to reservation, told to farm and have their crops destroyed, assured that the Government would ration them, then left to half starve, herded in the hot, malarial river bottoms of the Gila and San Carlos when they were mountain people? And above all they wondered if they would now be allowed to live in peace…four hundred innocent people, men, women, and children, who had kept the faith with us, punished for the guilt of barely one-fourth who had been lied to and frightened into leaving the Reservation. We have heard much talk of the treachery of the Indian. In treachery, in broken pledges on the part of high officials, lies, thievery, slaughter of defenseless women and children, and every crime in the catalogue of man's inhumanity to man the Indian was a mere amateur compared to the "noble white man."

So the war of words was on. Now citizens, advocates, senators and more lined up behind Welsh or behind the Administration and the public relations storm blew harder. The surrender of Geronimo continued to resurface with more explanations of promises made and not kept. Welsh distributed some of the official correspondence and made himself available for speaking engagements as he prodded the government to do better for the Apaches.

At Fort Pickens a reporter from the Chicago Tribune asked Naiche, "How do you like your quarters?" Naiche fired back, "Why is it I am asked how we like it here? People go around and see where I live, the fort, the waste of hot sands and water, the old guns, the guards ever armed, how we live, and what we evidently have to live for. I can't understand why we are asked such questions." In short, he told the reporter he and the other Apaches didn't come to Fort Pickens, they were brought. They were here not because they wanted to be, but because they had to be.

At Fort Pickens, tourists enjoyed seeing the captured Apaches, especially the blood-thirsty Geronimo and the Son of Cochise, Naiche. First, they had to obtain a pass from the Colonel and pay for a boat trip to the island. They would have seen the captives working seven days a week, clearing overgrown weeds, planting grass, stacking cannonballs and other important tasks. At least their conditions were better than those at Ft. Marion. Only one Apache died during their confinement, probably Nahin, Geronimo's fourth wife.

Colonel Langdon

Finally, in April 1887, more than 6 months after their arrival in Florida, the families of Geronimo and Naiche's men arrived from Fort Marion. Newspapers reported "Geronimo Happy." He ended up with three wives there; She-gah, Taayzslath and Ihtedda. Geronimo, the tourist attraction was doing great things for the City of Pensacola. He had an average of 20 visitors per day and on one day he had more than 459 visitors. In return, the Commander, Colonel Langdon, who had petitioned for the families to be re-united, authorized a corn dance to celebrate. 300 citizens of Pensacola attended and a grand time was had by all.

CHAPTER 47   Mt. Vernon

In 1887, shortly after the Welsh report, the government decided to move the Apaches out of Fort Marion, where 367 of 502 Indians had required medical attention, and from Fort Pickens. They claimed the decision was made because of the continuing fear of disease at the Florida prisons. Indeed, by that time more than 120 Apaches, nearly one-fourth of the population, had died from malaria, tuberculosis, yellow fever, pneumonia and hopelessness. One can only wonder whether the Welsh dust-up played an equal role. They were shipped to the Mount Vernon Barracks at Mobile, Alabama.

Mount Vernon Barracks, Alabama

The Mount Vernon Arsenal was built in 1828 to manufacture explosives. It was one of the Union's main ammunition plants until the Civil War when it was captured by the Confederacy. It became a prison with the arrival of the Apache prisoners of war. It was there that Walter Reed, an Army surgeon, confirmed that yellow fever is spread by mosquitoes.

As the government did with the children at the Carlisle School, the army now had the men line up to receive English first names to more easily identify them and to avoid mispronunciations of their Apache monikers.

"I was on the end of the line," said Chatto, "because I was a chief, so I got the name 'Albert.' Then the next man was named Bernard, and the next one was Carl—that was Mangus, then Fatty was named "David." That's how it went."

Naiche became "Christian," Gonaltsis was "Nelson," Kayitah became "Martin," and Martine became "Charles." Kaetenae became "Jacob," Kaydahzinne was "Tim." Only Geronimo, Chihuahua and Loco apparently escaped without having an English name tacked on to their identifications.

The relocation brought Chatto and Geronimo, with 376 of their Chiricahua followers, together again. If Chatto felt ostracized by Chihuahua and his band, it was doubled when Geronimo, Naiche, Kaetenae and their men arrived.

Geronimo looked Chatto over from head to toe. "You wanted to be a chief. And you are chief of a captive people."

"We are all captives," said Chatto, "our brothers from the warpath and our brothers from the reservation. It does not matter who was right or wrong. Now there are no sides among us. For the good of the people we eat the crow."

"Yes, it matters," said Geronimo, "You betrayed your people and we cannot take that away. But, because my family told me that you looked after them at Fort Marion, I will not kill you. Do not expect me to be your friend." He turned and stalked off.

Conditions at Mount Vernon were even worse than Florida according to some. It was in a low-lying area, nearly a bog where agriculture was out of the question. Helen told her grandchildren the Indians often captured frogs and ate their legs to survive. She also told them the dungeons at Fort Marion had, indeed, been used. Women were stashed there. Some were raped and there was routine mistreatment. She was glad to be at Mount Vernon. Apaches cut trees, built some log cabins and fought off swarms of flies and bugs. One

Apache, Eugene Chihuahua later reported, "It rained nearly all the time. On top of that the mosquitoes almost ate us alive. Babies died from their bites. Our people got the shaking sickness (malaria). We burned one minute and froze the next no matter how hot and muggy it was. No pile of blankets would keep us warm. We chilled and shook. We had our own Medicine Men, but none of them had the power over this."

Chatto lost his brother Gonaltsis at Mount Vernon. Gonaltsis had been wasting away and died from tuberculosis. Then word came that his son, Horace, had died at Carlisle from the same disease at nine years old. His niece, Gotsi's daughter Edith, died from pneumonia. Victorio's sister, Lozen, also suffered from tuberculosis. She died at Mount Vernon before she turned 50 years of age. The beautiful Dahteste contracted tuberculosis and pneumonia in Alabama, but she survived. Geronimo's oldest son, Chappo was discharged from Carlisle school due to illness and died shortly after arriving at Mt. Vernon. Still, overall, it was a better environment than the dank malarial, overcrowded prisons in Florida where more than 120 of the Indians had died by 1890. In 1889, partially because of the death toll, the Mescaleros among them were allowed to return to New Mexico. Geronimo sent his wife, Ihtedda, a Mescalero, and her two children to the reservation there and never saw her again.

And disease wasn't the only cause of death at Mount Vernon. The Warrior Fun, who had been sent by Geronimo to kill Lt. Davis and Chatto long ago, got into an argument with his wife, shot and wounded her. Then he went outside and killed a guard who was responding to the shots. Then he killed himself. Dutchy died violently. He and an Apache named Ditoin got into a drunken brawl with soldiers at the fort. The soldiers beat them to death. The warrior Cathla, (Colle), a former scout in Chatto's company, who had been with John Clum and Taza on their ill-fated trip to Washington, and with Ulzana on his raid, died in similar circumstances. He and a friend bought whiskey from a nearby farm. A quarrel developed and the other Indian killed Cathla with a broken beer bottle. Cathla had just been released from a New York Prison where he served time for stabbing a Mount Vernon interpreter in the neck.

If there were deaths, there were also marriages and births. Chatto and Helen had their first child, Morris, in 1891. Chatto's sister Gotsi married the warrior Eyelash, who had been her son-in-law before Edith died. Ihtedda, Geronimo's youngest wife, gave birth to Robert, perhaps after she arrived in New Mexico. There were many more.

To keep the minds of the men off their situation, a post commander, Lt. William Wotherspoon, formed Company I of his 12th Infantry Regiment at Mount Vernon. Chatto enlisted along with 46 of the most able-bodied men. Nana, Geronimo and Loco refrained because of their age and disposition. The Apaches marched, drilled and built additional housing. They were never involved in active duty.

General George Crook visited the Apaches at Mt. Vernon and a reporter wrote, "Chatto came out and went out to the General and gave him a warm greeting." Chatto started to hug the General around the neck, but then thought better of it. Still, it was clear Chatto was joyful to see the old soldier. He asked if the General knew anything more about his family. Crook told Chatto the Mexicans now claimed that Ishchosen and her children did not want to leave Mexico; they were happy in their current situation.

The General met with Chihuahua, Naiche, Kaetennae, Toclanny and interpreter George Wratten. He would not meet with Geronimo because he thought the medicine man was a liar. The General hated Geronimo because he had been so much trouble it cost him his job. Still, the General wrote to the Secretaries of War and Interior that: "I cannot too strongly urge that immediate steps be taken to secure a reservation for them where they could be settled on farms of their own, to work for themselves, and to receive for themselves the full benefit of their labors, for with red people as well as white, self-interest is the mainspring of progress. I would recommend that if possible they be sent as soon as practicable to some point in the Indian Territory." The Government accepted his recommendation, but left the Apaches to languish several more years at Mount Vernon before implementing it.

The Apaches at Mount Vernon held several conferences with the Indian Rights Association, missionaries and representatives of the government. Chatto was active speaking for his people, as were Chihuahua, Naiche and Loco, all of whom had submitted to the authority of the government but were now beseeching it to improve their situation.

Chatto spoke for the Apaches at a meeting sponsored by the Indian Rights Association, in the summer of 1889. Chatto urged a return to Arizona and said his people could be self-supporting there. If not, he was still plugging for the better reservation the Government had once promised. He was quoted as saying, "You can find some of the old people yet…the grandfathers and grandmothers…but most of them are dead. That is why I do not like it here. This country…yes there are lots of trees but there is nothing else. It seems as if the ground had something to bite you every time you step on it."

Chihuahua, who had adopted an Army uniform, top hat and a red cravat, said the Apaches needed immediate transfer to better facilities; the heat and lack of pure water were taking their toll. "I have a family…I want the change made for their sake, as I know they'll burn up if they remain here. When you take us away from here let it be to a place where we can stay forever, until all these people shall be old and gray headed."

Naiche had now come over to the whites, telling them that he now realized that he and his family would be better off following the rules and learning new ways of farming, building and selling. He stopped eating his meals while squatting on the ground and required his family to use a table and chairs with a white table-cloth. He taught himself to read, using an English primer, asking soldiers about proper pronunciations. He asked, in these conferences, why he had been trained to farm, use the implements, cut wood and make a living, but was not allowed to do so. He said, "This is a bad place for my people. They are dying around me. The sun rises on my friends; they are here. The sun sets and they are gone. Why is this?" He told the white representatives he believed they were good, not evil, but they should give the Apaches their farms and let them work for themselves.

Observers reported that Naiche was particularly despondent much of the time. A missionary said, "He is a magnificent looking man, but with a face so sorrow-stricken that, to me, it is painful to see him. His voice and manner were pathetic in the extreme."

Loco, who professed to like the white society, including the schooling of Apache children at Carlisle, spoke of his own despondency over prospects for the future. He said, "No white man can point to me and say there goes a bad man. My skin is dried up and drawn across the bones. Most of us have died since we came here. We thought we would do well, but it is like a road with deep cliffs on each side. They fall off on both sides. Nobody killed them. Sickness did it."

CHAPTER 48   Fort Sill

As Herbert Welsh and many others continued to keep pressure on the Government to let the Apaches go home to Arizona, the President, Grover Cleveland, resisted. In his annual message to Congress in December 1888 he said,

"I am not at all in sympathy with those benevolent but injudicious people who are constantly insisting that these Indians should be returned to their reservation. Their removal was an absolute necessity if the lives and property of citizens upon the frontier are to be at all regarded by the Government. Their continued restraint at a distance from the scene of their repeated and cruel murders and outrages is still necessary. It is a mistaken philanthropy, every way injurious, which prompts the desire to see these savages return to their old haunts. They are in their present location as the result of the best judgment of those having official responsibility in the matter, and who are by no means lacking in kind consideration for the Indians. A number of these prisoners have forfeited their lives to outraged law and humanity. Experience has proved that they are dangerous and cannot be trusted. This is true not only of those who on the warpath have heretofore actually been guilty of atrocious murder, but of their kindred and friends, who, while they remained upon their reservation, furnished aid and comfort to those absent with bloody intent. These prisoners should be treated kindly and kept in restraint far from the locality of their former reservation; they should be subjected to efforts calculated to lead to their improvement and the softening of their savage and cruel instincts, but their return to their old home should be persistently resisted."

Grover Cleveland, President, 1884

General Crook continued to publicly disagree. He loved his scouts and persisted, "they have been rewarded by captivity in a strange land." He was bitter that the scouts were imprisoned and he stayed that way until his death. On March 21, 1890, General George Crook suffered a heart attack and died in Chicago, Illinois, twenty four years before his scouts would taste freedom.

While Chatto and Geronimo were sweating it out in their Florida forts, in Arizona "The Apache Kid," one of the scouts not sent away because he was a White Mountain and not a Chiricahua Apache, was finding himself in deep trouble. His activities argued to authorities in Washington that President Cleveland was right; the imprisoned Apaches could still be a threat and needed to be closely held.

The Apache Kid had been left in charge of the scouts while Al Sieber and the Captain were away from Fort Apache on business and took the occasion to ride out and join in another of those whopping tiswin parties the Apaches loved so much. Things got out of hand and the Kid's father was killed by an Indian named Gonzizzie. The Kid's friends killed Gonzizzie in turn. Then the Kid went to Gonzizzie's brother's ranch and killed him.

There was going to be hell to pay when they returned to the reservation. A crowd gathered to see what would happen. Captain Pierce ordered the Kid and others to disarm and go to the guardhouse with his troopers. But someone fired a shot and then more shots were fired. Al Sieber took a big .45 caliber bullet in the ankle, which would cripple him for life. The Kid and four other scouts took off, grabbed horses and headed for the wilderness and maybe a dozen other Apaches followed with them. So if Geronimo thought he was the last of the renegades, maybe it was really The Apache Kid.

Naturally, the Army went after them while the area braced for another Apache outbreak and newspapers ran angry editorials. This didn't help things for Chatto and the other captives in the southeast. It just re-enforced the idea that Apaches would always revert to their warlike ways if allowed to run free. The Kid's Apaches led the cavalry a merry chase for about two weeks before Al Sieber's scouts led troopers to their hideout in the Rincon Mountains and captured their horses and equipment. The Indians escaped into the ravines but faced big problems without horses. The Kid sent a message to General Miles saying he and his friends would surrender if the General would call off the dogs. He did. And they did.

They went on trial and were found guilty of mutiny and desertion and sentenced to death by firing squad. General Miles thought this was too much. He thought ten years in Alcatraz was good enough. Even more fortunate, the Judge Advocate General's office reviewed the case and found the trial officers were prejudiced and the case ought to be re-tried. Then Secretary of War Endicott threw the case out and the defendants were back at Fort Apache in no time.

But it didn't end there. Herbert Welsh's Indian Rights Association sued the government and the court agreed that the federal government was wrong to incarcerate Apaches in state prisons and had all Apaches so situated released. Seven Indians held for murder were released to Fort Apache. The public raised billy-hell.

So, civil authorities got into the act. The Sheriff of Gila County had arrest warrants for most of the freed Apaches, including the

Apache Kid. The Kid and three others were tried and found guilty of assault to commit murder against Al Sieber. They were sentenced to seven years in the terribly hot and brutal territorial prison at Yuma.

On the stage-coach journey to prison the Apaches, although hand-cuffed to each other and shackled, overpowered their guards, killed two and wounded one. They unlocked their restraints with keys found on the guards and headed for the high-hills.

A bounty of five thousand dollars was put on the Apache Kid's head. Mickey Free, now a bounty hunter working with Al Sieber, tried to collect it, but couldn't find the Kid. At last word the Kid was seen here and there in Old Mexico up until the 1920s or 30s, but never for sure.

In 1894, after seven years at Mount Vernon, all 341 of Chatto's Apaches were shipped out again, this time to Fort Sill, Oklahoma.

General Phillip Sheridan had staked out Fort Sill in 1869, when he was campaigning against Indians in Oklahoma and Texas. Buffalo Bill Cody and Wild Bill Hickok had worked as scouts for Sheridan. Fort Sill had huge acreage with creeks lined with cottonwood where Chatto joined with others in putting up wickiups and forming twelve small villages scattered around the post. Chatto was head man in one of those villages. Eugene Chihuahua reported to Eve Ball that the villages were placed so that friendly people (Geronimo, Naiche, Chihuahua, Ulzana) were living close together and the "scouts we disliked" were kept at a distance. He said, "Nobody liked Chatto," indicating that the more volatile group stayed as far away from him as they could. Chatto lived nearer Kayitah, Toclanny, Kaetenae and Perico. Here, Chatto turned 40 and his 24 year old wife, Helen, gave birth to their second son, Blake, born in 1894.

A tract of an additional 24,000 acres was added around Fort Sill to accommodate the Indians, which included separating them from the Kiowas and Comanches there. This was later expanded to bring the land area to about 52,000 acres. And the government appropriated $15,000 for buildings, farm implements, animals, tools, utensils …essentials they would need.

After getting established, the Chiricahua built log houses or structures framed with timber. They discovered there was a Mesquite grove about 75 miles away and made many trips to pick the beans which had been a favorite food in Arizona. That, with the sagebrush and a view of some low mountains made it feel almost like home. Nalthchedah, long divorced from Chatto, married Dexter, the son of Loco and Chatto attended his first wife's wedding ceremony.

Meantime Geronimo, when he wasn't riding the four miles into Lawton, Oklahoma, for whiskey, was becoming a celebrity. Newspapers and dime novels had already made him one of the most famous Indians in the country. People had even cheered him on the train from Mount Vernon and he found they wanted to buy pictures of him, buttons from his jacket, hats, or whatever he had. He no longer represented the wild depraved murdering Apache, but rather something more robust, more admirable.

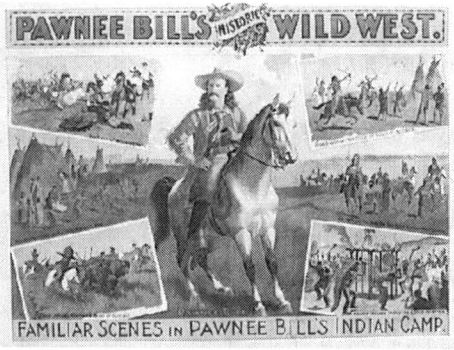

Having appeared at the Omaha World's Fair in 1898, and the Pan-American Exposition in Buffalo, New York in 1901, Geronimo got permission to travel with Pawnee Bill's Wild West Show, which was about to combine with the famous Buffalo Bill Cody's Wild West extravaganza. Geronimo was in his 70's by then and slowing down considerably. Nevertheless he hit the road with the likes of Frank Butler, Annie Oakley, and Calamity Jane. At 45, Chatto could still move around pretty well and was hired for some of the trips.

Buffalo Bill

Buffalo Bill Cody's show was world renown by that time, having played all over the United States and during eight tours of Europe, where it was viewed by Queen Victoria, Kaiser Wilhelm, the future King George V and other royalty. It played in England, France, Spain, Italy, Austria-Hungary, Germany and Belgium. After a career as a scout, hunter and entrepreneur, William Cody had started his show in 1883 while Geronimo was still terrorizing Sonora and while Chatto was staging his notorious Arizona raid. The European tours were taking place while both the Apaches were on lock-down at Forts Pickins and Marion, respectively. So, they were getting in on the tail end of the phenomenon.

Geronimo was asked to dress up in his best attire and be prepared to sell his photograph, have his picture taken, and sign autographs and hand out trinkets, which was about all he was up to at the time. Chatto, on the other hand, was relegated to some of the various scenes staged by the Bills Pawnee and Buffalo.

The shows always started with a parade featuring riders from horse-culture groups; U.S. Army Cavalry, Turks, Gauchos, Arabs, Chinese, and American Indians. Chatto looked a little plain in his Apache get-up next to some of those other cavalrymen. It didn't bother him; he was getting paid for it. In earlier shows, for about four months, Sitting Bull had appeared with 20 or so of his braves. But Sitting Bull was dead now; murdered at the Standing Rock Agency by soldiers.

Chatto's job was to help re-enact Indian attacks on wagon trains. The script usually called for him to end up dead, on the ground, in these scenarios. The finale of the show was a full-fledged Indian attack on a settler's cabin, with hoards of cowboys and cavalrymen riding to the rescue. Buffalo Bill, himself, would ride in with the cowboys and have a prominent role in saving the poor family from the savages. Chatto must have thought how good it would be just to do it for real again.

Pawnee Bill's Wild West Show. Is that Chatto on the ground?

Annie Oakley befriended Sitting Bull and he called her "Little Annie Sure Shot." It was a sweet thing. But she stayed away from Geronimo with his scarred face and Chatto with his plain clothes and rugged look. At least Buffalo Bill Cody had some sympathy for the Indians. Having shot thousands of buffalo himself, he later advocated for hunting seasons and a ban on hide hunters. And he is quoted as saying, "Every Indian outbreak that I have ever known has resulted from broken promises and broken treaties by the government." He paid his Indians pretty well and some, like Sitting Bull and Geronimo, became rich, by their standards, by selling signatures and doo-dads. Many of their family members travelled with the men and Cody encouraged wives and children to set up camp as they would at home. But, remember Cody was a show-man. He advertised this as a chance to see the other side of the "fierce warriors" and their cultures. And he wanted the public to pay to see this.

In 1895 Chatto got good news and bad about his family. The good news was the birth of Helen's third child, a boy named Cyril. The bad news came from the Mexican government saying there were no Apache captives anywhere in Chihuahua province, so the U.S. could stop asking for them. Ishchosen Bedisclove and Naboka were now lost to history.

Geronimo dressed for Wild West Show

In 1897, Chatto, Naiche and a few others enlisted as scouts in troop L, 7th Cavalry, Custers old outfit, now run by Captain and later General Hugh Scott who was an expert in Indian sign language and noted for promoting peace amongst the tribes. He had served in the Sioux wars in 1876 and was sent out to mark grave sites for the men killed in Custer's command at the Little Big Horn. He also warred against the Nez Perce in 1877. He was in direct charge of the Chiricahuas at Fort Still and was recognized as a friend of the Indians and did much toward their advancement. He went on to become the Chief of

Staff for the U.S. Army. There is no record that his Apache scouts at Fort Sill were involved in any real actions.

Chief Nana died of old age in 1896. He was 96 years old and became one of the first of many, many tribesmen buried at the Apache Prisoner of War Cemetery at Fort Sill.

Most of the other leaders were still active enough to participate in the great 1898 Trans-Mississippi and International Exposition in Omaha, Nebraska. It was held to showcase developments in the entire west and, face it, to bring big bucks into Omaha. Chatto didn't go. Some thought he was not invited because he was being ostracized for his support of the Army and his speeches about peace when, in fact, the peaceful Apaches were never much better off than the hostile ones. He claimed he was too busy. He was raising sorghum, melons, sweet potatoes, corn and a herd of cattle. His sister Bahnahtsi went, and Perico, in whose village Gotsi was living, and Naiche and his wife Haozinne and Geronimo attended. It was another proof that the Chiricahuas were contributing to society.

Chatto visited Perico's village often in the spring of 1902. His daughter Maude was living there with his sister, Bahnahtsi, when she got sick. Chatto had seen it too many times before, the fevers, the coughing. She was losing weight fast and not eating. At 29, she was the last vestige of his love for Ishchosen. He called upon Ussen and his new Christian God to save her. But it was not to be. The tuberculosis took her.

It was a hard time. His little son Cyril passed away before he turned three. With Maude gone, there were only his two sons, Morris and Blake remaining of his children. Blake had never been strong. He took ill after his 14th birthday and died there at Fort Sill.

Geronimo's generation continued to die out at Fort Sill. The son of Mangas Coloradas, Mangas, died in 1901. That same year Chief Chihuahua died. Chief Loco died there in 1905. Ulzana died in 1909. Geronimo buried three of his children there and his wife Taayzslath. Naiche lost two daughters and six sons. Chatto's sister, Gotsi, died from third degree burns at the Apache hospital in 1905. Details are uknown. And Helen's younger brother, James Holly, succumbed the same year. There were 300 others.

Geronimo and other Indian leaders were invited to ride in the inaugural parade of President Theodore Roosevelt and met the President. Chatto realized he did not have the star power of the Bedonkohe and was not invited. That was okay with him; it was time to plant the beans.

The Apaches had close to free rein around the fort. Chatto stuck to his farming and ranching. The reservation was building up an impressive herd of beef cattle. Asa Daklugie had spent significant time at the Carlisle school learning about cattle raising and became an expert.

Geronimo attempted an escape once, but was easily caught. He really had nowhere to go. During his eleven years at Fort Sill, Geronimo wrote his life story with the help of educator S.M. Barrett, who had to obtain special permission from President Teddy Roosevelt after the military forbad the project, fearing that Geronimo would say bad things about them…which he did. In 1909, at 84 years of age he was thrown off his horse during a night ride and was injured to the extent he couldn't get up. Some said he had been in Lawton, again, sipping whiskey. He lay in the wet and cold overnight. Almost immediately he contracted pneumonia. At the last he told a nephew, "I should have never surrendered. I should have fought until I was the last man alive."

On February 19th, 1909, the New York Times published a multi-column obituary headlined, "Old Apache Chief, Geronimo is Dead." The Times referred to Geronimo as "the leader of the warring Apaches of the Southwestern territories in pioneer days, Geronimo," it said, "gained a reputation for cruelty and cunning never surpassed by that of any other American Indian chief. For more than twenty years he and his men were the terror of the country, always leaving a trail of bloodshed and devastation. "

Chatto and Helen, he at 59 years old, she at about 44, and most of the Apaches farming at Fort Sill minded their business and stuck it out for 19 years. The U.S. Government promised they would own the lands surrounding the fort, but they never received them. The white population objected. Instead, the Apaches were eventually given an option; they would be given their "freedom" in 1913 and they could either remain at Fort Sill or go to the Mescalero Apache Reservation in New Mexico. Arizona was not a choice; the State of Arizona forbad the Chiricahua from returning. For Chatto, Naiche and 183 other Chiricahua, there was no choice, they opted for the Mescaleros. Chatto took Helen, Morris and his sister Bahnahtsi with him. Dahteste, who had spent all nineteen years at the military prison at Fort Sill, made the same choice. The seventy-eight or so Apaches who stayed in Oklahoma became known as the Fort Sill Apache Tribe. Their descendants still live in these places.

CHAPTER 49   Mescalero

The 463,000 acre Mescalero Reservation near Ruidoso, New Mexico, appealed to Chatto because it had mountains, pine forests, streams and plenty of elbow room. President Grant had set up the reservation in 1873. This was infinitely better than San Carlos, the Florida prisons or Oklahoma. The army recommended and Congress approved releasing the Chiricahua from their Prisoner of War status once in New Mexico. The government approved feeding and clothing them until their farm implements, horses and other equipment could be shipped by rail to them and they could get through their first crop year.

The Mescaleros were always close to the Chiricahua, cooperating and intermarrying more than raiding one another. They got their Spanish name from the staple food the women made from the mescal plant. By 1913 the reservation was in the business of ranching and before many years it would be attracting tourists not only to the flatlands, but to the four sacred mountains: Sierra Blanca, Guadalupe, Three Sisters and Mt. Oscura. Ski Apache, on Sierra Blanca, has become a world class ski and snowboarding resort. In its shadow is the four-diamond Inn of the Mountain Gods hotel, casino and gorgeous golf course that provide the economic base for the reservation, along with wood products and livestock.

The Chiricahuas coming from Fort Sill asked that their band have a place of its own, apart from the Mescaleros. They were allowed to ride the reservation and select where they wanted to be. Again those who had been closest to Geronimo, Chihuahua and Juh also wanted to be away from Chatto, the Benedict Arnold of the Chokonens. So, as that faction settled at White Tail, so named for its deer herds, Chatto chose Apache Summit, about ten miles east of the village of Mescalero. He operated on nearly 1,000 acres of prime land, covered with Penderosa Pine and sweet grazing grasses, which can be seen from the highway yet today if one knows where to look.

Daklugie, who had become a band leader based on his heritage from his father Juh, and his education at Carlisle, let the Mescaleros know that Chatto was unwelcome. Given the chance to talk about Chatto he was complimentary on the one hand, saying that Chatto was brave, intelligent and an excellent warrior, but criticizing him as an arch traitor, a shrewd and ambitious man who sought status in all the wrong places. Daklugie reported that Chatto was aware that he couldn't be the elected chief of the Chokonen band or those of the Warm Springs or Bedonkohe's. So, he decided to sidle up to the U.S. Army for whatever prestige that could bring. That seems too simple. It's not supported by any other reliable source.

Alfred Chatto lived on the Mescalaro Reservation for the 21 years remaining in his life and never lived down the stigma attached to him by the sons of the renegades. However, he was not burdened by that, remembering that he represented a strong majority in his tribe who had wanted peace and had practiced it. He remained a leader and contributed what he could to the success of the reservation.

Elderly Chatto

And successful it was. With the $170,000 from the sale of their cattle at Fort Sill and the payment of depts., the Chiricahuas had

$162,000 left to start a new herd on the Mescalero Reservation. They bought 2,000 grade heifers from various ranches and four registered bulls for each one-hundred cows and the investment paid off big-time. In 1914 the first roundup was held and the first calf crop branded. From those heifers they got 1,984 calves. Rancher Ted Sutherland said "I never saw such a good calf crop before." They were in business and it got better.

Two great-great grandsons are the only living descendants of Chatto; them and their children and grandchildren. They are the renowned artist and sculptor Vincent Kaydahzinne, and Freddie Kaydahzinne, recording artists and Curator of the Mescalero Culture Center, who I had the pleasure of meeting in November, 2014, and interviewing extensively in May, 2015.

Author with Freddie Kaydahzinne, Author's photo

The brothers Kaydahzinne are also the direct descendants of Cochise. Their great granddaddy, the warrior Kaydahzinne, married Cochise's daughter. Freddie and Vincent Kaydahzinne come down from Cochise on their father's side of the family and from Chatto on their mother's. The original Kaydahzinne was, according to Freddie, a runner for Geronimo and according to other histories, a scout in Chatto's company and for Lieutenant Britt Davis and Captain Wirt Davis. So Kaydahzinne is an old name to the Chiricahuas.

The brothers work to create and preserve their Apache heritage; Vincent through music and art. Freddie through the Culture Center and his own musical recordings. They follow the artistic footsteps of their grandmother, Helen Chatto, who was near them during the formative years of life, and their mother, Pauline, a renowned traditional basket weaver.

Freddie Kaydahzinne is a deeply spiritual man who preaches the Apache harmony with nature to friends and visitors. He is concerned that the young generations, with their I-pods and tablets, are not getting it, and that the language is fading away. He is one of the dwindling number of Athabaskan speakers who tries to pass along the language and the ceremonial songs of the tribe.

Apaches often feel constrained in delivering information about ancestors because of the Apache tradition of not talking about the dead. It was a sign of disrespect. Indeed this belief was cited by John Bourke in his book *"On the Border with Crook,"* And a fellow named Gillett Griswold, at Fort Sill, ran into that problem in the 1950's when he was trying to replace the old, rotten grave markers of the Apaches and make a record of who was buried where. Author Alicia Delgadillo mentions this as an impediment to her research for her book *From Fort Marion to Fort Sill.*

I remembered that the Duwamish Indians of the Northwest had a similar tradition. Chief Seattle begged white people not to name a city after him because at the mention of a dead Indian's name he or she would roll over in his/her grave. Chief Seattle had an awful mental image of spinning in his grave like an airplane propeller if a major city was named for him. Apaches feared any disrespect for the dead could result in their ghosts appearing in the form of bears or owls.

Freddie said, "Chatto was as bold and powerful a warrior as any. He didn't bow down to anybody. As a Medicine Man, the power he received from Ussen was equivalent to that of Geronimo." He agrees it took extraordinary strength for Chatto to have turned from war to peace and it was to save his people from obliteration.

The remainder of Chatto's generation died out at the Mescalero reservation, most from natural causes. Noche, Kaetenae, Naiche, and Martine died there between 1914 and 1937. Dahteste died of old age. A document showing the names of many Chiricahua families, compiled by a committee of Apaches, can be viewed at the Culture Center.

One afternoon in 1934, outside of Whitetail, New Mexico, a part of the reservation where practically nothing remains today to suggest a thriving village, Chatto ran his Model T Ford off the road. He was too injured to make it out of the car. He died at the scene. In his 80 years, Chatto spent only 20 of them as a free child and adult. He spent 33 years living on Indian reservations and 27 years as a prisoner of the U.S. Government.

After his death, Helen stayed on the land until the tribe took control of most of it and sent Helen Chatto to an old folks village on the reservation, where she became blind, absent effective medical care, and died in her sleep at a ripe old age. Fortunately, a goodly portion of the acreage was returned to the family and is now in the hands of Freddie and Vincent. Freddie has provided his portion to his son and three daughters, who have residences there. Vincent was building an art gallery on his land when I visited and it was almost completed.

I asked Freddie, "What percentage of the 5,000 Apaches living on the reservation today are Chiricahua?

He said, "It doesn't matter. They are all intermixed now, whether one is Chiricahua, Mescalero and or Lipan is of no consequence. We are all the Mescalero Apache Tribe."

I thought, then, the New Mexicans and Arizonans of old who wanted the Chiricahua exterminated, eventually got their way?

Not according to Freddie. "The bottom line is; we survived. We are doctors and lawyers and architects and scientists and competitive, honest, hard-working people who are very important in the fabric of modern society. And this," he says, "happens not as an exclusive product of assimilation, but while the tribe maintains its culture and identification. We are leaders here and in the world. We thrive."

And what became of some of the other characters in the story? After the dust settled a bit in his dealings with the Apaches, General Miles took Phil Sheridan's old job as the commander of the Military Division of the Missouri. This put him in charge of putting down the last of the Sioux resistance in Montana territory. This led to the murder of Sitting Bull and the horrible massacre of Indians at Wounded Knee. Miles was not directly involved and blamed others. He called Wounded Knee "an abominable criminal military blunder."

Again he rose to stand in Sheridan's boots as Commanding General of the U.S. Army, just in time for the Spanish-American war in Cuba and Puerto Rico. He commanded in Cuba and invaded Puerto Rico where, for a while, he was the first head of the military government. President Teddy Roosevelt referred to him as a "brave peacock."

Miles retired at the mandatory age of 64 and got a few votes for President at the Democratic National Convention. At 77, he volunteered for World War One, but President Wilson turned him down. He was 85 when he died from a heart attack while attending a circus with his grandchildren in Washington D.C. He is one of only two people buried in mausoleums at Arlington National Cemetery.

"Little Phil" Sheridan stayed on as the top General in the Army until 1888, when he was succeeded by Miles. During that time he is credited with saving Yellowstone as a national park against developers who wanted to sell lots there. And he was the first President of the National Rifle Association. But hard campaigning and even harder living led to a series of heart attacks. He loved good food and drink and had ballooned his weight to above 200 pounds; much too much for a man of his short stature. He died of heart failure at age 57 and was buried at Arlington National Cemetery.

After his Indian agent days, John Clum bought and ran the Tombstone Epitaph newspaper, where he sided with Wyatt Earp against Ike Clanton and the cowboys rustling gang and was Mayor in time for the shootout at the OK Corral. Clum may have stayed in Tombstone, but his friendship with the Earps and the cloud they stirred up made him a target. When somebody shot up the stagecoach and killed one of the horses when he was riding on his way to catch a train to see family in Washington D.C., Clum just knew it was an assassination attempt and he called it a day in Tombstone.

He got himself an appointment in Alaska, during gold rush days and headed to the far north as a Postal Inspector. While in Nome he met up with the operator of the Dexter Saloon; Wyatt Earp. After Alaska, he worked for the Southern Pacific Railroad, delivering hundreds of lectures to promote passenger service. In 1928 he moved to Los Angeles, where he hobnobbed with Wyatt Earp again and worked on a book dedicated mostly to himself. Wyatt Earp had died in January of 1929, Clum followed only three years later, in 1932. Both were 80 years old.

And what ever happened to Bonito? That is problematic. Posed photographs were taken of him in 1884. As a White Mountain Apache, he probably had been allowed to remain at the San Carlos reservation during the prison days. There is a brief notation on an Apache website that says he settled on the San Carlos reservation, presumably for life.

Chief of Scouts, Al Sieber was killed after the turn of the century during a construction accident at the San Carlos Reservation. He was leading an Apache work crew building a road to the new Roosevelt Dam when a boulder rolled on top of him. There was a rumor that Apaches intentionally rolled the rock. He was buried with military honors in Globe, Arizona.

Sieber's erstwhile lieutenant, Mickey Free, had been lucky in Leavenworth, Kansas. When Chatto, Loco and the rest of the D.C. delegation were shipped to prison, Mickey and another interpreter were allowed to go back to Arizona. Mickey stayed on the government payroll, basically as a bounty hunter, chasing escaped Indians like Massai and the Apache Kid and killing some in cold blood when he found them. He was pensioned in the summer of 1906, moved with his wife and kids to Fort Apache, and built a cabin from tin sheets which he filled with memorabilia, including scalps. He died in December, 1913.

Herbert Welsh never became as famous as some of the Native Americans he sought to help, but he was well known as an earnest advocate for the rights of Indians. "To deprive such men of liberty and all opportunity of engaging in useful and remunerative work, and to inure them on the same footing as those fresh from the war path, is a great hardship, and ought not to be continued longer than is unavoidable." Welsh served as corresponding secretary of the Indian Rights Association for 34 years and its President for 11 years. He urged, cajoled, and pressured Congress to provide education for Indian children and to extend civil law to their reservations. Prominent in Pennsylvania politics and always pressing for civic reform, he lectured on Indian problems, civil service reform, municipal government and more. Late in life he was also known for taking one month, a once a year, to hike the 400 miles from Philadelphia to his summer home in New Hampshire on behalf of forest preservation. He died of natural causes on June 28, 1941 in Montpelier, Vermont.

Epilogue

Geronimo and Chatto had much in common; their upbringing, their knowledge and skills, their raiding, stealing and killing. They also had great losses. Both lost wives to death or capture. Only two of Geronimo's children grew to an age to have children of their own. Of Chatto's seven offspring, all died young except for Maude and Morris. They may have reacted differently to those losses. It appears that they intensified Geronimo's hatred and stiffened his resistance. They may have torn away Chatto's resolve and turned him away from war.

For a long time the two Apache leaders shared a desire to rid themselves of enemies by visiting the most horrible acts upon them; submission through cruelty. It was a war plan reminiscent of Genghis Kahn sweeping through Asia, of the German Wehrmact against the Russian population, of the Japanese against the Chinese at Nanking. Wiping out villages and their total populations went back to Biblical times. Bourke points out "The Assyrians cut their conquered foes limb from limb; the Israelites spared neither parent nor child; the Romans crucified head downward the gladiators who revolted under Spartacus." This terror was utilized by the Apaches. It was also employed by the U.S. Government against Native Americans.

But why was Geronimo the most famous Apache, while Chatto faded into history? There are no buildings or street signs named for Chatto, except one street on the reservation, few if any books about him. Paratroopers don't scream his name jumping out of airplanes. Was it because Geronimo killed more people, burned more ranches, stole more horses? Or was it because he was the cruelest, nastiest, meanest Indian on the planet? Or was it because he was the last of the renegades to finally give up his rifle and end the Apache wars?

No, I think it was more than that. Geronimo became an icon; a symbol of independence and freedom and the will to fight against great odds for those ideals. Those are All-American ideals. We love heroes like this. Think Jesse James, Wyatt Earp and Billy the Kid, all somewhat twisted men who represented something we want to see in ourselves. In that way, and probably in that way alone, Geronimo became one of us.

Thus, Geronimo is represented in countless books, movies, posters, cards and bric-a-brac. He is a symbol of freedom-fighting. Authors don't write much about Geronimo the cruel sociopathic murderer, liar and hopeless alcoholic who led hundreds of Apaches to their own deaths. He is praised for eluding capture by thousands of troops but not criticized for his depravations and the heartbreak he fomented.

On the other hand, Chatto opted for peace. I don't know all the reasons. He may have just been selfish; not wanting to get killed and thinking the Government would come through to rescue his family.

But I have come to believe that it was more than that. I think he was a realist; a pragmatic man who saw the futility of battling a Goliath and determined that his people, the majority remaining in a band that was trying to live in peace, were best served by seeing the hand-writing on the wall, adopting the white man's way of life and making the best of it.

His actions indicate that once that decision was made, he was ready and able to fight for it. I believe his fight for peace was as strenuous and sometimes dangerous as the battles waged by the renegade Apaches out in the wilds of Mexico and Arizona. Once having turned away from the war-path, Chatto led his people, not through the destruction of war, but toward assimilation and acceptance. He may be seen as weak for throwing up his hands and lying down in front of the conqueror, or worse joining him. But I see him as a strong man, in the fashion of Martin Luther King, who went about protecting his people in a non-violent way. He was strong enough to withstand the hatred, even the murder plots of the Apaches who thought of him as a spy and collaborator. Perhaps history treats him differently because his advocacy of peace did not prevent the imprisonment of his people and the subsequent death by disease, the stealing of their children and the horrible conditions of the Florida fortresses. Still Chatto continued to advocate for the tribe while in custody and continued as tribal leader until the end. He just didn't get famous for it.

At least, in 2012, the Heard Museum in Phoenix staged an exhibit featuring Chatto, displaying his peace medal. Vincent Kaydahzinne was there arguing that his great great grandfather was anything but a turncoat…that he was thinking solely of how his people would benefit from an end to the cycle of vengeful violence. Even in this setting Geronimo stole the limelight. The Exhibit was entitled: "Geronimo, the Apache Experience," a title that probably brought in more attendees and made for a more interesting article in the June 12th edition of the Arizona Republic.

Geronimo was a war-maker. Chatto became a peace-maker. Each believed they were protecting their people and trying to insure their future. Geronimo preached resistance. Chatto urged submission. Resistance is much more exciting.

Chatto and Geronimo had another thing in common. They were both good examples of the race-based arrogance of the Europeans and what a government is capable of doing to the indigenous peoples of a land. The prison sentences of Geronimo and Naiche were perhaps understandable, given the times. Chatto's wasn't. If Chatto was to be imprisoned, why didn't they tell him at his surrender? How could they defeat him, take him into custody, enlist him and use him at the risk of his life, rely on him to keep the peace, write him letters of commendation, give him a medal, then put him in prison for 27 years? How could they promise him peace and a return to his home with tools and implements to work the land, then slap him in Fort Marion?

It's situational ethics. If you were an Apache in 1885, would you follow Geronimo or Chatto?

Bibliography

Aleshire, Peter, *The Fox and the Whirlwind: General George Crook and Geronimo*, Castle Books, 2000,

Ball, Eve. *Indeh*, University of Oklahoma Press, 1980

Barrett, Stephen. 1906 *Geronimo's Story of His Life*; as told to Stephen Melvil Barrett.: New York, Duffield & Company, Online at Webroots; Edition Oct 15, 2002

Bigelow, John Lt "*On the Bloody Trail of Geronimo*" New York: Tower Books 1958

Bourke, John G. *On the Border with Crook*. Lincoln: University of Nebraska Press, 1891

Capps, Benjamin. *The Indians*, Time Life Books, The Old West, NY 1976

Carroll, H. Bailey, " *Snively, Jacob*" Handbook of Texas Online, Texas State Historical Association

Carter, Forrest. "*Watch for Me on the Mountain*" Delta. 1990. (Originally entitled "Cry Geronimo".)

Davis, Britton "The *Truth about Geronimo*" New Haven: Yale Press 1929

Debo, Angie, *Geronimo: The Man, His Time, His Place*, Norman, OK: University of Oklahoma Press 1976

Delgadillo, Alicia, From *Fort Marion to Fort Apache,* University of Nebraska Press 2013.

Etulain, Richard W. *New Mexican Lives: A Biographical History*, University of New Mexico Center for the American West, University of New Mexico Press, 2002.

Faulk, Odie B. *The Geronimo Campaign*. Oxford University Press: New York, 1969.

Gatewood, Charles B. (Edited by Louis Kraft). *Lt. Charles Gatewood & His Apache Wars Memoir*. University of Nebraska Press 2005.

Geronimo (edited by Barrett) "*Geronimo, His Own Story*" New York: Ballantine Books 1971.

Gorenfeld, Will. *"The Battle of Cieneguilla." Wild West Magazine*, February, 2008.

Griffin-Pierce, Trudy. *Native Peoples of the Southwest*. University of New Mexico Press. 2000

Griffith, A. Kinney, *"Mickey Free, Manhunter."* Caxton Printers, Idaho 1969

Griswold, Gillette, *The Fort Sill Apaches; Their Vital Statistics, Tribal Origins and Antecedents,* filmed by Geneological Society of Utah, Salt Lake City, 1976.

Haley, James L. *Apaches: A History and Culture Portrait*. University of Oklahoma Press, 1997

Hammond, John Martin: *Quaint and Historic Forts of North America*, J.B. Lippencott Co. 1915.

Heard Museum, *Beyond Geronimo Exhibit,* http//archive.azcentral.com/arizonarepublic/ae/

Hodge, F. W. (Ed.). (1907). *Handbook of American Indians.* Washington.

Jones, Paul A., *Coronado and Quivira,* Lyons Publishing Co., Lyons KS. 1937

Kaydahzinne, Freddie. Interviews November 4, 2014, and May 4 and 5, 2015 on Mescalero Reservation. Subsequent communications.

Kaydahzinne, Vincent. Interview April 14, 2015, by telephone.

Kessel, William S. *Dragoons in Apacheland: Conquest and Resistance in Southern New Mexico, 1846,* University of Oklahoma Press, 2012

Lauer, Charles D. *Arrows, Bullets and Saddle Sores.* Golden West Publications, 2005

Leach, Mike, *Geronimo-Leadership Strategies of an American Warrior,* Gallery Books, N.Y. 2014

McChristian, Douglas, *Fort Bowie, Arizona,* University of Oklahoma Press, 2005

MilitaryHistoryOnline.com: *The Bascom Affair, Apache Pass February 4, 1861*

Rielly, Edward. *"Geronimo: The Warrior",* article for The Public Domain Review, 2011.

Roberts, David. *Once They Moved Like the Wind.* New York: Simon & Schuster, 1993

Robinson, Charles M., III. *"General Crook and the Western Frontier",* University of Oklahoma Press, 2001.

Schellie, Don, *"Vast Domain of Blood, The Story of the Camp Grant Massacre,"* Westernlore Press, L.A. 1968

Seymour, Deni J. *Various studies of Early Apaches*, Historical Archeology. University of Northern Colorado, 2004

Sharp, Jay, *Cochise and the Bascom Affair,* www.desertusa.com
Sheridan, Thomas E. *Arizona, A History.* University of Arizona Press, 1995

Simmons, Marc, *"Massacre on the Lordsburg Road,"* Texas A&M Press, 1984

Smithsonian, http://www.smithsonianmag.com/history/geronimos-decades-long-hunt-for-vengeance-

Sweeney, Edwin R. *Mangas Coloradas: Chief of the Chiricahua Apaches.* University of Oklahoma Press, 1998

Sweeney, Edwin R. *From Cochise to Geronimo,* University of Oklahoma Press, 2010

Terrell, John Upton. *Apache Chronicle,* World Publishing. 1972

Thrapp, Dan L. *The Conquest of Apacheria.* Norman: University of Oklahoma Press, 1967

Wallace, Robert, Time Life Books, The Old West; The Miners, 1973

Welsh, Herbert. *Apache Prisoners At Fort Marion.* Report by Indian Rights Assn. 1887

Wikipedia: Initial source for great number of subjects: Chatto, Apache, Cochise, Coloradas, Victorio, Juh, Nana, Apache Wars , George Crook, Nelson Miles, Phil Sheridan, Charles Gatewood, Chiricahua many more.

Worcester, Donald E. (1992). *The Apaches: Eagles of the Southwest',* University of Oklahoma Press, Norman, 1979

Index

A

Ake party, 71, 82
Aliso Creek Massacre, 156
Alma
    New Mexico, 10, 126, 157
Alope, 51, 53
Annie Oakley, 309, 311
Apache Kid, 230, 231, 305, 306, 307, 323
Apache Pass, 62, 64, 77, 79, 96, 105, 168, 330
Arizona Guards, 75
Arizpe, 53
Arthur
    President Chester, 164, 165, 171, 237
Askadodilges, 206, 214, 271

B

Bahnahtsi, 22, 51, 169, 313, 315
Bartlett
    John "Yank", 259, 260
Bascom
    Lt. George, 6, 56, 57, 58, 59, 60, 61, 62, 63, 64, 65, 330, 331
Battle of Cibecue Creek, 137
Bedisclove, 114, 201, 312
Belle Davis, 228
Beneactiney, 132, 169, 170
Betzinez
    Jason, 154, 155
Bisbee, 222
Bonito, 3, 7, 136, 140, 142, 145, 146, 147, 159, 161, 166, 168, 169, 172, 173, 175, 187, 188, 189, 190, 193, 196, 199, 201, 212, 215, 217, 219, 225, 226, 243, 263, 323

Bonneville
    Col Benjamin, 49
Bourke
    Capt John, 12, 13, 16, 68, 69, 93, 95, 102, 162, 204, 207, 215, 253, 254, 275, 288, 293, 319, 325, 328
Bowie
    Col. George, 79, 80, 96, 252, 276
Brown
    Maj. William, 99, 100
Buckley
    Corporal Michael, 62, 83, 84
Buffalo Bill Cody, 307, 309, 311
Buffalo Soldiers, 125, 260
Burro Mountains, 175
Bylas
    Richard, 147, 148

C

Calamity Jane, 309
Camp Grant Massacre, 331
Camp Verde, 65, 94, 101, 117
Cananea, 228
Carleton, 70
    Gen. J.H., 40, 78
Carlisle School, 15, 282
Carr
    Col. Eugene, 7, 137, 138, 139, 140, 141, 264
Carrasco
    Col. Jose, 52
Carson
    Kit, 69
Casas Grandes, 128, 145, 221
Chaffee
    Lt. Adna, 129
Chandler
    Lt. Col. Daniel, 9, 49

Chappo, 55, 159, 197, 198, 200, 203, 276, 300
Charleston, 170
Charlie
 McComas, 176, 183, 191, 219
Chief Joseph, 287
Chihuahua, 10, 30, 32, 33, 37, 125, 127, 129, 132, 136, 142, 145, 148, 159, 165, 167, 171, 187, 188, 189, 190, 194, 196, 198, 199, 208, 212, 214, 218, 221, 222, 223, 224, 226, 227, 228, 235, 237, 238, 239, 240, 241, 251, 252, 269, 287, 300, 313
Chiricahua Mountains, 9, 63, 78, 79, 105, 106, 112, 201, 238, 245
Chocolate Pass, 160
Cieneguilla, 329
Cleveland
 President Grover, 7, 237, 270, 272, 274, 277, 291, 304, 305
Cloverdale, 171
Clum
 John, 6, 109, 110, 111, 115, 116, 117, 118, 119, 120, 121, 122, 127, 134, 157, 322
Cochinay, 115
Cochise, 6, 8, 9, 10, 28, 31, 36, 39, 52, 53, 54, 56, 57, 58, 59, 60, 61, 62, 63, 64, 73, 75, 77, 78, 81, 82, 83, 85, 96, 104, 105, 106, 109, 111, 120, 134, 137, 142, 143, 144, 168, 169, 190, 296, 318, 331
Coloradas
 Mangas, 6, 10, 31, 33, 35, 36, 44, 52, 54, 56, 62, 75, 78, 79, 80, 81, 137, 142, 143, 167, 175, 313, 331
Comanches, 25, 30, 31, 185, 308
Compa
 Juan Jose, 33, 34, 35, 36, 37
Contention Mine, 170

Cooke's Canyon, 71, 72
Corredor
 Maj. Mauricio, 247, 248
Coyuntwa, 59, 60
Crawford
 Capt. Emmet, 7, 163, 164, 171, 187, 193, 197, 198, 199, 200, 201, 202, 208, 209, 210, 222, 224, 226, 227, 231, 232, 233, 244, 245, 246, 247, 248, 249, 265
Crazy Horse, 103, 162
Crook
 Gen. George, 6, 40, 91, 92, 93, 94, 95, 96, 98, 100, 101, 102, 103, 106, 135, 151, 162, 163, 164, 171, 174, 183, 184, 185, 186, 187, 188, 189, 190, 191, 193, 194, 198, 199, 200, 201, 202, 203, 204, 206, 208, 209, 210, 211, 212, 213, 215, 218, 222, 225, 235, 237, 238, 239, 242, 244, 249, 250, 251, 253, 254, 255, 257, 258, 263, 273, 275, 288, 289, 291, 292, 301, 302, 305, 319, 328, 330, 331
Culto, 25, 26, 82
Culver
 Charles, 58, 61, 62
Custer
 Gen George Armstrong, 162, 163, 257

D

Dahteste, 6, 124, 125, 143, 300, 315
Daklugie, 118, 131, 134, 191, 314, 317
Davis
 Captain Wirt, 151, 225, 226, 228
 Lt. Britton, 174, 199, 200, 202, 203, 205, 206, 207, 208, 210,

211, 212, 214, 217, 218, 220,
221, 222, 223, 224, 225, 231,
232, 233, 235, 249, 250, 256,
295, 328
Dawes
   Sen. Henry, 7, 237, 291, 293
Dawson
   Capt. Byron, 126
Deming
   New Mexico, 71, 234, 241, 242
Dibble
   Judge Henry, 171
Dodge
   Henry, 49
Dohn-say, 227
Douglas, Arizona, 169, 222, 258
Dragoon Mountains, 9, 77, 104, 105, 109
Drum
   Sec. R.C., 274, 281, 282, 283, 284, 286
Dutchy, 169, 172, 198, 219, 225, 294

E

Earp
   Wyatt, 157, 226, 322, 326
El Paso, 227, 234, 235
Elliot
   Lt. Charles, 232, 233
Endicott
   Sec. William, 236, 271, 274, 289, 290, 291, 306
Eskiminzin, 88
Eskinya, 109, 111
Ewell
   Capt. Richard, 50

F

Ford

   Charles D., 209, 210, 320
Forsyth
   Maj. George, 40, 150
Fort Apache, 137, 138, 140, 141, 145, 156, 163, 201, 203, 207, 210, 217, 218, 220, 223, 232, 234, 237, 240, 241, 242, 243, 244, 252, 263, 292, 323, 329
Fort Bliss, 58, 234
Fort Bowie, 6, 79, 80, 237, 244, 251, 276, 280, 287
Fort Breckenridge, 63
Fort Buchanan, 57, 63, 65, 82, 83, 84
Fort Filmore, 49
Fort Huachuca, 129, 170, 174, 264
Fort Leavenworth, 270, 284
Fort Marion, 3, 6, 12, 14, 15, 16, 18, 270, 274, 277, 279, 281, 282, 284, 286, 288, 290, 292, 293, 297, 298, 319, 327, 329, 331
Fort McDowell, 94
Fort Pickens, 277, 279, 290, 293, 296, 297, 298
Fort Sill, 5, 123, 307, 314, 319
Fort Tularosa, 126
Fort Wingate, 123
Fun, 152, 214

G

Galeana, 160
Garcia
   Gen. Lorenzo, 154
Gatewood
   Lt. Charles, 130, 163, 164, 187, 210, 211, 217, 223, 225, 263, 264, 265, 266, 267, 268, 276, 294, 329, 332
Geronimo, 6, 7, 10, 19, 20, 22, 26, 31, 36, 51, 52, 53, 54, 56, 62, 66, 80, 81, 96, 110, 111, 112, 113, 114,

118, 121, 122, 124, 125, 127, 128,
129, 132, 133, 135, 136, 137, 140,
142, 143, 144, 145, 146, 147, 148,
149, 150, 152, 153, 154, 155, 156,
157, 158, 159, 160, 161, 162, 165,
166, 167, 168, 171, 183, 187, 188,
189, 190, 193, 194, 195, 196, 197,
198, 200, 202, 203, 204, 206, 211,
212, 213, 214, 215, 217, 218, 219,
220, 221, 222, 223, 224, 225, 226,
227, 231, 232, 233, 234, 236, 237,
239, 240, 246, 248, 250, 251, 253,
257, 258, 261, 263, 264, 265, 266,
267, 269, 274, 276, 277, 278, 279,
280, 282, 285, 286, 287, 288, 290,
293, 294, 295, 296, 297, 299, 305,
306, 308, 309, 310, 311, 312, 314,
325, 326, 327, 328, 329, 330, 331
Gila City, 42, 43, 44
Gila Mountains, 234
Gonaltsis, 21, 22, 85, 97, 197, 199,
219, 271, 284, 299, 300
Gonzales
Col. Miguel, 195
Gordo, 109, 127, 133, 142, 143
Grant
Ulysses, 88, 89, 92, 94, 104, 115,
164, 185, 256, 316, 331
Guaynopa, 160, 165, 227

H

Hammond
John, 129, 329
Hart.
Lyman, 127
Hayt
Ezra, 128
Helen, Chatto, 16, 143, 283, 300, 301,
308, 311, 313, 314, 319, 320
Horn

Tom, 162, 257, 266
Howard
Gen. Oliver, 89, 104, 105
Huachuca Mountains, 112, 113, 170
Hunter
Capt. Sherod, 77, 78

I

Ihtedda, 23, 227, 249, 297, 300, 301
Indian Rights Association, 13, 16, 209,
288, 292, 307, 323
Irwin
Bernard, 64
Ishchosen, 73, 74, 94, 95, 98, 106,
107, 110, 112, 134, 142, 143, 158,
165, 194, 199, 201, 301, 312, 313

J

Janokla, 51, 190, 300
Janos, 3, 32, 37, 51, 53, 79, 158, 174,
234
Jeffords
Tom, 104, 105, 106, 108, 109
Jelikine, 149, 187, 189, 194
Johnson
John, 35
Juh, 6, 10, 53, 54, 109, 110, 111, 112,
113, 118, 129, 133, 136, 142, 143,
144, 145, 146, 156, 158, 159, 160,
161, 165, 166, 194, 195, 201, 227,
285, 331
Juniatta
McComas, 176, 177, 178

K

Kaetenae, 200, 203, 206, 207, 269,
271, 294, 320
Kaydahzinne, 223, 319

304

Freddie, 318, 319, 327
Vincent, 318
Kayitah, 150, 152, 159, 187, 195, 219, 265, 266, 287
Kaywaykla
 James, 15
Kirker
 James, 37, 38
Kit Carson, 69
Kitchen
 Pete, 129

L

Lamar
 Sec. Lucius, 271, 272, 273, 274, 289
Langdon
 Lt. Col. Loomis, 13
Las Cruces, 72
Lawton
 Capt. Henry, 264, 265, 267, 286, 308, 314
Lee, Robert E., 185, 256
Leslie
 Buckskin Frank, 226
Loco, 4, 7, 109, 114, 122, 124, 136, 142, 143, 145, 146, 147, 149, 150, 152, 153, 154, 155, 156, 160, 165, 190, 212, 215, 219, 225, 271, 313, 323
Lordsburg, 4, 175, 176, 180, 183, 331
Loring
 Col. William, 49, 50
Lozen, 6, 22, 124, 125, 143, 214, 258, 300
Lt. Dixon Miles, 49

M

Mangas, 6, 10, 25, 31, 33, 35, 36, 44, 45, 54, 56, 62, 75, 78, 80, 81, 82, 142, 167, 169, 175, 200, 208, 211, 212, 213, 214, 217, 218, 220, 221, 222, 225, 226, 227, 239, 240, 313, 331
Martine, 132, 219, 263, 265, 278, 287, 320
Massai, 277, 323
Mastin
 Capt. Tom, 75, 76
Maus
 Lt. Marion, 230, 247, 248, 251, 252
McComas
 Charley, 176, 180, 181, 182, 191, 271
 Judge Hamilton, 7, 176, 177, 178, 179, 180, 181, 182, 242, 274
McGinn
 Santiago, 234, 235
Mestas
 Victoriano, 147, 148
Mexican War, 39, 177
Mickey Free, 57, 60, 61, 65, 203, 219, 231, 236, 250, 307, 323, 329
Miles
 Gen. Nelson, 4, 50, 92, 244, 253, 255, 256, 257, 258, 263, 264, 267, 268, 270, 271, 273, 274, 276, 278, 279, 280, 281, 283, 284, 287, 290, 292, 294, 306, 321, 322, 332
Mimbres River
 Battle of, 45
Morrison
 Lt. Col Pitcain, 57
Mount Vernon, 5, 298, 299, 300, 301, 302, 307, 308

N

Naboka, 120, 134, 143, 156, 166, 201, 312
Nacori Chico, 146, 194
Naiche, 6, 109, 111, 120, 127, 128, 129, 133, 134, 136, 137, 140, 142, 143, 145, 147, 148, 149, 150, 154, 155, 158, 159, 160, 165, 169, 187, 188, 189, 193, 195, 198, 199, 212, 214, 218, 220, 221, 222, 225, 226, 228, 237, 238, 239, 246, 248, 251, 253, 258, 263, 265, 269, 278, 296, 315, 320, 327
Nalthchedah, 98, 110, 121, 142, 204, 243, 244, 245, 284, 308
Nana, 7, 10, 109, 122, 123, 124, 131, 132, 145, 190, 212, 214, 234, 237, 239, 251, 331
Nantaje, 99, 100
Na-tio-tisha, 144
Nock-ay-det-klinne, 137, 139, 140

O

Oatman
    family, 46
Ojo Caliente, 113, 114, 121, 122, 123, 129
Ortiz
    Juan Mata, 160, 161
Oury
    William, 88, 89

P

Paiutes, 92
Pawnee Bill, 309, 311
Pierce
    Capt. F.E., 210, 211, 306, 329
Pinos Altos, 3, 42, 44, 75, 76, 80, 221
Pionsenay, 111, 122
Prescott, 92, 94, 171
puberty rites, 74, 94

R

Randall
    Capt George, 101
Roosevelt
    Teddy, 144, 314, 321, 323
Roy Bean, 75
Rucker
    Lt. John, 112, 113

S

Safford
    Gov. A.P.K., 42, 89
Saint Augustine, 12, 284
San Bernardino, 198
San Buenaventura, 232, 233
San Carlos, 51, 93, 107, 108, 109, 110, 111, 114, 115, 116, 117, 119, 121, 122, 123, 124, 127, 128, 129, 130, 132, 133, 134, 136, 140, 141, 144, 145, 146, 147, 148, 150, 152, 153, 156, 157, 163, 169, 171, 172, 174, 189, 190, 193, 194, 197, 198, 200, 201, 203, 206, 210, 224, 227, 242, 243, 263, 272, 295, 306, 307, 316, 323
Santa Anna, 35
Santa Fe, 37, 46, 123
Santa Rita, 35, 37, 42, 44
Scott, General Hugh L., 312
Shanahan
    Phil, 259, 260
She-gah, 53, 157, 234, 235, 297
Sheridan
    Gen. Philip, 86, 92, 103, 184, 185, 236, 244, 250, 251, 253, 257,

270, 271, 273, 284, 288, 289,
   292, 307, 321, 322, 331, 332
Sherman
   Gen. William, 86, 91, 103, 141,
   184, 256, 257, 292
Shy
   John, 241
Sieber
   Albert, 65, 94, 151, 187, 222, 230,
   231, 233, 305, 306, 307, 323
Silver City, 6, 41, 42, 174, 175, 176,
   179, 182, 231, 234
Sitting Bull, 103, 287, 310, 311, 321
Skeleton Cave, 100
Smith
   Capt. Allen, 13, 14, 17, 67, 156,
   217, 218, 236, 260, 267
Snake Indians, 92
Snively
   Jacob, 6, 43, 44, 328
Southern Pacific Railroad, 322
St Louis, 178
Stanley
   Gen. David, 278, 279, 294
Stanton
   Capt. Henry W., 47
Stevens
   George, 129, 147
Stoddert
   Capt Richard, 50

T

Taayzslath, 194, 227, 297, 313
Taza, 109, 111, 119, 120, 134
Terahumara, 145, 168, 232, 248
Terrazas
   Col. Joaquin, 131
Tiffany
   Joseph, 136, 137, 162

tiswin, 19, 118, 128, 137, 204, 205,
   206, 207, 208, 211, 212, 213, 225,
   227, 287, 305
Tombstone, 9, 42, 92, 157, 170, 226,
   322
Tres Castillos, 131, 160
Tribolet
   Charles, 251
Trinidad Verdin, 258
Tubac, 3, 71
Tucson, 32, 44, 46, 57, 63, 72, 77, 82,
   88, 89, 92, 94, 107, 108, 129, 170,
   259, 294
Turkey Creek, 200, 201, 202, 206, 207,
   211, 214, 238, 243, 250
Tzoe
   Peaches, 150, 169, 173

U

Ulzana, 125, 132, 187, 224, 240, 241,
   242, 243, 244, 245, 252, 313

V

Victorio, 6, 10, 36, 109, 113, 122, 123,
   124, 125, 126, 129, 130, 131, 137,
   143, 144, 160, 237, 258, 264, 300,
   331

W

Wallace
   James, 58, 59, 61, 63, 64
Ward
   John, 56, 57, 58, 59, 65, 203
Ware
   Sen. Eugene, 178, 182
Welsh
   Herbert, 6, 12, 13, 14, 15, 16, 17,
   18, 19, 20, 21, 30, 104, 105,

107, 110, 121, 135, 142, 143,
144, 155, 168, 189, 190, 198,
203, 209, 211, 212, 215, 236,
273, 281, 282, 283, 284, 285,
286, 288, 289, 290, 292, 293,
294, 295, 298, 304, 307, 323,
331

West
   Gen. Joseph, 41, 57, 80, 81, 91,
164, 178, 185, 202, 255, 290,
309, 328, 329, 330

Whetstone Mountains, 170, 228

Whitman
   Lt. Royal, 88, 89

Wickenburg, 42, 44

Wilcox
   Philip, 163, 197, 198, 201

Wild Bill Hickok, 307

Willcox
   Gen. Orlando, 147

Winchester Mountains, 171

Wingfield
   Edward, 36

Y

Yeater
   Andy, 241, 242

Z

Zele, 31, 129, 158, 187, 189, 206

CPSIA information can be obtained at www.ICGtesting.com
Printed in the USA
LVOW06s0917050915

452965LV00028B/1746/P